Creative Explorations

How do you picture identity? What happens when you ask individuals to make visual representations of their own identities, influences, and relationships?

Drawing upon an array of disciplines from neuroscience to philosophy, and art to social theory, David Gauntlett explores the ways in which researchers can embrace people's everyday creativity in order to understand social experience.

Seeking an alternative to traditional interviews and focus groups, he outlines studies in which people have been asked to *make* visual things – such as video, collage, and drawing – and then interpret them. This leads to an innovative project in which Gauntlett asked people to build metaphorical models of their identities in Lego. This creative reflective method provides insights into how individuals present themselves, understand their own life story and connect with the social world.

Creative Explorations is a lively, readable and original discussion of identities, media influences and creativity, which will be of interest to both students and academics.

David Gauntlett is Professor of Media and Communications, University of Westminster, London. He is the author of several books on media audiences and identities, including *Media, Gender and Identity* (2002) and *Moving Experiences* (second edition, 2005). He produces the award-winning website on media and identities, Theory.org.uk, and the hub for creative methodologies, ArtLab.org.uk.

Creative Explorations

New approaches to identities
and audiences

David Gauntlett

 Routledge
Taylor & Francis Group

LONDON AND NEW YORK

First published 2007
by Routledge
2 Park Square, Milton Park, Abingdon, Oxon OX14 4RN

Simultaneously published in the USA and Canada
by Routledge
270 Madison Ave, New York, NY 10016

*Routledge is an imprint of the Taylor & Francis Group, an informa
business*

© 2007 David Gauntlett

Typeset in Garamond by
HWA Text and Data Management, Tunbridge Wells
Printed and bound in Great Britain by
TJ International Ltd, Padstow, Cornwall

British Library Cataloguing in Publication Data
A catalogue record for this book is available from the British
Library

Library of Congress Cataloging-in-Publication Data
A catalog record for this book has been requested

ISBN10: 0–415–39658–1 (hbk
ISBN10: 0–415–39659–X (pbk)
ISBN10: 0–203–96140–4 (ebk)

ISBN13: 978–0–415–39658–5 (hbk)
ISBN13: 978–0–415–39659–2 (pbk)
ISBN13: 978–0–203–96140–7 (ebk)

For Jenny, always

Contents

Figures

Acknowledgements

I have been developing the themes and ideas in this book over several years, and so I owe thanks to a number of people.

At Bournemouth Media School, I appreciated the support of Fiona Cownie, Barry Richards, Richard Berger, Stephen Jukes, Chris Wensley, Jon Wardle, and other colleagues. In my new institution, the University of Westminster, I am enjoying working with Annette Hill, Peter Goodwin, Colin Sparks, Sally Feldman, Jeanette Steemers, and many others.

At Lego, I have been very fortunate to work with Per Kristiansen, Director of Lego Serious Play, and his successor, Jesper Just Jensen, who have both backed my research with much enthusiasm. I also gratefully acknowledge the support of Lego Serious Play, part of the Lego Group, in terms of expenses, training and materials.

For helping to set up the Lego Serious Play sessions, I am grateful to Kat Jungnickel, Keri Kimber, Sandy Wilderspin, Marian Mayer, Sarah Goode, Knut Lundby, Anders Fagerjord, Ole Smørdal, Dagny Stuedahl, the staff of Indiefield, and especially Kristen Pedersen who helped with a number of the groups.

My colleagues on the Mediatized Stories project, funded by the Research Council of Norway and based at the University of Oslo have given me much to think about. In particular, the project director, Knut Lundby, has been very kind and made some excellent suggestions. I am very grateful to the Mediatized Stories project for funding the professional recruitment, and payment, of two unemployed groups in the Lego identity study. The Centre for Excellence in Media Practice at Bournemouth Media School also funded some of the fieldwork activity.

I would also like to thank Peter Holzwarth, Horst Niesyto, Sara Bragg, Ross Horsley, Jon Prosser, Nick Couldry, Nancy Thumim, Marc Bush, Paul Sweetman, David Buckingham, Darren Newbury, Elizabeth Chaplin, Stuart Nolan, Jenny Moon, and Julian Sefton-Green, for their help and ideas.

At Routledge, Natalie Foster and Charlotte Wood have been very supportive. Fatimah Awan and Jenny Gauntlett were kind enough to read through and comment on the whole manuscript, which was valuable, although all of the book's weaknesses remain, of course, my own. Finally I would like to add a big extra thanks and lots of love to Jenny for her help, creative ideas, and so much happiness.

Chapter 1

Introduction

Identity is complicated. Everybody thinks they've got one. Magazines and talk show hosts urge us to explore our 'identity'. Religious and national identities are at the heart of major international conflicts. Artists play with the idea of 'identity' in modern society. Blockbuster movie superheroes have emotional conflicts about their 'true' identity. And the average teenager can create three online 'identities' before breakfast.

Governments warn us about 'identity theft', but this involves the theft of external data: someone can make use of my electronic bank details, but even the most cunning thief cannot run off with the internal 'me'. And they probably wouldn't want it. Scientists, meanwhile, are developing 'The ultimate guide to self-knowledge', as *New Scientist* magazine called it (2006), using genome sequencing, genetic genealogy, intelligence tests and personal brain scans in order to understand human individuality. But these methods describe identity at the molecular, scannable or quantifiable level, which does not seem to really connect with our common conscious *experience* of actually being alive. Novelists, artists and musicians have managed to capture diverse aspects of human experience in evocative and imaginative forms. Sociology, though – including the study of media and culture in the world – recognises identity as a core concept but isn't really sure how to deal with this strange abstraction in practical terms. How do we find out about people's 'identities'? Is there not some empirical way in which we can explore this experience of being a 'self', of having an 'identity', somewhere between the scientist's microscope and the artist's brush, which remains true to the experience of being human?

That is what this book is about. We all have a complex matrix of ideas about ourselves, who we are and who we want to be. What can we say about this tapestry, this thing we call identity, including hopes and dreams, loneliness and love? In media studies and sociology we're interested in what influences identity, but before we can do that we need to look at *what identity means*. This book follows one path towards an answer, through a discussion of the ways in which creative, artistic and other 'making' activities, combined with time for reflection, can help us to better understand people's identities and social experiences.

It has long been understood that those people we call 'artists' make artworks in order to express, or communicate, something about their lives, feelings or experiences. For non-'artists', creative practices such as photography or weekend painting might be underpinned by a similar motivation, but are often regarded as little more than an attempt to make a 'nice' or 'realistic' picture. Other common activities such as blogging, poetry-writing, arrangement of artefacts and mementoes on a wall or desk, webpage design, clothing, and even speech, are all acts of more or less deliberate creative production and self-expression which are generally accepted as pretty normal (rather than being the exclusive province of an artistic 'master'). These are ways in which people can, and do, communicate messages or impressions to others about themselves.

Meanwhile, researchers have usually sought only to access people's experiences, or interpretations of their own experiences, through language. Interviews and focus groups are the most common qualitative methods which are supposed to provide researchers with 'deep' information about people's thoughts about social subject-matter, which may be politics, shopping, health, prejudice, dimensions of self-identity, or any of a wide range of issues. In my own area, media audience research, academics have used interviews in order to understand, for example, consumption of women's magazines (Hermes, 1995), science fiction fans (Tulloch and Jenkins, 1995), and women's use of video recorders (Gray, 1992), and focus groups to explore the reception of, for example, teenage romance magazines (Frazer, 1987), action movie audiences (Barker and Brooks, 1998; Hill, 1997, 2001), and men's magazines (Jackson, Stevenson and Brooks, 2001).

Figure 1.1 Searching for self-identity in popular magazines

These are not 'bad' examples – far from it – they may be classics of their kind, and are often helpfully reflective about their own limitations. Hermes, for example, likens her experience of interviewing readers about women's magazines to 'playing with weighted dice against crafty opponents' (1995: 143). She admits that her research set out to identify the meanings that magazines had for readers, but that 'readers told me that women's magazines have hardly any meaning at all' (ibid). The metaphorical dice would often land on one or two common answers – about either the 'cultural insignificance' or the 'practical use' of the magazines – although occasionally there would be a 'glimpse' of other sides of the dice. Overall one gets the impression that the researcher was asking individuals to generate opinions on something about which they did not previously have an opinion; and furthermore that her interviewees were actually trying to *resist* the academic drive to identify 'meanings' where they felt there really were none. We are able to discern this because Hermes is unusually frank and reflective about the problems she faced in her study; we can guess that other researchers might tend to play down such problems and instead present a set of 'findings' more strongly.

Hermes's problem – shared less explicitly by many other studies and researchers – was not simply that she was trying to get people to put into words something which they had not previously considered in any detail, or verbalised; it was also that she had preselected something as being of importance to people (magazines) and then wanted the people to explain why. This book is a response to both of these ideas: that researchers expect people to explain immediately, in words, things which are difficult to explain immediately in words; and that researchers often start with their own sense of a topic or problem (media, prejudice, economics or whatever) and then are frustrated when their pesky subjects do not seem to think that this subject-matter is as important as the researchers do.

Research methodology is often seen as a dry and technical topic. But it is only through research methods – ways of *finding things out* – that we *know* anything about the world. As sociologists (or scientists, journalists or anyone else), we cannot make claims about the social world without some kind of evidence, and that evidence always has a method. So methodology is crucially important. We cannot have 'knowledge' without it.

Creative Explorations therefore sets out to establish a somewhat different way of gathering knowledge – an approach which allows participants to spend *time* applying their playful or creative *attention* to the act of *making* something symbolic or metaphorical, and then *reflecting* on it. I sometimes call these approaches 'the new creative methods', but no approach can really be wholly 'new' of course, and a number of antecedents will be discussed throughout the book.

The kicking-off point

Many ideas and perspectives can be better understood by knowing what they are a response to. The new creative methods are obviously an alternative to language-driven qualitative research methods, as has already been mentioned. But my own work in this area developed, more broadly, out of a frustration with the ways in which media and communications researchers had sought to explore the relationship between the mass media and its audiences. The straightforward autobiographical version of this story is as follows.

In 1993–4, I was a new PhD student with a background in sociology, rather than media and communications studies. My project proposal had declared that I was going to see whether the coverage of environmental issues in children's television programmes in the early 1990s had led children to become more environmentally concerned. I had set myself this question with no particular awareness of the enormous problems at the heart of 'media effects' research – but I was soon to discover them. Because I was looking for some kind of media 'effect', it seemed to be a good starting-point to review this literature, even though much of it was concerned with the possible impact of media representations of *violence* on children. (A smaller number of studies concerned the effect of health and safety campaigns, and educational television programmes.)

The problems with these studies were of two kinds. First, a surprisingly high proportion of the studies seemed to have been simply done *badly*: inappropriate measures were used, data were distorted and participants were subject to inept instances of experimenter demand (for details see Gauntlett, 1995, 2005). A more fundamental problem was that they typically only gave participants the opportunity to either prove, or not-prove, a predetermined hypothesis. (I say 'not-prove' rather than 'disprove', because effects researchers seemed to assume that their predicted 'media effects' were always happening but, like cunning foxes, were not always easy to catch.)

Secondly, there was the even bigger problem that the whole idea of a 'media effect' as conceived in these studies – in which it was imagined that a person would view some media (such as a video showing scenes of violence) and as a consequence would behave differently (such as becoming more violent themselves) – was terribly simple-minded. On the one hand, when set up in this way, a media effect should be quite straightforward to detect. On the other hand, it made no sense because any media influence would surely be cumulative, developing over a matter of years, and would be so mixed up with a massive range of other influences (parents, friends, school) that it would be impossible to single out the 'media' component anyway. The flipside of this point is that if a single video or film clip *did* have the power to make people behave anti-socially, then any typical media diet would have correspondingly turned most of the population into full-time thugs. Crime statistics show that this is not generally the case.

My detailed literature review took key studies apart one by one (and became the book *Moving Experiences*, Gauntlett, 1995, 2005), but I also tried to summarise the broader problems with this approach in the article 'Ten Things Wrong with the "Effects Model"' (Gauntlett, 1998, also in 2005). The term 'effects model' refers to the general approach and assumptions, as well as the particular studies, of the many researchers who have engaged with the idea of media cause-and-effect. I won't reproduce the arguments here in much detail, but the 'ten things wrong' were as follows (summarised from Gauntlett, 1998):

1 The effects model tackles social problems 'backwards' – because it begins by assuming the 'cause' is known already (the media), rather than starting with an exploration of the phenomenon in question (such as crime and violence).
2 The effects model treats children as inadequate – it does not assume that children are able to make meaningful sense of the media themselves.
3 Assumptions within the effects model are characterised by barely concealed conservative ideology.
4 The effects model inadequately defines its own objects of study – for example, very mild and very strong representations of violence would be bundled together as 'violence', as would the physical breaking of objects to achieve positive goals within the narrative.
5 The effects model is often based on artificial elements and assumptions within studies – such as the assumption that hitting a doll in an observed experiment is the same as hitting a person in real life.
6 The effects model is often based on studies with misapplied methodology (numerous examples).
7 The effects model is selective in its criticisms of media depictions of violence – for example, violence in entertainment films is reviled but distressing real-life violence in the news is usually not.
8 The effects model assumes superiority to the masses – because researchers, teachers and well-educated adults are taken to be immune, whilst some distant 'other' group of children and the underclass are at risk from its messages.
9 The effects model makes no attempt to understand meanings of the media – the context of incidents within stories is not considered at all.
10 The effects model is not grounded in theory – there is no underlying meaningful model of *why* people's behaviour should be changed just because they have seen things on a screen.

In short, this was not a research tradition you'd want to buy into, and a research tradition which barely even made sense. But meanwhile, I was still meant to be doing a PhD about the influence of TV on children's awareness of environmental issues. It was therefore clear that I had to do *something else*. Being based in a well-equipped media department, and having always admired community art and photography projects, my solution was to take video cameras into primary schools and work with groups of children to make videos about 'the environment'. Although not tackling the 'effects' question in a direct way, this gave me a sideways entry-point into understanding what the children felt about their environment, what mattered to them and some insights into how the media had steered these thoughts in certain directions. The study is described in more detail in Chapter 6. For now, I just want to highlight two points. First, each group produced a video film by the end of six weeks, and this was usually an informative and entertaining summary of their concerns. However, the video *itself* was not the crucial piece of sociological 'data'. The most valuable data gathered was the observation of the *process* of each video's production – the discussions, the choices, what was put in and what was left out. This provided a rich seam of qualitative information based around a specified creative task.

Second, my first meeting with each group of children was like a focus group where they apparently told me their feelings about environmental issues. However, the 'findings' of any of those first-week sessions were revealed, by the end of each six-week video-making process, to have been very poor accounts of what actually concerned the participants. In the first-week discussions, the children were typically excited about the environment as an issue (even cheering 'hooray!' when it was first mentioned) and could name various dimensions of environmental concern, and suggest solutions. Their enthusiasm was clear but unrefined – and an interviewer can't say, 'Okay, but what do you *really* care about?' when faced with interviewees who have already said that they care about everything. A lot of research is based on just one encounter – and it is assumed that one focus group provides useful qualitative data. This study enabled me to *compare* focus group responses, from the first week, with richer and less 'performed' data gathered over the following weeks; and this showed that one-off focus groups can have significant limitations and, in these particular cases at least, were not especially useful at all.

This experience, then, established for me the value of research activities which allow time for participants to reflect; which get them doing or making something; and which do not expect that responses to a research topic can necessarily be articulated straight away in language. The value of the video-making method led me to take an interest in other artistic, construction and media-making activities that could be used as part of social research; and so led, in time, to this book.

Two more starting-points

A couple of other kicking-off points are worth a mention, both 'classics' in media audience studies if only for the *problems* that they raise. First, there is Ien Ang's influential *Watching Dallas* (1985), which was one of the earliest studies to get responses from media audiences in unconventional ways. Her study was based on the 42 letters she received in response to an advert placed in the Dutch magazine *Viva*, which asked readers to 'write and tell me why you like watching [*Dallas*] ... or dislike it' (p. 10). Ang was reasonably cautious and circumspect in her treatment of her data, and qualitative researchers can be allowed some leeway in how they find willing participants. Nevertheless, we are obliged to note that this was – to be polite – a *distinctly whimsical* form of sampling or recruitment, since it gives us only the responses of a very particular self-selected group of people who happened to see Ang's advert, and then had both the time and the motivation to write down their thoughts about this TV show and post it to an unknown researcher. If Ang had wanted to treat this group as a good sample of *Dallas* viewers, and show what they had in common, she would have been in terrible trouble. However, her study has a different orientation and is reasonably able to identify *diversity*: she finds that each viewer relates to *Dallas* differently. It is especially significant that Ang does not feel that the letter-writers' motives can be read off from their letters:

What people say or write about their experiences, preferences, habits, etc., cannot be taken entirely at face value, for in the routine of daily life they do not demand rational consciousness; they go unnoticed, as it were. They are commonsensical, self-evident; they require no further explanations. This means that we cannot let the letters speak for themselves, but they should be read 'symptomatically': we must search for what is behind the explicitly written, for the presuppositions and accepted attitudes concealed within them.

(Ang, 1985: 11)

Disappointingly, of course, Ang has no particular method with which to achieve this (informed guesswork notwithstanding). Attitudes which are *actually expressed* are fine: if a letter-writer was to say 'Like most Dutch people, I hate the Americans', then we would be able to see both a personal attitude being expressed, and also a presupposition about how this attitude sits within the context of other national views. But how do we find the 'concealed' attitudes, the views which (by definition) are not included in the words actually written down? If 'we cannot let the letters speak for themselves', then what *can* we do? I don't have the answers to these questions, by the way; I am not sure they are answerable. When you can only 'know' a person from a single text which they have posted to you, how can you judge them on anything except ... the single text which they have posted to you?

My second starting-point in this section is David Buckingham's (1993a) discussion of his attempts to explore young males' relationships with television. In this study, Buckingham and colleagues had interviewed small groups of boys aged 8 to 12 about a range of film and television programmes, but found that the interviews could not straightforwardly be said to reveal 'information' about this topic. Instead, the data represented a set of *performances* of masculinity, produced by each boy for the others in the group, and (perhaps secondarily) for the researcher. Therefore, brash and confident talk about action and horror films, for example, was more likely to be produced because it would create a positive impression amongst peers. Furthermore, each performance was 'policed' by the others, whose keen eye for potential humiliations would lead them to swoop in on any instance of apparently 'feminine' attitudes, or signs of sexual feeling. Therefore, for example, there was no sense in which a boy could admit to liking a female star or soap character, without being made fun of. If he claimed to admire her *as a person* then he would be teased for this suspiciously effeminate view; if he appeared to like her in a sexual sense – to 'fancy' someone – this would be even more taboo. In fact no such viewpoint would ever be expressed in any detail, as the continuous 'policing' process would detect even a hint of controversial material and head it off at the pass. Buckingham observes that in the interview discussions, 'there is a sense in which the boys are constantly putting themselves at risk – primarily of humiliation or ridicule by each other – and then rapidly withdrawing' (p. 103).

Unable to hide from the difficulties of analysing this data, Buckingham makes those problems the very *point* of his article. Focus groups, he suggests, may provide researchers with useful insights regarding the performances which participants are willing to generate in particular contexts – which may, in themselves, be interesting – but not direct access to individual beliefs.

> Rather than regarding masculinity as something simply fixed or given, I want to suggest that it is, at least to some extent, actively defined in social interaction and in discourse … Rather than regarding talk as a transparent reflection of what goes on in people's heads, I have attempted to analyse talk as a *social act* which serves specific social functions and purposes.
>
> (Buckingham, 1993a: 92)

Just as Ang was stuck with 'just' the contents of her letters, Buckingham effectively admits to being stuck with the talk generated in particular research situations, unable to say with any certainty whether his data represent 'real' views, entirely fake 'performances' or something in between. His study also raises the idea that these apparently opposite positions (authentic 'truth' versus performed 'fiction') may be rather indistinguishable and intertwined: could there be a meaningful separation between how I communicate my self to others, and the self that I 'actually' have? Buckingham notes that masculinity is not a 'unitary or fixed' characteristic which would be simply *conveyed* through speech; rather, 'masculinity is actively produced and sustained through talk

... subject to negotiation and redefinition as the talk proceeds ... Masculinity, we might say, is achieved rather than given' (p. 97).

We can broaden this point to note that the whole presentation of identity is a dynamic process, an active production, continually achieved through verbal and non-verbal communication. Researchers cannot escape this fact; any research activity has to accept it and work with it. These two studies by Ang, and Buckingham – the former less intentionally and the latter more explicitly – remind us that researchers always have to work with certain kinds of data, gathered in particular ways; and that this data will usually have a mangled relationship with the stuff that was originally in participants' heads.

Thinking about modern identities: Anthony Giddens and Tracey Emin

This book also builds upon ideas which I associate with two people who are not an obvious pairing: the sociologist Anthony Giddens and the controversial contemporary artist, Tracey Emin. Let's begin with the academic. Anthony Giddens established (or, arguably, drew together and popularised) a model of how self-identity is an especially important and active concept for everyone living in developed Western societies. I devoted a whole chapter to Giddens's ideas about this theme in *Media, Gender and Identity* (Gauntlett, 2002), so here I will only set out the highlights which are important to us for this book.

Giddens argues that we are living in a period of 'late modernity', within which all social activity has become the object of reflection and analysis, at all levels from everyday romantic relationships to, say, the workings of government and industry. In traditional societies, social roles were more or less 'given', but in the post-traditional age, responsibilities and expectations become more fluid and subject to negotiation (Giddens, 1991, 1992). At the same time, of course, *other people's expectations* have a strong influence upon behaviour, and social actors continue to have a strong and sometimes very pointed sense of 'normal' conduct, reinforced by the discourses of tabloid newspapers, radio DJs, TV presenters and everything that gossip magazines find 'shocking' or 'embarrassing'. At the same time – even within the same moments – the media contribute significantly to our awareness of social changes and different ways of living.

Perhaps the most significant consequence of this heightened reflexivity is that all social actors have to think about their identity: it becomes inescapable. 'Thinking about identity' may sound like the province of a therapy-going elite, or an activity for the readers of self-help books, and therefore not something done by everyone across the social spectrum. But Giddens points out that today we are increasingly aware of choices and alternatives, so that even the most predictable and commonplace way of living is necessarily a choice to not do something else. Critics observe that, if you're a single parent living in a tower block with no money, a world of playful choices seems like a bourgeois fantasy. I think Giddens would reply that, although many such people face very harsh constraints, the idea of thinking about lifestyle and identity is still put onto their agenda repeatedly by popular discourses, circulated by the media. As Giddens (1991: 70) puts it:

> What to do? How to act? Who to be? These are focal questions for everyone living in circumstances of late modernity – and ones which, on some level or another, all of us answer, either discursively or through day-to-day social behaviour.
>
> (Giddens, 1991: 70)

This does not mean that people are in a continual state of 'identity crisis'. It is rather that the brain's back-burner is aware of these questions and choices, more than ever before, and that this has important implications for society: Giddens developed the idea of 'structuration', which binds together everyday behaviour and broad social forces in one model, which will be discussed in Chapter 4.

The inescapable nature of identity questions perhaps explains the popularity of artists such as Tracey Emin, who have caught the public imagination by dealing with intimate autobiographical issues. Emin became well-known in the UK in the late 1990s, and continues to fascinate popular media audiences (or, at least, producers). Although she did not win the 1999 Turner Prize, her show in the accompanying exhibition of shortlisted artists at Tate Britain was consistently the most packed, as the public marvelled at her autobiographical artefacts, including handwritten texts, tapestries, videos, sketches, and *My Bed*, the notorious exhibit of her actual bed as seen at the end of a period of depression surrounded by discarded pregnancy tests, vodka bottles, polaroids and cigarette packets. Emin tells stories about her life which are at once apparently 'spontaneous' eruptions of intimate information and also very carefully constructed ruminations on memory and personal history and a kind of battle for self-identity. She has said, 'There should be something revelatory about art. It should be totally creative and open doors for new thoughts and experiences' (European Graduate School, 2005). Emin has become a significant 'celebrity' in the UK – attracting attention from the tabloids, unusually for an artist – but (or perhaps, *therefore*) much that has been written about her seems to dwell on her personality rather than her work. After interviewing her in 2002, Melanie McGrath seems to have got to grips with the connection between the two:

> This brings me to something important about Emin and her work. It's important but it's difficult to say without being misconstrued. You see, Tracey Emin is narcissistic. And by that I don't mean that she loves herself.

I mean that Tracey Emin loves an image which may or may not be herself but of which she can never be sure. I mean that Emin only half recognises her own projection. And this, of course, is why her work is so lonely, so furious and so demanding of attention. When you look at Tracey Emin's work you see the artist struggling to reach herself, compelled by her own self-consciousness to fail and condemned by the self-same thing to begin again. What you see up on the wall or in the bed or on the screen is Emin's own reflection, exiled.

(McGrath, 2002)

Emin's work therefore represents an extreme case of the idea that making artistic work gives a person the opportunity to externalise, and therefore diffuse, their personal pain. McGrath's point is that the fascination lies in the artist's repeated failure to achieve this kind of resolution. On the other hand, given the range of problems Emin has faced, we can see from many interviews that her artistic output (and the level of professional success and recognition which it has attained) *has* helped her to become happier, and that she 'needs' her art to sustain her existence. The fact that this work has caught the public imagination, rather than being an isolated therapeutic project, is partly because Emin herself has made this personal material public, and proudly sought fame and success; but must also be because we, the public, are also constructing narratives of our intimate lives and so have an immediate engagement with art which is so directly about that topic.

Outline of the book

The following chapter begins to consider individuality and identity, and discusses their expression through creativity, before looking at the ways in which some well-known artists have engaged with ideas about personal identity in their work. As this book is about embracing people's creativity within *empirical research* about identity – rather than just artistic self-expression – I take a step back in Chapter 3 to consider the philosophy of science. In other words, I look at debates about what we can reasonably say about the world, and what counts as evidence. Chapter 4 considers the sociological debates about the degree to which individuals are free to create their own social realities, and the extent to which we can make use of their own accounts of their experiences. The concern in both of these chapters is the question of whether necessarily 'subjective' and 'artistic' data can form part of a scientific study of human life. Continuing this interest in combining social theory with scientific realism, in Chapter 5 I look at perspectives from neuroscience on what consciousness, and therefore awareness of personal identity, really means.

Having established a set of principles in the first half of the book, in Chapters 6 and 7 I look at previous studies which have used visual and creative methods, including a couple of my own, and I consider the emerging fields of 'visual sociology' and 'visual culture'. In Chapter 8 I unveil the research study to which, in a sense, all of the preceding chapters have been building up. In this project, participants were led through a process which encouraged them to reflect upon identities and metaphors, and ultimately asked them to build a metaphorical model of their own identity in Lego. The chapter outlines the Lego Serious Play consultancy process upon which this research method was based (in a research collaboration with the Educational Division of the Lego Group), its underlying psychology and philosophy, and the use of metaphors in research, including examples of metaphors created by participants in the study. Chapter 9 discusses the meaning of the identity models built within the study, and connects these with Paul Ricoeur's arguments about narrative identity. Finally, Chapter 10 sets out a number of conclusions and findings, about creative research methods, social experience and identities, and media audiences.

Chapter 2

The self and creativity

Thinking about self-identity and individuality can cause some anxiety – at least in cultures where individuals are encouraged to value their personal uniqueness. Each of us would like to think – to some extent – that we have special, personal qualities, which make us distinctive and valuable to the other people in our lives (or potential *future* friends). But does this mean anything? Is individuality just an illusion? Maybe we are all incredibly similar, but are programmed to value miniscule bits of differentiation. The first part of this chapter begins to look at these questions, with brief reference to both science and literature. Then I go on to consider creativity, which is where human individuality perhaps seems most observable and meaningful. A creative achievement means that someone not only *thinks* they are a distinctive individual, but has actually got something to show for it. I therefore proceed to consider the works of some noted artists, to see how they have worked with ideas about the individual identity in a social world.

Isolated individuals?

For those who want to believe in their personal uniqueness, science can be quite reassuring. At the level of the biological formation of the brain – a rather simple level, which doesn't tell us much about what the mind actually *does* – we can be sure that we are all different. As neuroscientist Antonio Damasio notes, 'Because our encounters with the environment are unique, the brain circuitries are shaped somewhat differently in each of us' (2001: 59). Even twins do not have the same neural wiring.

In the past, sociologists would often choose to ignore or be dismissive about neuroscience, because we would tend to assume that the philosophical implications of everyday life cannot be worked out by looking at brain scans; because of an insecurity about what is and is not regarded as 'science'; and because we are rightly anxious about the possible stench of sociobiology – the idea entertained by racists and others that we can distinguish (and therefore discriminate) between different social groups on a biological basis. Indeed, brain science would obviously be problematic if it was trying to argue that the brains of people in group A are different to the brains of people in group B, and that therefore we should treat the As and Bs differently. But if brain science is merely suggesting to us that people's brains are generally somewhat diverse, this can be worth knowing, if only to comfort ourselves that individuality is not just a psychological illusion but is biologically meaningful as well.

Indeed, we might begin to bridge the traditional divide between the natural sciences and the arts and humanities by making use of recent findings in the neurosciences which give us foundational information upon which we can build theories. If a social or philosophical theory, however complex, sits coherently on top of the building-blocks of neuroscience as currently understood, then both sides can be happy; whereas if a social theory has no correspondence with what science tells us about the brain – if it makes assumptions about how people tick which neuroscience would actually say are *wrong* – then we might be a little worried, even though we are sure that science doesn't have all the answers.

To readers of sociological and philosophical theory, a lot of modern neuroscience can seem surprisingly simplistic (even though the scientific procedures are highly advanced). It can seem strange, and rather old-fashioned, that scientists are still working out which bits of the brain process which types of information. Nevertheless, neuroscientists are typically modest about the limits of their work – unlike cultural theorists, who usually manage to get away with grandiose abstractions. Indeed, the modesty of much high-level contemporary science compares favourably with the arrogance of some of our most celebrated broad-brush social theories. Not all science is lovely, and it is not value-free; but there's no escaping the fact that no scientist could get away with shooting out the kind of cool-sounding randomness which brought attention and status to cultural theorists like Jean Baudrillard or Camille Paglia. This is not to say that all science should be embraced, but rather that we can at least try to see where its propositions may be philosophically fruitful. Neurobiologist and philosopher of science Gunther Stent offers a good example:

> Structuralism provided the insight … that knowledge about the world of phenomena enters the mind not as raw data but in an already highly abstract form, namely as 'structures'. In the preconscious process of converting the primary sensory data, step by step, into structures, information is necessarily lost because the creation of structures, or the recognition of patterns, is nothing other than the selective destruction of information. The mind creates a pattern from the mass of sensory data by throwing away this, throwing away that. Finally, what's left of the data is a structure in which the mind perceives something meaningful.
>
> (Stent, 2001: 36)

Stent notes that this 'eliminative view of cognition' has received support from recent neuroscientific research, and it is certainly provocative for the sociologist. Stent himself adds: 'I think this is one of the few philosophical implications neurobiology has so far produced' (ibid). If people make sense of the world through a process of destroying a mass of 'data' at high speed, and slotting it into established patterns and categories by which we can recognise what is left, this could form part of an explanation of many social phenomena from, for example, religion (which offers a set of ready-made structures to help people make sense of the world) to prejudice (which occurs when ready-made structures are imposed without reflective thought). To think about this neuroscientific finding in a different way, one could remark that if people are smashing environmental and sensory data into bits to make sense of it – and discarding most of it – it is amazing that we manage to end up with any compatible worldviews at all.

This returns us to the matter of the uniqueness of each individual consciousness. William James, the American pioneer of psychology, discussed it in these terms, in 1890:

> In this room – this lecture room, say – there are a multitude of thoughts, yours and mine, some of which cohere mutually, and some not. They are as little each-for-itself and reciprocally independent as they are all-belonging-together. They are neither: no one of them is separate, but each belongs with certain others and with none beside. My thought belongs with my other thoughts and your thought with your other thoughts. Whether anywhere in the room there be a mere thought, which is nobody's thought, we have no means of ascertaining, for we have no experience of the like. The only states of consciousness that we naturally deal with are found in personal consciousness, minds, selves, concrete particular I's and you's.
>
> (James, [1890] 1950: 225–6)

Our thoughts, then, are unique and never directly connect or match with those of another, in the way that, say, a USB cable can move files directly from one computer to another. Nevertheless, through language and other forms of self-expression (formations of the body, such as gestures or facial expression, or products of the body, such as drawings) we can make communications about our consciousness and our sense of being in the world which others can connect with and feel that we are living within a set of collective understandings and share some sense of collective experience.

The comfort of shared sensations

Literature frequently deals with these issues – not least of all because each instance of literature is an example of a person seeking to create a representation of consciousness, outside of themselves, which others may be able to connect with. Ian McEwan's best-selling novel *Saturday* (2005), for example, is a detailed description of one man's consciousness during one day (of course, this is not new in itself – see *Ulysses* by James Joyce (1922) and *Mrs Dalloway* by Virginia Woolf (1925), for instance). Here, at the start of the day, for example, Henry Perowne is getting on with getting up while still struggling to wake up:

> He's trying to locate a quite different source of shame, or guilt, or something far milder, like the memory of some embarrassment or foolishness. It passed through his thoughts only minutes ago, and now what remains is the feeling without its rationale. A sense of having behaved or spoken laughably. Of having been a fool. Without the memory of it, he can't talk himself out of it … The grandeur. He must have hallucinated the phrase out of the hairdryer's drone, and confused it with the radio news. The luxury of being half asleep, exploring the fringes of psychosis in safety.
>
> (McEwan, 2005: 57)

I suppose I selected this bit because I was comforted to find my own inability to straightforwardly 'file' all of my thoughts was being echoed by another. So I am pleased to find that my brain functions may have something in common with those of the interesting and successful writer Ian McEwan. (I am assuming that McEwan's character's brain-functionings are not wholly imagined, but are based on his own.) So a connection is made. Whereas, in perhaps the most telling, and arguably most frightening, bit of *American Psycho* by Bret Easton Ellis (1991), the narrator referred to in the title, Patrick Bateman, indicates that, in his case, this kind of connection is not going to be possible.

> There is an idea of a Patrick Bateman, some kind of abstraction, but there is no real me, only an entity, something illusory, and though I can hide my cold gaze and you can shake my hand and feel flesh gripping yours and maybe you can even sense our lifestyles are probably comparable: *I simply am not there*… . I am a noncontingent human being… . But even after admitting this – and I have, countless times, in just about every act I've committed – and coming face-to-face with these truths, there is no catharsis. I gain no deeper knowledge about myself, no new understanding can be extracted from my telling.
>
> (Easton Ellis, 1991: 376–7)

I have quoted this in a previous book about identity, and make no apologies for repeating it here, because it reminds us in a rather eerie way of the reliance which we have on the *assumption*, for which we usually have no evidence, that our experience of the world is similar to other people's, and that the consciousness behind someone else's eyes is more or less knowable and not wildly different to our own. Personally, when I was younger, and even today, one of my comforts from the mass media is the sense that it can help me come to know people, through stories, and feel some sense of commonality. (Even if they are fictional characters, they are usually intended to be recognisable as possible people.) Put like that, it may sound a bit odd – perhaps I am unusually insecure! – but the popularity of storytelling through the ages suggests that this urge to connect with a shared sense of experience is common.

Putting together experience

Another aspect of experience that we take for granted is that the brain will put together a mass of data, in any one moment, continuously, to provide us with one complete (but ever-changing) sense of what's going on. As the Nobel Prize-winning neuroscientist Gerald Edelman observes, we apprehend the world, in each moment, as a 'unitary scene', although the scene may change continuously as we receive new stimuli or have new thoughts.

> The number of such differentiated scenes seems endless, yet each is unitary. The scene … can contain many disparate elements – sensations, perceptions, images, memories, thoughts, emotions, aches, pains, vague feelings, and so on. Looked at from the inside, consciousness seems continually to change, yet at each moment is all of a piece – what I have called 'the remembered present' – reflecting the fact that all my past experience is engaged in forming my integrated awareness of this single moment.
>
> (Edelman, 2005: 8)

At the same time, we have an ongoing sense of self which seems more permanent, an underlying identity which experiences all these moments but is not usually changed by them. We are happy to accept that a person's emotions or even attitudes can change quite quickly, as a result of external inputs or internal thoughts; but change to the underlying identity is assumed to be far more gradual and incremental; we look doubtfully at someone who says they feel like a completely different person to who they were last week, or last month.

It is common in contemporary sociology to assume that this sense of self-identity is a construction; something we like to believe in to make life more tolerable and comprehensible. For instance, Anthony Giddens, mentioned in the previous chapter, makes the argument that in contemporary modern societies, individuals create a 'narrative of the self' to explain their journey through the social world and their sense of who they are (1991, 1992). Michel Foucault showed that individuals are required to create a sense of an ethical self, and that different cultures – historically, or geographically – might conceive of this in markedly different ways (1990, 2000). And as we will see in Chapter 9, Paul Ricoeur argued that we make use of stories, from literature and popular culture, to help us assemble the narrative of our own lives (1984, 1988, 1992).

These arguments are convincing, but can lead us to become derailed if we misunderstand their implications. There is a tendency to think that the idea that self-identity is socially constructed is the same as saying that it doesn't really exist, that it is just an illusion. But that does not follow. Of course your identity is 'all in your mind' – where else would it be? – and is influenced by social discourses – how could it not be? Nevertheless, the sense of a reasonably consistent self-identity is very important to each of us. I have talked about identity with many people – students, friends and acquaintances, academics and research participants across a broad spectrum – and have not come across anyone who wants to claim that they have *no identity at all*. Although academic argument may say that identity is just a set of stories that we tell ourselves, I haven't met anyone who says that they have no particular identity or set of core values (although, of course, certain individuals may exist who *do* say that). A socially constructed identity is one which has been, as the phrase suggests, built, and brought into being. If a sense of identity is common, and central to human experience, then any amount of discussion about where this comes from is secondary to the fact that it *is* common and central to human experience.

Individuality and the unique properties of identity are often seen to reach their zenith in human creativity – the amazing expressive or technological things we are able to *make* in the world. The achievements of great composers, writers, engineers and scientists seem to 'prove' the enterprising power of the independent human spirit – or the capacity of several such spirits working in collaboration. On a more everyday level, individuals tend to feel a special sense of accomplishment when we have made something solid and visible – external proof of our own personal vitality. So here I turn to a discussion of creativity.

What is creativity?

Creativity seems often to be considered on two different levels. First there is the 'grand' level of creativity – the high profile kind of creativity which wins you a Nobel Prize for your unique contribution to human knowledge. Such distinctive performance is relatively straightforward to identify, especially if it is defined as a level of achievement which has been socially *recognised*. This kind of high-impact creativity has been studied by Mihaly Csikszentmihalyi, whose book *Creativity* is based on interviews with 91 highly successful creative people (14 of whom actually *had* won Nobel Prizes, and 'many of the others' accomplishments were of the same order': 1997: 13), and by Howard Gardner, whose even more selective method is helpfully summarised in the title of his book, *Creating Minds: An Anatomy of Creativity Seen through the Lives of Freud, Einstein, Picasso, Stravinsky, Eliot, Graham, and Gandhi* (1993). By looking at the most extreme instances of creativity, writers such as Csikszentmihalyi and Gardner hope to find clues towards the identification of factors which enable creative accomplishments to emerge. Their sociological approach tends, as we will see shortly, to find that creative achievements appear in certain circumstances and environments; creative impact arises from someone doing something clever at the right place and at the right time. The 'something clever' is likely to be a valuable and unique contribution – the specialness of their idea is not to be denied – but it is not the product of sheer magic; it is more usually the result of hard work in a supportive environment.

The second form of creativity is much more commonplace. Most of us feel that we have done numerous 'creative' things in our lives, even though the Nobel Prize committee has never invited us round for dinner, nor even looked up our telephone number. We might feel that we do several creative things every day. Creativity in this sense is not limited to certain exceptional individuals, nor to certain memorable products – so, in your own life, it is not just that painting you did on your 16th birthday, that jug you made in a pottery class, or the card you made for your partner last Christmas. Creativity in this broad sense can include everyday ideas, writing, making, management, self-presentation and even creative speech or thought.

The cut-off line for creativity, when we get down to this level, is necessarily fuzzy, subjective and relative. As I write this text, maybe I have to accept that the sentence about the Nobel Prize committee coming round for dinner was more creative than, say, this one, which merely repeats a line from earlier up the page. If something as apparently mundane as a choice of clothing can be 'creative', you might feel that the outfit you wore on Saturday was quite creative, but that today's is not. You could argue endlessly, if you wanted to be rather trivial, about whether one thing 'is' and another thing 'is not' creative. But that's not really the point. The point is that creativity is widely dispersed and, more importantly, is one of the most central aspects of being human.

When we think of 'creative' activities we often pick 'artistic' examples – as I did above, with the painting and the pot and the Christmas card. But of course creativity, and its communication, can take many forms. The composer Bruce Adolphe tells this story:

> I was at a music festival a number of years ago. Because I was there as a composer, I was not directly involved in rehearsals and would sit outside on the porch and listen to the music. This particular day, I happened to be sitting next to someone who turned to me and asked, 'Aren't you a composer with the festival?' 'Yes,' I answered. 'Well,' he remarked, 'we both do the same thing, we project abstract thought into a logical format, making it available.' 'Oh,' I said, 'what kind of music do you write?' And he answered, 'I design weapons systems'.

> (Adolphe, 2001: 69)

That these two forms of creativity – making music and making weapons – should be equated seems rather shocking and is, of course, the humorous/ disturbing point of the anecdote. Creativity is traditionally seen as the domain of artists rather than, say, managers, government agents or scientists. Indeed the debate between artistic and scientific notions of creativity appears in various contributions to the book *The Origins of Creativity*, edited by Karl Pfenninger and Valerie Shubik (2001). Gunther Stent argues that art and science are fundamentally similar, as they both 'seek to discover and communicate novel truths about the world' (2001: 35). He notes that we tend to judge science on the ideas or discoveries involved, whereas in art it is the *form* of their communication which preoccupies us. So we admire Watson and Crick's paper revealing the structure of DNA because of this discovery itself, not because of how it was written up; whereas we admire Shakespeare's play *Timon of Athens* because of the unique way in which the Bard has brought to life Timon's tribulations, in words, and not because of the story itself, which is unremarkable and which, in any case, was not original to Shakespeare, who had borrowed it from a book of classic stories (Stent, 2001: 34). Creative works of art *or* science make propositions about the world, albeit in different ways.

Thomas Cech, however, replies in the same book by pointing out that scientists and artists have quite different intentions. A number of scientists working on the same problem are striving towards the same goal – they want to reach the one 'perfect' explanation, which the field (the audience of scientists and other interested parties) will agree is the correct one. Whereas a number of artists working on the same 'problem' – which in this case might be, say, the nature of identity or memory – will expect to produce strikingly *different* 'answers' to this issue and would be embarrassed if their proposition was very similar to someone else's.

Perhaps we can take from this that 'creativity' can mean different things – unsurprisingly. For scientists a 'creative' breakthrough might mean seeing something in an entirely new light; for artists, it might be a form of presentation which is successful because it enables some of its *audience* to see something in a new light. You could say that scientists seek to 'discover' fact, whilst artists seek to 'discover' feeling. But both, as Stent noted, are about making inventive propositions, and trying to say something new about the world. The painter Françoise Gilot says that art is 'a kind of mediation between the individual, nature and society ... through which we can find an order that will enrich the imagination and lead to new, more complex truths' (2001: 176). This seems fair enough and, although subjective, seems to be a reasonable inductive explanation for the fact of the enduring role of art in human societies.

Summarising the neuroscientific perspective, Pfenninger and Shubik offer this definition or outline of creativity:

Creativity must be the ability to generate in one's brain (the association cortex), novel contexts and representations that elicit associations with symbols and principles of order ... Creativity further must include the ability to translate the selected representations into a work of art or science.

(Pfenninger and Shubik, 2001: 235)

To see creativity as the generation of new contexts and representations, and the application of them to something, is fine but doesn't really seem to tell us anything new. This ability has been cultivated through both evolution and culture. The evolution of the association cortex in humans, which suggests connections between things, holds them in memory and enables us to work on them, is important; so too is the cultural learning about art and ideas and their contexts, which provide an essential foundation to our thinking. 'Advances in modern neuroscience have demystified creativity', then, as Pfenninger and Shubik say (2001: 236), but none of it seems like a revelation. Maybe then we should return to the studies of the Nobel Prize winners after all, to see what this can tell us about creativity more generally.

What can we learn from the grand creatives?

As mentioned above, Mihaly Csikszentmihalyi (1997) and Howard Gardner (1993, 2001) have explored creativity by looking at extreme cases – people whose creative contribution to the world has been celebrated at the international level. This approach identifies a 'creative triangle' which affects the emergence of creative potential, and its acceptance within the culture. Of course, these studies, by choosing to look at widely recognised cases of creativity, leave out those possibly brilliant creative people who have not, for whatever reason, achieved recognition in the culture. This is not an accident, or a problem, since this perspective holds that creativity is a culturally constructed phenomenon: therefore creativity that goes unrecognised doesn't really count.

The creative triangle connects three dimensions: the *individual*, the *domain* (the particular symbolic system in which the individual works) and the *field* (other people working in the domain). So imagine, for example, a sculptor called Kate. To assess Kate's chances of becoming recognised as a highly creative artist, we need to consider not only Kate's own talent and originality (the individual), but also the history and current state of sculpture, in particular the kind of sculpture that Kate produces (the domain), and her connections with curators, journalists, critics, art buyers and other gatekeepers (the field) who contribute to establishing who becomes recognised and celebrated. Without a knowledge of the domain, and connection with the field, Kate is unlikely to make an impact.

Because of this approach, Csikszentmihalyi's and Gardner's studies are good on how creative people manage to break through to national and international success, and give very interesting insights into the individual working methods and approaches of highly creative individuals. They are necessarily less good, though, on the 'raw' nature of creativity unfettered by the demands of what you might call the creativity marketplace. Nevertheless, interesting points emerge about the nature of creativity in general; here I have selected four of them.

A recursive process

Csikszentmihalyi notes that there is a traditional view of the creative process, which describes a five-step process from preparation and incubation, to insight, evaluation and elaboration. This is too simple and linear, he notes (1997: 78–81). These stages – or something like them – do develop, but recursively, with insights and reflections from 'later' parts of the process feeding back into 'earlier' stages and then leading to further insights, and so on. Different parts of the process can take minutes or months, and a set of creative cycles may add up to a summer of invention, or a whole lifetime. An important part of the process is the next feature:

The 'underground' incubation

The writer Douglas Adams prevaricated terribly when he was supposed to be writing, and famously commented, 'I love deadlines – I love the whooshing noise they make as they go by'. Although months or even years would pass before he was eventually locked in a hotel room by his publisher and forced to write, the non-writing time was not 'wasted' time, but was an essential part of the creative process. Although perhaps an extreme case, this 'underground' incubation seems to be common. Csikszentmihalyi notes, 'Our respondents unanimously agree that it is important to let problems simmer below the threshold of consciousness for a time' (1997: 98), and they report insights appearing whilst gardening, jogging, having a shower, driving, or as they wake up.

There are different psychological accounts of how this can be, ranging from the psychoanalytic to the cognitive, but it is commonly assumed that, as Csikszentmihalyi puts it, 'some kind of information processing keeps going on in the mind even when we are not aware of it, even when we are asleep' (1997: 101), and that this kind of processing, freed from the more plodding rational rules followed by the conscious mind, can make connections and link together ideas in a potentially fruitful way – eventually appearing in consciousness as a sudden, brilliant burst of 'inspiration'.

Csikszentmihalyi found that 'most of the people in our sample' could clearly recall an '"Aha!" moment' when the solution to a problem crystallised in their minds (1997: 103–4). So although the idea of an '"Aha!" moment' sounds rather magical and unscientific, there is a lot of evidence for it happening – even if we suspect that sometimes the dull reality may have been transformed into a more exciting anecdote – and it is certainly consistent with contemporary psychology and neuroscience, which accept that unconscious processing takes place even though there are debates about the form and function of these processes (as we will see in Chapter 5).

There is obviously a connection between these unconscious processes and the assumptions of the creative research methods discussed later in this book (and also, of course, art therapy), where it is hoped that an engagement in creative activity – rather than the more everyday activity of speech-generation – will prompt some of the ideas which 'simmer below the threshold of consciousness' to surface in the creative work.

Crossing boundaries

Creativity often takes place where one perspective meets another, or where the insights of one paradigm have a playful engagement with the subject-area of another. Csikszentmihalyi reports:

> A large majority of our respondents were inspired by a tension in their domain that became obvious when looked at from the perspective of another domain. Even though they do not think of themselves as interdisciplinary, their best work bridges realms of ideas. Their histories tend to cast doubt on the wisdom of overspecialisation, where bright young people are trained to become exclusive experts in one field and shun breadth like the plague.
>
> (Csikszentmihalyi, 1997: 89)

These creative masters may not *perceive* themselves as interdisciplinary, perhaps because their linking of spheres has been so successful that those areas are no longer thought of as distinct. In Gardner's study, Freud stands out as being a person who actually created a whole domain – namely psychoanalysis – and a field – the colleagues and followers who supported and governed the development of psychoanalysis. Others, such as Picasso, worked within a well established domain (in this case, visual art), but extended the borders of the domain by adding new dimensions, and challenged the field to see in a new way. Creating or transforming whole domains is highly unusual, but the creative stars in Gardner's and Csikszentmihalyi's studies are typically people who have crossed borders between fields, played provocatively in the margins of accepted knowledge, or made links between previously separate systems or ideas.

Being in flow

In earlier work, Csikszentmihalyi had already established the idea of 'flow' – the optimal sense of an effortless but highly focused state of consciousness which means that a person can gain great enjoyment from 'work' activity (see Csikszentmihalyi, [1990] 2002). As the author explains, these are states of optimal experience,

> in which attention can be freely invested to achieve a person's goals, because there is no disorder to straighten out, no threat for the self to defend against. We have called this state the *flow experience*, because this is the term many of the people we interviewed had used in their descriptions of how it felt to be in top form: 'It was like floating,' 'I was carried along by the flow'.
>
> (Csikszentmihalyi, [1990] 2002: 40)

Unsurprisingly, the author finds that in his *Creativity* study, 'it is easy to recognise the conditions of flow in the accounts of our respondents'. These include: having a clear goal or problem to solve; ability to discern how well one is doing; struggling forward in the face of challenges until 'the creative process begins to hum' and one is 'lost' in the task; and enjoying the activity for its own sake (1997: 113–26).

In everyday life, just as it is for famous creatives, 'flow' activities are those which are somewhat challenging. A person can fall out of flow if the task is too difficult, causing anxiety, or too simple, causing boredom. Rewarding self-contained activities can enhance the sense of flow in everyday life. As it happens, Csikszentmihalyi influenced the development of Lego Serious Play (see Chapter 8) and participants absorbed in the Lego building process are good examples of individuals 'in flow'.

Back to everyday creativity

The 'symptoms' of creativity identified by Csikszentmihalyi are surely present in more everyday manifestations of creative activity. However, it perhaps remains unclear what everyday creativity looks like. The 'grand creative' behaviour is much easier to spot: when I unveil my latest experimental painting, invite you to my new ballet, or indeed show you the weapons system I've just built, we can probably agree that these are pretty straightforward cases of creative production. But when I've made a joke, or a sandwich, or arranged some cups in an unusual style, and if I am known not as 'an artist' or 'a designer', but as 'an accountant' or 'a builder' or 'a nurse', we are then less certain about whether we can label my stuff as creative.

So what is the common form of creativity? Psychometric tests are used by employers and schools to assess how creative a person is, on the everyday level. These tests are usually underpinned by the assumption that creativity is about divergent thinking – being able to think of several different answers to a question. A 'creativity test' might show you an unusual object and ask you to list possible uses for it, for example, or ask you to list the consequences of people no longer needing to sleep (Plucker and Renzulli, 1999). These kinds of tests measure *something*, but arguably they might show that someone is quite quick and 'free' in their thought, but may not show whether they are able to create suggestions which are especially insightful, useful, original or beautiful. It remains debatable whether any of these things are important for creativity per se.

In terms of how we should *study* creativity, a number of contributors to the state-of-the-field volume *Handbook of Creativity* (Sternberg, 1999) suggest that creativity is complex and cannot be studied by one method alone: a multidimensional, interdisciplinary approach is required. It probably helps to be similarly inclusive about acceptable definitions of creativity itself.

Lumsden (1999) considered a range of definitions from leading figures, and concluded that 'the "definitions" of creativity I have seen in the literature … carry the unique imprint of their progenitors while suggesting some mild degree of consensus: creativity as a kind of capacity to think up something new that people find significant' (p. 153). This audience dimension – that 'people' should find the creative output to be somehow 'significant' – is indeed a frequent aspect of definitions of creativity.

When talking about 'creative methods' myself, I am simply referring to methods in which people express themselves in non-traditional (non-verbal) ways, through making something. So this is a very basic interpretation of creativity – that it involves *creating* a physical thing – although it fits with common-sense usage. 'Very creative!', we say, when our friend has decorated a cake nicely, indicating that an element of surprising revelation is also involved (even in this banal example) – which connects with the need for a positive audience response, mentioned above. If our friend decorated cakes in the same way every day, however, we certainly *wouldn't* exclaim 'Very creative!' each time. So this particular understanding of creativity involves the physical making of something, leading to some form of communication, expression or revelation. Of course, creativity means lots of other things too – there are other forms, and other kinds, of creativity. But then it gets more fuzzy, and can start to seem meaningless. In this context, going with a 'common-sense' interpretation of the term is probably as good as any, and will not be inconsistent with common expectations.

Why creativity?

If we have made a start on the definition of creativity – the 'what' – we are perhaps still left with the question of the 'why'. Why do we like to create? Creative activity seems to give people a special buzz. It is perhaps self-evident that making something new should be rewarding – whether this is a painting, a machine or just a humorous remark made in conversation. David Bohm, regarded as one of the greatest physicists of the twentieth century, suggests that something underlies human creative activity, whether it be in the sciences or the arts:

> Man has a fundamental need to *assimilate* all his experience, both of the external environment and of his internal psychological process. Failing to do so is like not properly digesting food … Psychological experiences that are not properly 'digested' can work in the mind as viruses do in the body, to produce a 'snow-balling' state of ever-growing disharmony and conflict, which tends to destroy the mind as effectively as unassimilated proteins can destroy the body.
>
> (Bohm, [1968] 1998: 27)

Science is a desire to understand the universe, then, and to feel 'at home' in it, and making art can similarly be seen as a way of thinking through our place in existence. Bohm adds that religion also represents the desire for a holistic understanding of the universe; and that science, art and religion all look for a kind of *beauty*. Creative activity may thus be driven by a drive for assimilation, beauty and wholeness. It is also seen by Bohm as essential to human progress:

> Creativity is essential not only for science, but for the whole of life. If you get stuck in a mechanical repetitious order, then you will degenerate. That is one of the problems that has grounded every civilisation: a certain repetition.
>
> (Bohm, [1989] 1998: 108)

People have certainly been engaged in everyday creative expression for a very long time.* The Chauvet-Pont-d'Arc cave in southern France, for example, provides direct evidence of drawings that are at least 31,000 years old (Lewis-Williams, 2002; Clottes and Féruglio, 2004), and museums around the world contain tools, weapons, pots, art, inventions and writings from across the centuries. There is a lot of evidence that people like *making stuff*, in new and original ways, not only for its utility but because creativity carries its own rewards.

Friedrich Nietzsche suggested that human beings, since ancient times, have felt the need to make marks to represent their lives and experiences, not simply as a reflection of private dreams, or to communicate instrumental facts about survival, but as a kind of necessary celebration of existence: an 'impulse which calls art into being, as the complement and consummation of existence,

---

* Some of the examples in this particular section appeared previously in Chapter 11 of Gauntlett (2005).

seducing one to a continuation of life' ([1872] 1967: 43). This connects with Bohm's idea that creativity is about the assimilation of experience, but brings in the notion that it is also about *creating the circumstances in which life can carry on.*

For many centuries the purpose of art was generally seen as being the attempt to reflect the beauty of nature – stemming back to Aristotle's notion (*c*.384–322 BC) that the purpose of art should be the imitation of nature (*mimesis*). This would apply on the everyday as well as 'masterpiece' levels, and did not mean that art should strive for photographic reproduction of reality; rather, art should offer, as Richard Eldridge puts it, the 'presentation of a subject matter as a focus for thought, fused to perceptual experience of the work' (2003: 29), with truthfulness at a psychological or emotional level. This meant that music, for example, fitted this definition very well, despite being unable to provide a literal picture of the visible grandeur of nature. Furthermore, in *Poetics*, Aristotle argued that art arises because 'representation is natural to human beings from childhood', and because 'everyone delights in representations' and we like to learn from them (2004 : 4). He also stated that the function of art is 'not to relate things that have happened, but things that may happen, i.e. that are possible in accordance with probability or necessity' (p. 12), thereby suggesting that art is about possibilities, and perhaps a thinking through of ideas about ways of living.

Creativity and the inner world

Ancient ideas about art, then, were often quite sophisticated, but did not place special emphasis on the psychology of the artist themselves. It was only in the Romantic era, from the second half of the eighteenth century, that the idea was established that art should primarily be self-expression of the artist: feelings, emotion and experience. The groundwork had been laid by George Berkeley, who in *An Essay Towards a New Theory of Vision* (1709) proposed the idea that we can only have mental representations of things, and not fully 'know' a thing in itself. An artwork, then, could not be about the world, but about a person's experience of the world. Romantic critics built on this idea to celebrate artistic expression, and the mind's creative power, as superior to the 'accurate' but unfermented view of the world produced by a camera obscura.

'In the light of this,' Julian Bell explains in his elegant *What is Painting?*, 'eighteenth-century artistic theory turned from how the painting related to the world towards how the painting related to the painter' (1999: 56). Although an artist's individual skill would previously have been admired, and their personality may have been seen to influence their work, the inner life of the artist themselves had not previously been what art was *about*.

The artist David Hockney, whose work includes a range of experiments with representation – in particular rejecting the conventional Western approach to perspective – says that artistic depiction 'is not an attempt to re-create something, but an account of seeing it' (Hockney and Joyce, 2002: 58). Cubism, in the early twentieth century, made this explicit, with paintings of objects seen from several angles at once. Hockney cites Cézanne, whose paintings in the later part of the nineteenth century made the experience of seeing especially apparent: 'He wasn't concerned with apples, but with his *perception* of apples. That's clear from his work' (ibid). Arthur C. Danto makes a similar point in *The Transfiguration of the Commonplace* (1981): 'It is as if a work of art were like an externalisation of the artist's consciousness, as if we could see his way of seeing and not merely what he saw' (p. 164).

In an attempt to provide an even broader account of creative production, Richard Eldridge suggests that the motive of all creators and artists is 'To express, and in expressing to clarify, inner emotions and attitudes – their own and others' – in relation to the common materials of outer life' (2003: 100). This useful phrase highlights the working through of feelings and ideas, and the way in which creative activity is *itself* where the thinking through and the self-expression takes place, *as well as* being a process which creates an artefact which represents the outcome of those thinking and feeling processes.

Indeed, many key thinkers on the meaning of art have similarly seen artistic making as an act which reflects, and works through, human experience. In his *Introductory Lectures on Aesthetics*, originally delivered in the 1820s, Hegel describes the making of artworks in terms of a universal human need to consider one's own existence:

> The universal and absolute need out of which art, on its formal side, arises has its source in the fact that man is a thinking consciousness, i.e. that he draws out of himself, and makes explicit for himself, that which he is... The things of nature are only *immediate and single*, but man as mind *reduplicates* himself, inasmuch as prima facie he *is* like the things of nature, but in the second place just as really is *for* himself, perceives himself, has ideas of himself, thinks himself, and only thus is active self-realizedness.
>
> (Hegel, 2004: 35)

Making 'external things' upon which a person inevitably 'impresses the seal of his inner being' gives that person the opportunity to reflect upon their selfhood; 'the inner and outer world' is projected into 'an object in which he recognises his own self' (p. 36). Hegel's implication that something made by a person will *necessarily* express something about its creator interestingly predates Freud's suggestion, which would emerge almost 100 years later and in a quite different tradition, that art works – along with dreams, slips of the tongue and most other products of the brain – will reflect aspects of conscious or unconscious personality.

Novelist Leo Tolstoy also felt that art communicated selfhood, but his model anticipates more deliberate action. In 1896, he wrote: 'Art is a human activity [in which] one man consciously by means of certain signs, hands onto others feelings he has lived through, and that others are infected by those feelings and also experience them' (1960: 51). Although Tolstoy's transmission model – where feelings are implanted into a work by its creator and then 'infect' its audiences – seems rather simplistic, his point is that art should primarily be about the communication of genuinely felt emotions. On this basis, he rejected numerous highly regarded works of art, including many of his own, as decadent and 'counterfeit', because they were based on spectacle and an attempt to capture beauty or sentiment, rather than stemming from truly felt emotions. Only works with this authentic base in feeling (whatever its character – joy or despair, love or hate) would be able to evoke a matching experience of such feelings in the audience.

In the twentieth century, John Dewey, in *Art as Experience* ([1934] 1980), argued that looking at art works – or at least, particular works of art that are meaningful to us – 'elicits and accentuates' the experience of wholeness and connection with the wider universe beyond ourselves (p. 195). Dewey does not mean famous 'masterpieces' in particular (although those are likely to have become celebrated because of these properties, at least in part); for Dewey, art is part of everyday experience. 'The understanding of art and of its role in civilisation is not furthered by setting out with eulogies of it nor by occupying ourselves exclusively at the outset with great works of art recognised as such' (p. 10). Dewey suggests that understanding an artistic experience is like understanding how a flower grows – rather than simply noticing that it is pretty – and therefore involves an understanding of 'the soil, air, and light' which have contributed to the aetiology of the work and which will be reflected in it (p. 12). This means that, just as we associate a botanist with the study of flowers, we could expect to associate a sociologist with the exploration of art works and other elements of visual culture – an insight which would pop up 100 years later in a clutch of 'visual culture' books such as Sturken and Cartwright (2001), Elkins (2003), and Mirzoeff (1999).

Furthermore, Dewey suggests that art can introduce us 'into a world beyond this world which is nevertheless the deeper reality of the world in which we live in our ordinary experiences'. This may sound rather spiritual, but Dewey's concerns are pragmatic: 'I can see no psychological ground for such properties of an experience, save that, somehow, the work of art operates to deepen and to raise to great clarity that sense of an enveloping undefined whole that accompanies every normal experience'. This brings 'a peculiarly satisfying sense of unity in itself and with ourselves' (p. 195). Therefore, simply put, making or looking at a work of art encourages reflection upon ourselves and our place in the world.

This in turn connects with the renewal of interest in drawing. This arguably began with Betty Edwards's book *Drawing on the Right Side of the Brain*, first published in 1979, which became an international bestseller not only because it helped people to make better drawings, but also because it promised to foster 'specific, visual, perceptual ways of thinking' which when combined with the more traditional numerical and analytical modes of thought enabled people to comprehend details and also 'see' the whole picture, which – as the author asserts – is 'vital for critical-thinking skills, extrapolation of meaning, and problem solving' (Edwards, 2001: p. xiii). This kind of idea would not traditionally be found in a book about 'how to draw'. In a collection of essays entitled *Drawing: The Process* (edited by Duff and Davies, 2005), Leo Duff argues that today drawing is seen as an 'assistant to thinking and problem-solving', whereas until recent decades it was generally thought of in terms of 'seeing more clearly' and 'perfecting realism' (2005: 2). She also alludes to the mysterious/experimental sense in which drawing can pull ideas up from the unconscious: 'The fascination with drawing … is the inconclusive way in which it works within, yet moves our practice forward' (ibid). In the same volume, John Vernon Lord asserts that 'Drawings have a lot to do with trying to make sense of the world as we know it, and what we have seen, thought about, or remembered. They are proposals and thoughts turned into vision' (Lord, 2005: 30).

These theories all suggest, albeit with different emphases and nuances, that creativity and artistic production are driven by a desire to communicate feelings and ideas; and that such works will almost inevitably tell us something about their creator. In particular, artistic works are a thinking through and reflection of social and psychological experience.

Self-exploration in art

Many of the theories discussed above stem from writers thinking about particular recognised artists and art works. Although this book is more concerned with everyday creativity, and artefacts made by people who probably *don't* call themselves 'artists', it is worth looking at a selection of examples from the world of recognised art and artists to see how they have felt that art-making plays a role in the construction or expression of selfhood and identity.

All works of art are likely to (arguably) have *some* kind of autobiographical or expressive dimension, so my personal selection of examples may seem arbitrary almost to the point of randomness, but that's probably inevitable. Limiting ourselves to the past couple of centuries, let's begin with Édouard Manet (1832–83), who rejected traditional mythological, religious and historical subjects, and painted scenes of everyday life in Paris. His paintings show people drinking, dancing, enjoying music, chatting flirtatiously, in crowds, taking pleasure in urban social life. His use of black outlines, 'photographic' lighting, and a somewhat rough painting technique, do not attempt to hide the process of painting itself. His famous *Olympia* (1863), showing a prostitute with a defiant gaze in a composition mirroring Titian's classical *Venus of Urbino* (1538), shocked visitors to the Paris Salon of 1865 – not in the trivial sense in which *Daily Mail* readers pretend to be shocked by things today, but apparently being genuinely appalled, 'terrified, shocked, disgusted' and 'moved to a kind of pity' by the work (according to contemporary accounts quoted by Clark, 1999: 83). The painting reflected changes in society – prostitutes were at this time stepping from the shadows to become visible in Parisian cultural life, stirring the boundaries between the margins and the mainstream – and at the same time the character of the painting itself, with its ambiguous intent and unfinished style, destabilised conventional ideas of representation; so that *Olympia* became 'the founding monument of modern art', as T. J. Clark puts it in his seminal book on Manet and his followers, *The Painting of Modern Life* (1999: 79). Although Manet had not sought to offend, his particular way of painting prostitutes and railways and bars positioned his work at the heart of a social tornado which was happening *anyway*, but which dragged him into its eye and spoke with his voice. Manet 'told the truth about modern life but made it momentous' (Johnson, 2003: 588). Matisse said of him: 'He was the first to act on reflex and thus simplify the painter's business … expressing only what directly touched his senses' (quoted in Néret, 2003: 7).

Why does Manet's work seem so pregnant with purpose, and seem to so uniquely capture the coming of modernity? Clark reflects on this in the new preface to his book, written ten years after its first publication, and wonders 'why I ever believed my story could be told the way it is, by looking mainly at paintings'. His answer begins with the following:

> One thing that makes oil painting interesting, as far as I am concerned, is that usually it is done slowly. The interest becomes greater the more the surrounding culture puts its stress on speed and immediacy.
>
> (Clark, 1999: xix)

Although Clark is here most concerned with how a painting captures a moment, and simultaneously is able to hold steady elements which are in tension, such as pathos and delight, or nostalgic desires and future dreams; but he also raises the point central to this book – and it is interesting that he would bring it up here, in this context, I think – of the *time* needed to process experience and turn it into a visual representation. He goes on:

> Painting is (again, potentially) a means of investigation; it is a way of discovering what the values and excitements of the world amount to, by finding in practice what it takes to make a painting of them — what kind of play between flatness and depth, what kind of stress on the picture's limits, what sorts of insistence, ellipsis, showmanship, restraint? If *these* are the means needed to give such and such a scene or world of emotion convincing form, then what does this tell us about the scene or emotion?
>
> (Clark, 1999: xxi)

Manet's work therefore is a meditation on changes in society, and art, but we can't get to know much about Manet from his pictures, except that he wanted to test these things. In the work of Vincent Van Gogh (1853–90), by contrast, we can see the passionate, 'tortured soul' of the artist in the paint itself – and of course it is a cliché to say so. Van Gogh was clearly possessed by a relentless drive to make pictures, producing 900 paintings and 1,100 drawings in the ten years before his suicide. His letters reveal thoughtfulness about colour composition and the effects he wanted to achieve, but his words alone cannot convey the ardent fury of his actual painting. Van Gogh's paintings are perhaps the most brilliant examples of how the rendering of an image can be so much more significant and expressive than the subject-matter itself. We 'know' about Vincent from the mythologies and books and films, but we also know about him from the particular way in which his pictures of 'ordinary' things (some fields, a bedroom, a sky), are *painted*. He wrote to his brother Theo in 1889:

> When the thing represented is, in point of character, absolutely in agreement and one with manner of representing it, isn't it just that which gives a work of art its quality?
>
> (Van Gogh, 1958: 179)

Although typically categorised as a post-impressionist, Van Gogh seems to be the most popular and brilliant embodiment of expressionism – the distortion of conventional realism to achieve an emotional effect (or, more broadly, art which is meant to convey intense emotion). His thick oils and dashes of vibrant colour seem to be an insistent cry from within the artist himself, and his several self-portraits (even if partly produced for the convenience of having himself as a model) – some 35 of them produced in his last five years – vary in colour and composition but all seem to be driven by an intense and burning exploration of self.

Max Beckmann (1884–1950), the German artist seen as an archetypal expressionist even though he rejected the term himself, was another intense and troubled character, and painted a remarkable number of self-portraits throughout his life. His 1938 lecture, 'On my Painting', offers a lucid and very modern account of his motivations:

> What I want to show in my work is the idea which hides itself behind so-called reality. I am seeking for the bridge which leads from the visible to the invisible, like the famous cabalist who once said: 'If you wish to get hold of the invisible you must penetrate as deeply as possible into the visible'... .
>
> Self-realisation is the urge of all objective spirits. It is this self which I am searching in my life and in my art... . I am immersed in the phenomenon of the Individual, the so-called whole Individual, and I

try in every way to explain it and present it. What are you? What am I? Those are the questions that constantly persecute and torment me and perhaps also play some part in my art.

(Beckmann, 1968: 187–91)

Again, we see the idea of self-exploration through *making pictures*. Of course, this is common to many – perhaps almost all – visual artists, in some way. In the above quotation, we also see an artist in the 1930s asking questions about identity which mirror those raised by sociologists such as Anthony Giddens in the 1980s and 1990s, mentioned in the previous chapter. More specifically, Beckmann is saying that he has to face questions about himself which Giddens says in modern times we *all* have to face about ourselves. And in his work the artist can be seen thinking through these questions about 'who to be' quite literally, through his numerous self-portraits in which he presents himself in a range of roles including as a prisoner, a clown, a fortune-teller, a sailor, a medical attendant and a socialite.

Although she had a very different artistic style and background, the Mexican artist Frida Kahlo (1907–54) similarly used self-portraits to explore different dimensions of her life and biography. As she explained in a letter in 1939:

> Since my subjects have always been my sensations, my states of mind and the profound reactions that life has prompted in me, I have often objectified all this in figures of myself, which were the most real, most sincere thing I could do to express what I felt within and outside myself.
>
> (Kahlo, 1939, quoted in Tibol, 2005: 185)

Although there is a romantic discourse around Kahlo's work suggesting that her complex and painful personal life led to the spontaneous, 'naïve' production of expressive paintings, it is more likely that her diverse imagery was chosen rather carefully. As Gannit Ankori notes,

> Kahlo produced over one hundred images that explore aspects of her complex identity in relation to her body, to her genealogy, to her childhood, to social structures, to national, religious and cultural contexts, and to nature. Thus, she scrutinised her physical and psychological process of becoming and decomposing as it unfolded through time, imaging herself as a zygote, a foetus, a child, an adult and a disintegrating mortal being.
>
> (Ankori, 2005: 31)

Kahlo pictured herself in traditional female roles, as Wife and Mother, and explored alternative 'evil' roles, sexual ambiguities and hybrid roles where the self joined with nature. She had a strong drive to make pictures expressing her troubled relationship with her physical body, her husband, and miscarriages, as well as politics and folklore, so that all of her life and interests are exposed and reimagined in different symbolic forms on her canvases.

Surprising drive for emotional communication

More recently, Howard Hodgkin (b. 1932) has developed his own visual language, making paintings which represent emotions and memories. The works have specific titles, such as *In Paris with You* and *Patrick in Italy*, but represent *feelings* stemming from thinking about those scenes, rather than the scenes themselves. Hodgkin says, 'I don't think you can have a successful work of art of any sort which doesn't contain the maximum amount of feeling. I'm not going to try any harder to define art than that' (interviewed in Illuminations, 2002: 45). Andrew Graham-Dixon notes that 'Hodgkin's pictures … often seem loaded with a significance that cannot be exactly articulated – as if what survives, after the transmutation of memory into art, is the intensity of a feeling without the incidental paraphernalia of its narration' (2001: 39). We can sense the emotion in the work, and can add our own fragments of narrative; but the absence of obvious representations reminds us that other people's stories are unknowable in any case, and that we only have our own. For instance, one painting, *Discarded Clothes* (1985–90), prompts this typically lyrical passage from Graham-Dixon:

> *Discarded Clothes* acknowledges the inevitable imperfection of every representational picture: its inability to be more than a painted surrogate for a fraction of the life of the person who brought it into being. But defeat can also contain the possibility of success, because these ambiguities and deliberate omissions are the source of another kind of truth to reality. They suggest that our definitions of ourselves, the identities we invent to negotiate a way through life, are as imperfect and impartial a reflection of the truth as paintings … Hodgkin's bright puzzles have the character of an insinuation. They remind us how little any of us know, about ourselves or others.
>
> (Graham-Dixon, 2001: 51–2)

Everywhere we see artists trying to *communicate* – even those contemporary artists who are commonly thought of as being extreme, elite or incomprehensible. Gilbert and George, for example, have for over 30 years produced art works which have been seen as shocking, and which middle-brow critics have dismissed as being outside the bounds of good taste. But the artists do not seek to alienate people; on the contrary, their statement 'What our Art Means' (1986) is headed 'ART FOR ALL':

> We want our art to speak across the barriers of knowledge directly to People about their Life and not about their knowledge of art. The 20th

century has been cursed with an art that cannot be understood. The decadent artists stand for themselves and their chosen few, laughing at and dismissing the normal outsider. We say that puzzling, obscure and form-obsessed art is decadent and a cruel denial of the Life of People.

(Gilbert and George, [1986] 1997: 149)

Their large-scale photo-montage grids obviously differ from traditional paintings, but make use of contemporary techniques, in the style of advertising, to communicate in what the artists hope is an 'accessible' form:

We want the most accessible modern form with which to create the most modern speaking visual pictures of our time. The art-material must be subservient to the meaning and purpose of the picture. Our reason for making pictures is to change people and not to congratulate them on being how they are.

(Gilbert and George, [1986] 1997: 149)

Similarly, the artist Martin Creed may be thought of as an extreme minimalist – an arch-intellectual making 'clever' and therefore rather cold works, such as *Work No. 200, Half the air in a given space* (1998), in which half of the air in a room is contained in balloons, and *Work No. 227, The lights going on and off*, the self-explanatory work that he installed for the 2001 Turner Prize show. Whilst such work can seem highly abstract and conceptual, in interviews the artist reveals a sensitive, thoughtful side and an artistic ambition continually confounded by a deep insecurity about what to make and whether it is worthwhile.* For example:

The only thing I feel like I know is that I want to make things. Other than that, I feel like I don't know. So the problem is in trying to make something without knowing what I want… . I think it's all to do with wanting to communicate. I mean, I think I want to make things because I want to communicate with people, because I want to be loved, because I want to express myself.

(Creed interviewed in Illuminations, 2002: 97–8)

Creed says that he makes art works not as part of an academic exploration of conceptual art, but rather from a wish to connect with people, 'wanting to communicate and wanting to say hello'. The work is therefore primarily emotional:

---

*   Sharp-eyed Wikipedia users may find that this bit of text is strangely similar to part of Wikipedia's entry on Martin Creed; that's because I wrote a chunk of that Wikipedia article – as can be seen in its 'History' page – and then wanted to say and quote similar things here.

To me it's emotional. Aye. To me that's the starting point. I mean, I do it because I want to make something. I think that's a desire, you know, or a need. I think that I recognise that I want to make something, and so I try to make something. But then you get to thinking about it and that's where the problems start because you can't help thinking about it, wondering whether it's good or bad. But to me it's emotional more than anything else.

(Ibid: 100–1)

Tracey Emin also, as we saw in Chapter 1, emphasises emotional honesty in a much more explicit way, through a rigorous programme of self-exposure which has fascinated her audiences. Artists across the centuries, then, have made representations of selfhood, of being and seeing in the world, and their works have delighted, infuriated and moved people. They also provide some perhaps rather quirky documents of everyday life, and consciousness, for the historian. But for the social scientist who wants to use the visual products of human creativity as research data – can this be justified? What kinds of claims can we make about the world based on that kind of material? That is what I will consider in the next chapter.

Chapter 3

Science and what we can say about the world

This book, as you will know if you started at the beginning, is about finding new ways of generating knowledge about the (social) world. This chapter begins to get to grips with the philosophical nitty-gritty of how we can do that. It begins with a short discussion about how much we can 'generalise' – draw broader conclusions about the world – from the findings of qualitative research. This leads us into an (even) bigger debate from the philosophy of science, about whether science can tell us facts about the world, and the extent to which we can rely on those claims to truth. Rather than collapse into an entirely relativistic or postmodern puddle of woe, I arrive at a middle-ground suggestion for how we can proceed. All of this discussion arises, of course, from the fact that we want to be able to say that a study in which people *make* things – such as a collage, drawing, video or model – might ultimately be able to offer some scientific knowledge about the world, rather than being just a nice set of individual instances of subjective self-expression.

Generalisability

Quantitative research is often designed specifically so that generalisations can be made on the basis of the data. A sample is used which is representative of the broader population being studied: for example, a study of teenagers' attitudes to drugs in the UK might involve structured interviews with 1,000 teenagers, spread across ages 13–19 and with proportions of females and males, and ethnic minorities, which mirror the actual population of teenagers in the country (who actually number, according to the 2001 UK Census, over five million individuals).

Qualitative research *can* be based on large and carefully assembled samples, in just the same way, which would enable reasonable and statistically satisfactory generalisations to be made, precisely because the sample was of a good size and was designed to represent the broader population. However, because of the expense of qualitative research in terms of both time and resources, it usually does not involve systematic sampling, or several hundred participants.

Instead, researchers tend to work with small groups, and argue that their aim is to reach an *in-depth* understanding of the views of a particular set of social actors, rather than a large-scale, generalisable, but rather superficial overview of people's stated views. So for example the quantitative study of teenagers' attitudes, mentioned above, would lead to results in the form of percentages which would record teenagers' responses to multiple-choice questions about their attitudes and behaviour in relation to drugs.

Such studies are not without value: it is worth knowing what a representative sample say about these things, even if their answers provided to researchers may not be entirely reliable. Different people may play down, or may exaggerate, their behaviour and attitudes to illegal substances, but we are still likely to assume that what they say to a researcher has some connection with reality – partly, when the question is about *behaviour*, because of an assumption that most people will try to give an answer which is at least *plausible*, even if not precisely true. So the fact that we live in a society where (for example) 80 per cent of teenagers – rather than 30 or 60 per cent of teenagers – thought it would be plausible to tell a researcher that they had tried a particular drug, is worth knowing.

In the case of *attitudes*, surveys are on even stronger ground, because most people, normally – with some exceptions – have little motivation to lie about their beliefs. So if 80 per cent of the teenagers had said that they thought that a certain drug should be legalised, then this is probably what 80 per cent of them think. We don't know, of course, what this gut-reaction response really represents: we cannot tell whether this apparently widely held view is based on a good understanding of the issues and their implications, or is purely inspired by an attempt to give the 'cool' answer, or something else. Nevertheless, a stated view is a stated view, and it is worth knowing how these views are distributed through the population.

A qualitative study on the same topic, meanwhile, would perhaps work with a selection of groups of young people (for instance, groups of teenagers living on a Manchester estate, divided into groups by gender and ethnic background) and would seek to explore in detail the meaning of drugs, or the idea of drugs, in their lives. The authors of such a study would typically acknowledge that their findings could not be generalised to a wider population, although they might be likely to suggest that some of their findings could be fruitful for researchers trying to understand, or policy-makers trying to combat, the appeal of illegal drugs.

Payne and Williams's challenge

These differences between quantitative and qualitative research, and what you can reasonably claim to do with the findings of each, are well-known and widely understood. However, in an article published in the journal *Sociology* in 2005, Geoff Payne and Malcolm Williams pointed out that qualitative sociologists routinely ignore these boundaries. To illustrate their point, the authors analysed all articles published in the 2003 volume (volume 37) of the journal *Sociology* itself. The four issues published that year included 38 peer-reviewed articles. Of those, 17 used qualitative methods, covering a wide range of procedures ('a total of 34 qualitative research techniques comprising 11 different types of qualitative method', Payne and Williams, 2005: 300). On their selection of this particular journal, the authors say:

> Volume 37 of *Sociology* ... does not provide a representative sample of all sociological activity but as the official, general sociology journal of the British Sociological Association, and one of the leading English language journals in the discipline, it is hard to argue that *Sociology* does not reflect mainstream tendencies in British sociology.
>
> (Payne and Williams, 2005: 299)

Their assessment of the journal's standing is fair enough, and it would be fair to assume that the research published in *Sociology* represents the kind of work seen by an international audience as being of good quality and, in methodological terms, 'best practice'. Whilst it might not be too surprising to find that one or two researchers occasionally stretch a little beyond their evidential base, Payne and Williams's finding is much more stark:

> The numbers of informants/sources varied (and was not always clear) but with two exceptions, data were collected from relatively few people: between eight and about 60. In almost all cases, the reader was given very little methodological information about why or how the specific informants had been recruited [... and] there was almost no explicit discussion of the grounds on which findings might be generalised beyond the research setting. Despite this, *all the 17 articles made generalisations*, albeit of different kinds.
>
> (Payne and Williams, 2005: 300; emphasis in original)

The authors note that the articles usually did not discuss the issue of generalisability at all, and wryly note specific cases such as Samantha Punch, author of a paper entitled 'Childhoods in the Majority World', who they find 'made generalising claims but also denied making them'.

Payne and Williams have a solution for qualitative researchers who are not able to make the kind of grand generalisations which quantitative researchers can more easily defend: the '*moderatum* generalisation'. This is 'an intermediate type of limited generalisation' (p. 296), which must be carefully formulated and explicitly discussed. Having noted the tendency of qualitative sociologists to say that they are not interested in generalisation, but then to do it anyway, Payne and Williams emphasise that possible generalisability must be explicitly considered at the point of research design, especially when people or sites to be researched are being selected. Even so, in most qualitative research the generalisations must necessarily be modest:

> The qualitative papers in Volume 37 of *Sociology* are best described as being based on small selections of units which are acknowledged to be part of wider universes but not chosen primarily to represent them directly... There is no means of knowing, let alone mathematically calculating, the probability that what is found in these samples is reflected in their wider universes. Although as we noted earlier, their authors do draw such inferences, there are no formal grounds for so doing.
> (Payne and Williams, 2005: 305–6)

Therefore, it is suggested, researchers should moderate their generalisations. They should be cautious in terms of *breadth*, making sure that such statements do not generalise to a population more wide or diverse than can be justified; and should be cautious in terms of *time period*, and avoid assuming that findings will apply too much into the past or future. Payne and Williams also suggest that researchers could make modest observations of 'basic patterns, or tendencies, so that other studies are likely to find something similar but not identical' (p. 306).

From their analysis of the qualitative research published in volume 37 of *Sociology*, Payne and Williams note that in most cases the research sites and subjects seem to be chosen on the basis of convenience and ease of access. 'In calling for more considered generalisation,' they write, 'we are not asking for larger, quasi-statistical samples' (p. 309), but they suggest that, if any kind of generalisation is to be attempted (which is a common aspiration for most researchers, apart from those studying unique scenarios *as unique scenarios*), researchers should try to use a range of hopefully representative participants as well as exercising caution about their representativeness. Most of the qualitative articles they studied, however, did not do this.

Making social-scientific statements

Payne and Williams seemed to find that social scientists at the most method-ologically 'free' end of their craft, qualitative research, were failing to adhere to the most basic principles which would justify their methods. To explore this issue a little further, we can turn to the philosophy of science itself.

There is a well-known debate between the positivist view of science, typically represented by Karl Popper, which suggests faith in the reliability of 'pure' scientific methods, and a much more social-constructionist view, typically represented by Thomas Kuhn, which sees science as a cultural construction created by the actors in that field, namely scientists. Although the arguments are often seen as being in stark opposition to each other, I think that they – or a version of them – can be married, or at least can manage to cohabit. But let us consider each view in turn.

First we need a bit of background from the philosophy of science: the problem of deductive versus inductive reasoning. Deductive reasoning occurs when we draw a conclusion based on premises which we know to be true. So, for example, I know that steel is a hard metal, so if you give me a table made of steel, I can be confident that the table will not feel soft and spongey, and that if I walk into it at some speed then I might sustain an injury. As long as the premise (steel is a hard metal) is true then I can be sure that my conclusions are also true. Inductive reasoning, on the other hand, makes 'logical' assumptions or predictions based on past experience. For example, I have observed that watering my plant every week helps it to grow, so I conclude that water is always good news for plants; or, I have spent time with many people and they have never just vanished into thin air, so I conclude that people do not spontaneously vanish. These inferences move from that which I have observed (my pot plant, hundreds of people) to that which I have not observed (*every* instance of water being added to plants, *all* people). In these particular examples, what I *actually* believe is that I would be wrong about the first one – a severe flood, for example, would destroy most plants, rather than being good for them – but probably correct about the second, based on past experience.

But that's the problem: 'based on past experience'. Inductive reasoning seems to be based on a faith that what was true in the past will remain true in the present and future, as philosopher David Hume noted in his *Enquiry Concerning Human Understanding* of 1748. Most scientific reasoning is inductive, moving from a *sample* of cases to conclusions about *all* cases. The 'sample' may be all cases so far observed: for example, our knowledge about a particular virus or disease will be based, ideally, on all observed cases. But we don't *absolutely* know that our knowledge about its characteristics will be true tomorrow, although we assume it probably will be. Even my example of deductive reasoning above is imperfect because we wouldn't *really* know that steel would *always* feel hard; maybe in certain atmospheres or circumstances, it would not be (and indeed I already happen to know that if I was admiring my table whilst it was in a furnace, it would not be hard at all). This is what led Hume to assert that, although we all use induction all the time, it cannot be rationally justified. We cannot *prove*, and cannot be *certain*, that the scientific 'laws' which appear to be true today will still be true tomorrow, even though – as Hume was happy to admit – we all tend to have complete faith in them. But the idea that science is dependent on any kind of 'faith' seems rather shocking.

Popper's optimistic solution

It was to this problem that Karl Popper addressed himself. He was uncomfortable with science being founded on faith in inductive reasoning, but proposed that there could be a solution which relied only on deductive reasoning – simple observations. He noted that although we cannot permanently 'prove' that something is true, we can clearly prove that a hypothesis is *not* true simply by pointing to one example of it being false. This is Popper's famous notion of *falsifiability*. Observation of any number of green apples does not *prove* that all apples are green, although it's fine as a hypothesis. But if you can show me one apple that is red, then we have to rethink our conclusion about apples. Through a process of scientific dialogue we would have to decide to accept either that my hypothesis was wrong – not all apples are green – or that there is another explanation – for example, that all apples *are* green, and that the fruit you have shown me is a different kind of red-coloured fruit for which we will need to create a new category. Thus, we can advance knowledge simply by making clear and potentially falsifiable statements.

This could be seen as a quite radical model of science: it accepts that our current body of knowledge is a provisional stack of claims about the world, each waiting to be disproved. Popper clearly says this in *The Logic of Scientific Discovery* (first published 1934). Any theory leads to logical deductions, which can then be tested, resulting in a positive decision (verification) or a negative one (falsification). But Popper reminds us that this knowledge is only provisional:

> It should be noticed that a positive decision can only temporarily support the theory, for subsequent negative decisions may always overthrow it. So long as theory withstands detailed and severe tests and is not superseded by another theory in the course of scientific progress, we may say that it has 'proved its mettle' or that it is 'corroborated' by past experience.
>
> (Popper, [1959] 2002: 10)

Rather than being a defender of an unattainable model of scientific 'truth', then – which he is sometimes characterised as – Popper is here arguing that any scientific statement is merely 'the best we can say at the moment'. He is not saying that science is a handed-down set of fictions, or a mere belief system, though. Rather, he seems to be offering a model by which honest scientists can work towards having a fuller understanding of the world.

This kind of optimism doesn't always play well in the sociological world, where we like to be disappointed with scientists for inventing nuclear bombs, chemical weapons, thalidomide and other things that look less than altruistic. But science, as a knowledge-gathering process, can't be blamed for the numerous unpleasant *applications* of science (although we can of course look critically at the individuals and groups who practise science). It is perhaps best to let Popper explain his basic intentions himself. He does it clearly enough in the 'Preface to the First English Edition, 1959' of *The Logic of Scientific Discovery*, beginning with a sideswipe at a prevailing school of linguistic philosophers who saw the business of philosophy as being all to do with language. Popper clearly thought there were bigger issues to be dealt with:

> Language analysts believe that there are no genuine philosophical problems, or that the problems of philosophy, if any, are problems of linguistic usage, or of the meaning of words. I, however, believe that there is at least one philosophical problem in which all thinking [people] are interested. It is the problem of cosmology: *the problem of understanding the world – including ourselves, and our knowledge, as part of the world*. All science is cosmology, I believe, and for me the interest of philosophy, no less than of science, lies solely in the contributions it has made to it.
>
> (Popper, [1959] 2002: xvii; emphasis in original)

This is good stuff, addressing the crucial question of how we can – as scientists, or social scientists, or philosophers – claim to 'know' anything. Popper is not quite talking about finding 'the meaning of life' itself, but rather is interested in the approaches we might use to establish knowledge about the world we live in.

> Philosophers are as free as others to use any method in searching for the truth … And yet, I am quite ready to admit that there is a method which might be described as 'the one method of philosophy'. But it is not characteristic of philosophy alone: it is, rather, the one method of all *rational discussion*, and therefore of the natural sciences as well as of philosophy. The method I have in mind is that of stating one's problem clearly and of examining its various proposed situations *critically*.
>
> (Ibid: xix; emphasis in original)

This is Popper's way of introducing the notion of falsifiability. He makes it clear that his model rests not only on it being *possible* for a theory to be shown to be wrong, but that enthusiastic effort should be put into the testing:

> The point is that, whenever we propose a solution to a problem, we ought to try as hard as we can to overthrow our solution, rather than defend it. Few of us, unfortunately, practice this precept; but other people, fortunately, will supply the criticism for us if we fail to supply it ourselves. Yet criticism will be fruitful only if we state our problem as clearly as we can and put our solution in a sufficiently definite form – a form in which it can be critically discussed.
>
> (Ibid: xix)

It is worth noting that Popper does not emphasise any particular method. In the social sciences, Popper is equated with positivism, which in turn is equated with quantitative methods – clear-cut surveys and statistics – rather than anything more imaginative. But Popper's basic principles would accept any method as long as it was clear and transparent and enabled claims to be falsified – or provisionally verified. The message which we can take from Popper, then, is that natural and social scientists can be enormously imaginative and, indeed, *say anything*, as long as it's a clear claim which others can seek to falsify. Indeed, the 'scientific anarchist' Paul Feyerabend – who argued that science should be bound by no methodological rules, and that 'anything goes' was the only acceptable and humanitarian approach – was originally inspired by Popper (see Feyerabend, [1975] 1993).

Popper not popular

Popper's model of falsifiability seems to be a reasonable model for how knowledge can advance and be developed. However, in modern philosophy Popper is lacking fans. For example in his generally useful introductory book, *Philosophy of Science*, Samir Okasha gives Popper's model of falsifiability short shrift:

> The weakness of Popper's argument is obvious. For scientists are not only interested in showing that certain theories are false. When a scientist collects experimental data, her aim might be to show that a particular theory – her arch-rival's theory perhaps – is false. But much more likely, she is trying to convince people that her own theory is true. And in order to do that, she will have to resort to inductive reasoning of some sort. So Popper's attempt to show that science can get by without induction does not succeed.
>
> (Okasha, 2002: 23)

This is, at best, pedantic and ungenerous in its interpretation of Popper's argument. Popper is not *against* claims made on the basis of inductive reasoning; on the contrary, he *welcomes* such claims – as we have seen in the quotes above, he wants scientists to make clear predictive statements which can then be tested. Philosophically, he notes that we can never be certain that a 'scientific law' will always be true, although it is possible to have a body of knowledge in which we have some confidence because it is open to falsifiability and yet no one has (so far) shown it to be false. This seems to be a valid and convincing argument – and even includes the challenging view, which would become taken for granted as part of postmodernism some decades later, that science is not a body of 'truth' after all, but is merely a set of accounts which scientists have, more or less, for the moment, managed to agree upon.

This is clear in, for example, Popper's discussion of Einstein, where Popper is not merely comfortable with, but absolutely delighted about, the provisional nature of Einstein's theories and Einstein's own lack of certainty in them:

> It is interesting, moreover, that Einstein himself had an extremely critical attitude to his own theory of gravitation. Although none of the experimental tests (all proposed by himself) proved unfavourable to his theory, he regarded it as not fully satisfactory on theoretical grounds. He was perfectly well aware that his theory, like all theories in natural science, was a *provisional attempt at a solution* and therefore had a *hypothetical* character. But he went into greater detail than that. He gave *reasons* why his own theory should be seen as incomplete, and as inadequate for his own research programme. And he listed a set of requirements that an adequate theory would have to fulfil.
>
> (Popper, [1972] 2001: 18; emphasis in original)

Unlike many postmodernists, Popper presumes that there is an underlying truth that we can work towards – science should always be seeking 'a better approximation to the truth', he says (ibid). But Popper shares with postmodernists the view of science as a bunch of competing narratives.

Therefore I was puzzled as to why an expert in the philosophy of science such as Samir Okasha would be so quick to dismiss Popper. Thanks to the internet – one product of scientific progress – I was able to email and ask him. The problem, Okasha replied, was that, in a number of works, Popper dug his heels in on the point that you couldn't ultimately-and-forever confirm a theory just by subjecting it to severe tests.

> This immediately leads to a problem, for at any one time, there will be an infinite number of theories that haven't been falsified. How do we choose between them? Popper provides no advice.
>
> (Okasha, 2006: email)

This objection seems quite good, but actually there will not normally be an 'infinite number' of theories which have not been – or could not easily be – falsified. For example I could make up any number of theories about gravity, to explain why an apple falls to the ground – it is because apples are magnetic; it is because apples seek to be underneath oxygen; it is because the clouds in the sky are pushing downwards – but you could falsify all of these quite easily. In reality we can probably only think of three or four theories of gravity which are not obviously wrong. And then you *would* want to follow the 'advice' that Popper does provide – you would try to falsify these theories until you were left with one (or two) that seemed to survive. If you are left with two which both appear to work, well, Popper would seem to be right that you can't really tell which one is correct. If you are left with one, and nobody can suggest a better one, then that's the best we can do for now.

Okasha clarified his reservation:

> At root, the problem is that Popper was torn. He knew perfectly well that passing severe tests *does* confirm a theory, and this is the essence of science. But he had talked himself into accepting a philosophical position which implies that confirmation is impossible. Hence his persistent, and unsuccessful attempts to wriggle out of the problem, often by highly disingenuous means.
>
> (Okasha, 2006: email)

But this doesn't seem like a big problem. Philosophically speaking, confirmation of all laws for all time *is* impossible, surely. And in any case, Popper is here seen as having been too radical for his own good, which is odd because poor old Popper more often appears in textbooks as the conservative voice of positivism, and representing a naïve faith in the honourable pursuit of science.

Popper also runs into difficulties, I think, because he is basically describing an 'ideal type'. His prescriptions for the advancement of science optimistically assume a 'pure' kind of scientific environment where all ideas are freely tested in a drive to find the best explanations, with ideology and personal or group bias playing no role whatsoever. This aspirational view contains a decent ideal, but also opens the door for more socially realistic critics to point out that this is not how the world works. Which is where Thomas Kuhn comes in.

Kuhn's more pessimistic proposal

In his classic work, *The Structure of Scientific Revolutions*, first published in 1963, Kuhn showed that if we look at the history of science, it is difficult to see it as a happy accumulation of knowledge, shaped and perfected through empirical testing. Rather, scientists tend to buy into the status quo – the current 'paradigm' of understanding – and, Kuhn suggests, are extremely resistant to change. Normally, he says, scientists only want to develop the current mode of understanding and are unhappy to find anomalies. In Kuhn's version, scientists seek to prop up the current paradigm, which only collapses when there are so many anomalies that it cannot be supported. Only at that point do the scientists have to give up on, say, their idea that the earth is at the centre of the universe, and accept that we are in a solar system, going around the sun, instead.

This more pessimistic model of scientific progress seems to chime with part of what we may already suspect about human nature – that there may be a certain conservatism in established systems, and that people are not keen on change. On the other hand, it does not fit with another expectation about human nature – that ambitious young scientists would want to establish their reputations by making surprising claims, showing the established ideas to be wrong and proposing new models. It seems unlikely that scientists launch into their careers motivated by a desire to merely confirm existing orthodoxies. Kuhn suggests, though, that social factors such as peer pressure, and a desire to be accepted by senior scientists, mean that challenges to the prevailing paradigm are often softened or silenced.

This relatively 'irrational' model of scientific development was controversial when it first appeared, but has had a huge impact on the philosophy of science. As we have seen, Kuhn highlighted social and interpersonal factors, and the faith of scientists in their own narratives. In particular his account was taken as evidence that Popper's model of scientific progress was over-optimistic and a bit foolish.

However, Popper clearly recognises that there have been significant scientific disputes over explanations, and interpretation of data. Although he does not highlight personality factors as such, he clearly knows well that negotiations have to take place between the proponents of different scientific views until one prevails – indeed, he even entered into such debates himself, such as one with Einstein about probabilities (where, incidentally, they failed to agree (Popper, 2002: 481–8)), and rows with Marxists and Freudians (who he thought did not offer a falsifiable science, since they could offer an 'explanation' for everything, but one which was 'simply non-testable, irrefutable'). So Popper was clearly aware that there are controversies and discussions in science – rather than just the discovery of a fact followed by discovery of another fact; and indeed, his approach rather depends on scientists trying to shoot each other down. 'The scientific method is not cumulative ... it is fundamentally *revolutionary*', Popper states (2001: 11); 'Scientific progress essentially consists in the replacement of earlier theories by later theories'. So Popper and Kuhn share a vision of science proceeding in revolutionary steps, and both use Darwinian evolutionary analogies. In his 1963 publication, Kuhn appeared to be somewhat agnostic about whether a new paradigm would be superior to its predecessor. He notes that Darwin saw nature becoming more complex but not necessarily 'better', as neither God nor nature had a particular goal in mind (Kuhn, 1996: 172). In the postscript to the 1969 edition, however, Kuhn put it a little differently: he observes that problem-solving ability is highly valued in the sciences, and therefore that science will evolve in a way where the fittest problem-solving theory will survive. This is stated clearly:

> Later scientific theories are better than earlier ones for solving puzzles in the often quite different environments to which they are applied. That is not a relativist's position, and it displays the sense in which I am a firm believer in scientific progress.
>
> (Kuhn, 1996: 206)

Kuhn qualifies this by saying that problem-solving is not everything, however; a paradigm may be better than another at solving problems but not necessarily be a better way of capturing what nature 'is really like', he suggests (ibid). One may or may not follow Kuhn on this point, but let's not get stuck on that here. In general, and if we can avoid being too pedantic, I would argue that particular interpretations of Kuhn and Popper can sit together quite happily; Kuhn emphasising the social conventions which affect how science works, and Popper emphasising the rational possibility of different schools of thought using evidence to reach agreement and move forward. Kuhn scores points for having highlighted the significance of interpersonal relationships, loyalty and even belief, in the historical and cultural construction of science; but ultimately, it's easy to be cynical. Popper's approach may be more 'naïve' but retains a pleasant optimism that knowledge can get us somewhere. Popper begins *The Logic of Scientific Discovery* with the epigram, attributed to the German philosopher Novalis: 'Hypotheses are nets: only he who casts will catch'. This seems to underline the spirit of enquiry and even playfulness that Popper favoured.

The need for another solution

In the discussion above I generally seemed to prefer Popper's noble optimism to Kuhn's easy cynicism. In my own reading – which others might disagree with – Popper wishes for a range of interesting and creative views to be brought onto the playing-field of knowledge, to be kicked around until the weaker ones are forced to retire to the sidelines. Kuhn, meanwhile, makes good critical observations but doesn't necessarily give us a useful model to work with. However, it is clear that there are problems with both approaches. In particular, the idea of falsifiability works if you are happy to allow the false premises to emerge over time, from various tests; but if you want to be very rigid about it – as philosophers such as Okasha want to be when comparing ideas (which is reasonable enough, and could be seen as consistent with Popper's own approach) – it simply doesn't work, because there are various instances in the history of science where something we now agree to be true appeared to be false. Popper's argument that 'falsified' theories should be discarded would not have been helpful in these cases. Paul Feyerabend points out that such an approach 'would wipe out science as we know it and would never have permitted it to start' ([1975] 1993: 155); but he also notes that this interpretation of falsificationism is 'strict' and 'naïve'. (Not that Feyerabend is especially forgiving: 'falsificationism is not a solution', he says grandly (p. 261), but by assuming that all theories of knowledge should offer a solution to the problems of humanity, he may have been setting the bar a little high.)

An example will help us to consider the problems with simple-minded or short-term falsificationism. At the start of the nineteenth century it could be observed that the orbit of the planet Uranus was not consistent with Newton's theory of gravitation. Therefore, we could consider Newton's theory to be falsified; according to a strict reading of Popper, we would have to cast Newton aside and go looking for a different theory to explain our observations. But what actually happened was that Newton's model was used to predict the existence of *another* planet, which affected the orbit of Uranus. The theory enabled astronomers to estimate the size and location of the as-yet unseen body, which led to the discovery of the planet which was named Neptune in 1846.

As an objection to Popper, a case such as this (which I have borrowed from Proctor and Capaldi, 2006: 16) may be seen as more or less serious. It's embarrassing for Popper if you actually think he would have intended that Newton's theory should be chucked out completely on the basis of Uranus's apparently inconsistent orbit. (Proctor and Capaldi seem to believe this.) I think a fairer reading of Popper would be that Uranus's orbit would create discomfort in the field until an explanation could be found; you could even say that Newton's theory was temporarily falsified until a new, winning, non-falsifiable account could be presented – which it duly was. This new explanation happened to show that Newton had actually been fine all along, because of the existence of Neptune (indeed, Newton's theory had *helped* astronomers to locate the planet, so Newton wins bonus points). If Neptune had *not* been found, however, then the apparent falsification of Newton would have had to stand. So a case such as this doesn't really knock down Popper, unless you believe that Popper wished that as soon as one apparently contradictory observation was made, a whole mostly convincing seeming paradigm would be instantly thrown out of the window and permanently forgotten about. But that is surely a parody of what Popper really intended.

A third way?: abductive reasoning

Nevertheless, if there are problems with both induction and deduction (through falsification), is there not a third way? In the book *Why Science Matters*, Proctor and Capaldi (2006) suggest *abduction*, 'which is a widely employed, extremely important method in science whose strengths and weaknesses are seldom explicitly discussed' (p. 18). Proctor and Capaldi's text is profoundly irritating in parts, in particular when the authors wheel on a simplified, patronising and bad-cherry-picked version of qualitative methodology in one chapter, so that they can rubbish it in the next. Knocking down a 'straw man' like this is not really a model of 'scientific' fairness. Nevertheless, the authors helpfully draw our attention to the model of abduction.

Abduction was first prominently discussed by philosopher C. S. Pierce in the late nineteenth century. The idea of abduction is that the scientist observes a number of cases and proposes a causal explanation for what is observed. This is different from induction, because the speculation is not about future cases but rather is a (proposed) explanation for the observed cases. And it is different from deduction, because the account is not necessarily 'read' directly from the observations, but proposes a *cause* of these observations. So a typical abduction might be along the lines of, 'We can note [this characteristic] of [this thing], and [that characteristic] of [that thing], and this is because of [explanation X]'. It remains to be seen whether explanation X is a useful causal explanation in other cases, but of course it needs to be a reasonable-looking explanation of the cases in hand.

An abduction therefore leads to a hypothesis, but rather than being tested in isolation, this hypothesis is considered in the context of competing hypotheses. This recognises the fact that any theory is always considered in the light of its rivals. The leading theory in a particular field may not be able to explain all aspects of that field, but has probably gained its status by offering better explanations of a greater number of things than competing theories. This approach differs from Popper's more 'true or false' model, which assumed we could judge a theory in isolation. In common with Popper, though, it is assumed we are working towards 'the best available explanation' (and we can assume that this prize will not be won by a theory which is observably wrong). Interestingly, Proctor and Capaldi think a 'best explanation' is good to have – because it's the best we've got – even if it does not seem wholly convincing.

> Just as one should not accept theories in isolation, one should not reject them in isolation. A theory cannot be rejected in absolute terms but only relative to some other theory. Even a bad theory, for which problems are known to exist, is better than a worse theory or no theory. Although this approach of arguing to the best explanation is seldom explicitly stated, we believe that it is observed implicitly in practice by most psychologists in particular and scientists in general.
>
> (Proctor and Capaldi, 2006: 76)

Note, incidentally, that if you are thinking that this sounds like a relativist point of view ('a theory cannot be rejected in absolute terms but only relative to some other theory'), it is not. Problematic theories only survive here by being the best available. So my theory that the moon is made of cheese *would* be rejected, quickly and entirely, in the face of much better evidence-based argument that the moon is not made of cheese but is made of dust and rock.

Factors that contribute to a 'best explanation' include fruitfulness (whether the theory helps make new predictions), innovation, scope, as well as internal and external consistency. Superior theories are likely to tick more of these boxes than their competitors. This abduction model, then, whilst perhaps less logically decisive than induction or deduction – since it allows several balls to be in play at once, only gradually pointing towards one winner – is a workable model which we can proceed with, and indeed which is probably the underlying model of most progress in science and social science.

The limits of big theories: a dappled world?

The abduction model is helped by its contingent and specific nature. Although it could be employed by those searching for one holistic body of 'truth', this is not emphasised; instead, we are looking for 'the best available explanation' in a particular sphere. One of the problems for Popper, in the discussion above, was that his critics were looking at his work as a description of a science which aspired to account for *everything*. This is not necessarily unfair; Popper's style invited such a view. On the one hand, he invited researchers to be playful, to make any argument and use any method as long as the hypotheses could be tested; and he emphasised that knowledge was always provisional. On the other hand, falsificationism was meant to lead a drive to increasingly precise knowledge and the ability of science to explain an ever-growing number of phenomena. Because of this grand aspiration for science, as we saw above, Popper could be knocked down for failing to notice the socially mediated aspects of scientific progress and for not actually suggesting a model which could, in itself, explain much.

Counter to the grand view of an overarching science is Nancy Cartwright's notion of 'the dappled world' (Cartwright, 1999). Cartwright is a philosopher of science with a background in advanced mathematics; she has the kind of scientific expertise that enables her to conduct detailed critiques of pure physics and quantum theory. She is not 'anti-science', but rather prefers a model of science which can deal realistically with the real world we inhabit.

Cartwright points out that even the most precise scientific theories can usually only be demonstrated in very tightly controlled experimental environments; outside of those rigid conditions, additional real-world factors typically mess things up. Meanwhile, everyday life runs on a set of assumptions which are fuzzy and imprecise in scientific terms, but which are relied upon on a daily basis. For example, we might think of items of 'general knowledge' where we know things about gardening, cooking, navigation, or health:

> I know these facts even though they are vague and imprecise, and I have no reason to assume that that can be improved on … But I want to insist that these items are items of knowledge. They are, of course, like all genuine items of knowledge … defeasible and open to revision in the light of further evidence and argument. But if I do not know these things, what do I know and how can I come to know anything?
> (Cartwright, 1999: 24)

Cartwright argues that the search for a unified 'theory of everything' is misguided. The search for an all-explaining theory has become a fashionable idea, especially in physics, and this is reflected in the titles of popular science bestsellers such as *The Theory of Everything: The Origin and Fate of the Universe* (Hawking, 2006), *The Elegant Universe: Superstrings, Hidden Dimensions, and the Quest for the Ultimate Theory* (Greene, 2000), and *Universe on a T-Shirt: The Quest for the Theory of Everything* (Falk, 2005). But Cartwright argues that the universe is not really like that, and cannot be usefully understood in that way. Rather than a 'fundamentalism' of scientific laws which are expected to apply in every situation, Cartwright proposes a 'patchwork' of laws, pulling together our best available knowledge in particular spheres. This is expressed simply at the beginning of her book, *The Dappled World: A Study of the Boundaries of Science*:

> This book supposes that, as appearances suggest, we live in a dappled world, a world rich in different things, with different natures, behaving in different ways. The laws that describe this world are a patchwork, not a pyramid.
>
> (Cartwright, 1999: 1)

The 'pyramid' model represents the idea of the unity of science, which has the social sciences at its base, up through biology and chemistry, to physics at the peak. In contrast to this, Cartwright advocates a view, based on a model by Otto Neurath, which sees the natural and social sciences (or perhaps even their subdisciplines) as balloons, tied to the same material world, but separate and with boundaries. Relations between the balloons are not fixed, and their boundaries can change, expand and overlap; and they can be tied together in different ways. But they do not add up to one whole science. The idea of the 'dappled world' is that we will have different kinds of explanations for different spheres of nature and social experience. In each case – to bring us back to the discussions above – we would employ 'the best available explanation' for a particular problem or sphere, but would not necessarily hope that this was going to one day explain everything else. This approach, for Cartwright, reflects the complex nature of the real world – and leads to a new problem:

> To me this [is] the great challenge that now faces philosophy of science: to develop methodologies, not for life in the laboratory where conditions can be set as one likes, but methodologies for life in the messy world that we invariably inhabit.
>
> (Cartwright, 1999: 18)

The fact that science does not usually try to identify 'messy world' explanations, but is more often concerned with finding 'pure' and overarching theories which can at least be shown to work in hyperclean and superprecise testing environments, would be seen by Cartwright as part of the problem.

In conclusion

In this chapter I began with Payne and Williams's challenge to qualitative researchers. Their quarrel was not with qualitative research itself, but with those academics who conducted small-scale studies of particular social spheres and then – sometimes whilst saying 'of course, we cannot generalise from such a small and unscientific sample' – would go and make generalisations anyway. Thus, for example, a study of primary school teachers in the Scottish Highlands would be taken to 'probably' tell us about the challenges faced by educationalists around the world. Payne and Williams made the point that whilst such suggestions could be floated, researchers should be very careful to make moderate generalisations which do not reach too far beyond the original context, should make very clear the nature of generalising statements, and should clearly state the basis upon which such claims are made.

This not unreasonable scientific challenge to qualitative research procedures led us onto bigger questions from the philosophy of social science. Karl Popper, in my own sociological education, had typically been wheeled in as the arch curmudgeon – always ready to dampen the dreams of imaginative researchers with his relentless empiricism. Looking at his own words here, though, we found a Popper who was quite playful, within limits, and happy with any methodological approach as long as it eventually produced hypotheses which could be tested. Which seems fair enough. Thomas Kuhn, on the other hand – normally seen as a pretty cool guy by sociology teachers – emerged as the more persistent miserabilist, proposing a model of how science really works which is probably a decent critical description, but which still doesn't help us work out how we might reasonably claim to 'know' anything.

Both of these approaches had problems, so we therefore considered a slightly different approach: the idea of 'abduction', a causal explanation offered on the basis of cases observed. An abduction therefore suggests a hypothesis which fits with what has already been observed, but does not seek to make claims about future potential observations. Rather than being assessed in isolation, this hypothesis is then compared with competing theories, so that we can hope to arrive at 'the best available explanation' in the light of available evidence.

In keeping with this somewhat more modest aspiration, we also considered Nancy Cartwright's notion of 'the dappled world', an approach which would never assume that the findings or methods of one discipline would be necessarily applicable in another. Whether or not one agrees with Cartwright's radically non-universal angle, her focus on the real-world and everyday aspects of knowledge – 'messy' as they may be – is provocative.

In terms of the overall concerns of this book, this detour into the philosophies of science reminds us that:

- Science does not simply produce 'facts'; instead it offers propositions about the world.
- Even Popper, representing the 'strong' wing of positivist empiricism, does not want to prescribe particular methods or approaches; he merely asks that the propositions, arrived at through whichever method, can be *tested*.
- These propositions should draw upon (at least) a present set of observations, and will be assessed in competition with other hypotheses.
- There are continuing debates about the extent to which scientific knowledge can be abstracted from everyday reality. A prevalent view is that science should produce overarching explanations characterised by unity, purity, interconnectedness and universality, but another view disputes this.

If we want visual methods in social science to be defensible as reasonable scientific practice – fitting at least *somewhere* within the scientific development of knowledge – then these points offer some comfort. We can offer propositions, drawn from data, which can be considered by others.

Not everyone cares about this: some cultural theorists are happy to regard the scientific process as just another 'discourse'. I would agree that *fruitful ideas* are much more valuable than *data*; but it's still good if ideas and real-world experience can be brought together (especially since ideas that have no connection with real-world experiences, or possibilities, are likely to be a complete waste of time). Having considered the scientific context, in the next chapter we consider the connected discussions of knowledge in the social sciences specifically.

Chapter 4

Social science and social experience

In the previous chapter, we considered the debates within the philosophy of science about how we can claim to 'know' something, and the appropriate way in which researchers can proceed to develop knowledge. There are debates within social science, too, about how we can 'know' things about the social world in particular, and whether we can base our explanations on what people themselves have to say about social experience – or, alternatively, whether the 'reality' of social life exists somewhere above and beyond the experience of individual citizens. Indeed, these are matters which were grappled with by the 'founding fathers' of sociology, so it is relevant and appropriate to start with them. First we will consider the macro sociology of Emile Durkheim (which has much in common with that of Karl Marx, despite carrying different political implications), and then the methodological writings of Max Weber, which are more concerned with individual experience.

Classical sociology: Durkheim and 'social facts'

As the founder of the first European university department of sociology (in 1895), and the pioneering journal *L'Année Sociologique* (in 1896), Durkheim was keen to pin down what sociology *is*, and what it is *about*. He argued that sociology could play a scientific role through the study of 'social facts'. These are phenomena which are not part of individual psychology, but are nevertheless social, and are therefore the natural subject-matter of sociology. As Durkheim explains in *The Rules of Sociological Method*:

> There is in every society a certain group of phenomena which may be differentiated from those studied by the other natural sciences. When I fulfil my obligations as brother, husband, or citizen, when I execute my contracts, I perform duties which are defined, externally to myself and my acts, in law and in custom.
>
> (Durkheim, [1895] 1938: 1)

There are expected ways of behaving within professions, families, religions, consumer activity and social life which are part of everyday reality for individuals, but are felt by each individual to be external to themselves. In other words, people often slip into 'roles' which seem to be ready-made for them, rather than the products of spontaneous invention. Such social activities and duties may be engaged in happily, or with some reluctance, but they form solid blocs of behaviour which are clearly cultural – they are likely to vary across different times and different places – but which nevertheless for Durkheim constituted particular 'social facts' which could be studied more or less like other scientific phenomena, such as weather systems, or the behaviour of bees.

Durkheim accepts that not everybody knows what all the rules are – in fact it's part of his evidence that we sometimes have to consult family, friends or colleagues about what the 'done thing' is in a particular situation (ibid: 1). We mostly want to fit in, then, although Durkheim recognises that we do not always conform; again, it's part of his evidence that we will typically feel subject to, if not a strong punishment, then at least some kind of social disapproval, ridicule or shame, when we do not comply with regular behaviour (ibid: 2).

> Here, then, is a category of facts with very distinctive characteristics: it consists of ways of acting, thinking, and feeling, external to the individual, and endowed with a power of coercion, by reason of which they control him.
>
> (Durkheim, 1938: 3)

This 'control' is not, of course, direct, and is not 'strong' control. But Durkheim means that through the 'soft' control of social expectations – and the associated risk of social embarrassment, contempt or isolation – we are kept in line by these 'social facts', and that these therefore feel as 'real' to individuals as the laws set by government, or by physics.

As mentioned above, these 'facts' are clearly cultural, and indeed cultural difference gave Durkheim's new 'science' something to get its teeth into. For example, his famous study *Suicide* ([1897] 2002) took as its starting-point the observation that, in different countries or social groups, the suicide rate would typically be quite stable, year by year, but might be massively different to that of another country or group. From this observation he built a model which described suicide not as a consequence of individual psychological problems but as the product of particular 'social facts' in different societies. Features of the social framework – such as family integration, religion and military obligations – would produce a certain level of suicide, which for example in the mid-nineteenth century was consistently high in Denmark (around 260 suicides per one million inhabitants) and consistently low in Italy (around 34 suicides per one million inhabitants) – principally, Durkheim would say, because of the power of Catholic strictures, and correspondingly strong family values, in Italy (Durkheim, 2002: 105–25). This is a fundamental example of Durkheim's perspective and its methodological implications. A psychologist, he notes, could study each individual case, find that the victim was penniless, broken-hearted, depressed or otherwise lacking the will to go on, and deduce a motive for the suicide.

> But ... this motive does not cause people to kill themselves, nor, especially, cause a definite number to kill themselves in each society in a definite period of time. The productive cause of the phenomenon naturally escapes the observer of individuals only; for it lies outside individuals. To discover it, one must raise his point of view above individual suicides and perceive what gives them unity.
>
> (Durkheim, [1897] 2002: 288)

From his macro perspective, Durkheim is able to draw valuable conclusions about the levels of social integration in different societies. These are not simplistic: Durkheim does not merely conclude that low-suicide societies are happier, or have stronger family ties, than their high-suicide counterparts. Instead, he maps a network of connections that an individual may have with society, including nuances such as the level of individualism within different religions, expectations about family responsibilities and political stability. Suicide is not always equated with despair or disconnection, either: his category of 'altruistic suicide' – when a person kills themselves to avoid being a burden, or bringing shame, on their family or community – is a consequence of *too much* social integration, rather than not enough. (Durkheim refers to a range of anthropological studies to show traditions where men who are elderly or sick nobly commit suicide; where women kill themselves after their husband has died; and where followers or servants commit suicide when their chief has died; [1897] 2002: 176–86.)

Critics have pointed out, amongst other things, that Durkheim was relying on official statistics, which could be flawed in various ways. A published suicide statistic is not a straightforward record of how many suicides have taken place; rather, it is the result of a complex interplay of interpretations made by family, police and other authorities. In theory, cultural attitudes to suicide might mean that two societies with identical 'actual' rates of suicide might end up with quite different published statistics. You may or may not think that Durkheim's 'scientific' aspirations are spoilt by his inability to avoid this technicality.

Hoping to mimic scientific 'laws' whilst using scientifically imprecise evidence might seem odd, but I think that Durkheim's demonstration of a macro approach to sociology, whilst rather 'broad brush' in its approach, is compelling. Sociology *should* rise above the study of individual cases and tell us something broader about social existence in different societies. The problems with an individual psychological perspective have come up in my own work before – for example, the psychologists who were aware of individual cases of young people who had been upset by certain things they had seen on television, and therefore concluded that television was responsible for a range of complex social problems, were clearly guilty of a failure to 'raise their point of view', as Durkheim would put it; they were not paying attention to the bigger picture, where sociological and criminological evidence showed that various social and cultural factors were much more likely to predict antisocial behaviour than levels of television viewing (Gauntlett, 1995, 1997, 2005). Indeed, Durkheim put his finger on this very problem:

> The group thinks, feels, and acts quite differently from the way in which its members would were they isolated. If, then, we begin with the individual, we shall be able to understand nothing of what takes place in the group. In a word, there is between psychology and sociology the same break in continuity as between biology and the physicochemical sciences. Consequently, every time that a social phenomenon is directly explained by a psychological phenomenon, we may be sure that the explanation is false.
>
> ([1895] 1938: 104)

Whether or not one shares this dismissive view, it is clear that Durkheimian macro sociology can offer valuable insights into phenomena, as seen in the *Suicide* study, which simply could not be accessed if we stayed at the level of individuals and their personal interpretations of action.

Classical sociology: Weber and individual meanings

Having satisfied ourselves that Durkheim was able to demonstrate the power of sociology as a form of macro analysis, which need not concern itself too much with personal psychological dimensions, this is a good point at which to turn to Weber's emphasis on the *meanings* which actors ascribe to actions. Weber might just persuade us of the opposite point of view.

In his writings on methodology, Weber pointed out that if we merely observe behaviour but do not know the meaning ascribed to it by the individual, we are lacking the critical dimension which can lead to understanding. Suicide is an excellent example of this, as it is a deliberate meaningful act, and indeed is one which is *defined* by its meaning for the individual concerned – by the *intention* to kill oneself. Peter drives his car over a cliff, plunging the vehicle into the ocean, where he dies. Kate drives her car over the same cliff, plunging into the ocean, where she also dies. These two acts *appear* to be the same; it is only when we know their meanings that we can begin to usefully consider them. When we learn that Peter is happy but a very clumsy driver, whilst Kate is a great driver but one who has despaired and made a decision to end her life, the two same-looking acts become two considerably different tragedies.

Weber's emphasis on the importance of such distinctions was part of a much broader project. Like Durkheim, Weber reacted against Marx's economic determinism, and sought to establish his own approach to social life which considered the meanings of the political, religious and legal spheres of society, as well as the economic dimension. Unlike Durkheim, he felt that there were crucial differences between the social and natural sciences. Sociology could not simply set itself up as another branch of science, since people's behaviour would not be explainable in terms of fixed, predictive laws. As social life consists of people's individual actions, which are based on values, Weber felt that the social sciences must seek to understand how values underpin social action. This is clear from his very definition of sociology, presented at the start of his two-volume masterwork *Economy and Society* (this part written around 1919):

> Sociology (in the sense in which this highly ambiguous word is used here) is a science concerning itself with the interpretive understanding of social action and thereby with a causal explanation of its course and consequences. We shall speak of 'action' insofar as the acting individual attaches a subjective meaning to his behaviour – be it overt or covert, omission or acquiescence. Action is 'social' insofar as its subjective meaning takes account of the behaviour of others and is thereby oriented in its course.
>
> (Weber, 1978: 4)

Although Durkheim is not mentioned in the book, this definition was produced more than 25 years after his *Rules* were first published (in French), and Weber was carrying forward a rejection of Durkheimian positivism which had been initiated in Germany by Windelband in the 1890s, and Rickert after that (see Morrison, 1995, for a clear account of the debates which influenced Weber). By placing the *subjective meaning* of behaviour at the heart of his definition of sociology, Weber was clearly signalling the centrality of unique human experiences. In his fleshing out of this definition, under the heading 'Methodological foundations', Weber places particular emphasis on *Verstehen* – 'human understanding' – and the centrality of understandings and interpretations of meanings and intentions in human affairs. It is this which make the social sciences different from the natural sciences, and which explains why the methods of the natural sciences cannot be copied across to sociology. As Ken Morrison puts it:

> Stated simply, the *Verstehen* thesis is based on the idea that meaning precedes action; or more specifically, meaning is a causal component of action since we cannot act unless we know the meaning of other acts. This

meaning, Weber thought, constitutes a positive basis to make distinctions between the natural and social sciences, since the objects studied by the physical sciences do not have 'understanding'.

(Morrison, 1995: 278)

This emphasis on the particular meanings of social acts looks like the 'opposite' of Durkheim's approach: if Durkheim stands for big broad social theory – which wouldn't need to concern itself with such details – then Weber must stand for individualistic psychological case studies. But that's not what Weber intended. Weber produced broad-sweep studies of capitalism, bureaucracy, economics, law and religion, even though he did not seek to produce 'laws' of human behaviour. However, his model of social science, which builds from people's everyday experiences up to the level of social theory and analysis, is much more of a precursor to today's common understanding of sociology than Durkheim's attempted mirroring of the natural sciences.

Nevertheless, in Weber's work it is not entirely clear how the theoretical emphasis on personal interpretations connects up with the 'big picture' analyses of social life, especially since the latter are not based on any kind of social research seeking to explore people's perceptions of actions, or attributions of meaning to action. Part of Weber's answer lies in his use of 'ideal types', which are akin to thought experiments, used to explore certain models of social action and reality. An 'ideal type' does not present a description of reality, but rather accentuates key features of an area of society, or sphere of social action, so that we can understand it better, and compare it with others. So, for example, we might consider an 'ideal type' of a system of democracy, or a particular religion, so that we can consider the consequences of its 'ultimate' form without having to worry about the muddier reality, which can involve personalities causing problems for the system, or the system not working as well as it should due to resistance, incompetence or apathy. The 'ideal type' gives Weber a way of seeming to incorporate people's affective responses without having to actually research these in reality. Nevertheless, there seems to be a gap between the supposed emphasis on real people's meanings and interpretations, and the broader social theorising. We are still left with a sociology which could deal with ground-level studies of communication and interactions, or grand theoretical accounts of the development of social life, economics or religion, but not really connect up these levels meaningfully within one theory.

A modern solution: Giddens and structuration theory

One solution to this has been suggested by Anthony Giddens, writing some 65 years later. Giddens's theory of 'structuration' makes a connection between micro-level studies of people's everyday interpretations, and macro-level discussion of social structures and social forces, by proposing a circular model where one feeds into the other, and we can't understand one without the other. The repetition of 'expected' social attitudes and behaviour is what gives them form and, therefore, reproduces the social structure. The invisible 'social forces', which Durkheim talked about, turn out to be a set of commonly held expectations about behaviour – in other words, the meanings and interpretations of action that Weber highlighted. In *The Constitution of Society* (1984) Giddens noted that the development of social theory had been dominated by the 'empire-building endeavours' of functionalism and structuralism on the one hand, and interpretive sociologies on the other. The former, like Durkheim, emphasise the power of social structures, and the latter, like Weber, emphasise action and meaning. Giddens's structuration model potentially brings this competition to an end, and adds fruitful meaning to both perspectives, by sealing them in a loop:

> The basic domain of study of the social sciences, according to the theory of structuration, is neither the experience of the individual actor, nor the existence of any form of societal totality, but social practices ordered across space and time. Human social activities, like some self-reproducing items in nature, are recursive. That is to say, they are not brought into being by social actors but continually recreated by them via the very means whereby they express themselves *as* actors. In and through their activities agents reproduce the conditions that make these activities possible.
>
> (Giddens, 1984: 2)

This idea is both simple and complex. We can see it happening on both small and large scales, but the small-scale examples help us to picture how it can occur in broader terms too. So, for example, think of life in a community of anarchist environmentalists. The everyday practices of the people living there shape an overarching idea of how life is to be lived, in that context, which then informs how newcomers and general residents are to behave and to think and to express themselves. This example has an obvious ideological dimension, but the same would apply in a totally different context, such as life in a well-heeled retirement home in a conservative town by the seaside. Here, again – and in just the same way, even though the content of the ideas may be totally different – the everyday behaviour of residents shapes a common understanding of how life is to be lived there, which then – to repeat this same formula in the different context – informs how newcomers and general residents are to behave and to think and to express themselves. As Giddens puts it:

> I don't want to discard the Durkheimian point that society is a structured phenomenon and that the structural properties of a group or a society have

effects upon the way people act, feel and think. But when we look at what those structures are, they are obviously not like the physical qualities of the external world. They depend upon regularities of social reproduction. Language has this incredibly fixed form. You can't go against even the most apparently minute rules of the English language without getting very strong reactions from other speakers. But at the same time, language doesn't exist anywhere, or it only exists in its instantiations in writing or speaking. Much the same thing is true for social life in general. That is, society only has form and that form only has effects on people in so far as structure is produced and reproduced in what people do.

(Interviewed in Giddens and Pierson, 1998: 77)

Giddens therefore bridges the gap between Durkheim and Weber (and/or the gap between Weber's methodological prescriptions and his own theoretical practice). Giddens's model also shows how social structures can, over time, change: since these structures are reproduced through the actions of individuals, this means that, as people make individual decisions to live life a little differently, this can lead to macro-level social change.

Indeed, the emphasis on the possibility of change is an important and distinctive part of Giddens's overall model. As we saw in Chapter 1, Giddens highlights that modern Western societies are increasingly characterised by greater levels of personal (and institutional) reflexivity – thinking about identity and lifestyle has become an everyday dimension of social existence, reinforced by contemporary media. As ties to traditional roles becomes weaker, individuals at all levels of society necessarily think more about their 'aspirations', 'goals' and what they'd like to do with their lives. In the connected-up structuration model, this micro-level hubbub of conversations, ideas, magazine articles, TV shows and stories about personal identity and self-fulfilment feeds into the macro level of, for example, governmental policies which affect lifestyle, health and the family, and the ways in which large corporations find opportunities to profit from the ways in which people live their lives.

Giddens's value is enhanced because his eclectic approach makes use of concepts from diverse fields – such as the notion of the *unconscious*, which is avoided by some sociologists because it's too difficult to talk about empirically (that is, you can never give someone a questionnaire about the contents of their unconscious). Traditional sociologies often struggle to take individual meanings and motivations on board, whilst not allowing anything that might seem too 'psychological'. Giddens's structuration theory, however, *requires* us to accept levels of consciousness lying beneath the kinds of meanings and motivations which research participants can discuss in interviews. Indeed, in Giddens's three-level model of the consciousness of social actors, only the top level – 'discursive consciousness' – is of the kind that could be reported and discussed by interviewees (1984: 6–7). Below that is 'practical consciousness', which refers to the everyday knowledge held by social actors which incorporates 'the capability to "go on" within the routines of social life' (p. 4), but which is not usually made explicit and so does not become part of discursive consciousness (although there is no barrier between the two, and practical consciousness can become part of discursive consciousness whenever an individual chooses to consider or reflect on their normally taken-for-granted behaviour). Below that is the unconscious. Giddens does not follow a strictly Freudian line on the nature of the unconscious, but he says that there are barriers, 'centred principally upon repression', between discursive consciousness and the unconscious (p. 7). (This model, I would suggest, could just as usefully be adopted with a different take on the unconscious, such as the Jungian view which sees the unconscious less in terms of repression, and more as a positive source of creativity.)

Structuration theory necessarily invokes these less-than-fully-conscious levels of experience because it assumes that a great deal of social life goes on in a routine way, without being consciously deliberated over. Social systems are reproduced because people casually reproduce conventions, partly because it's not necessary to think about them too much, and partly because it's often unnecessarily taxing to challenge them (even if you wanted to) and, anyway, social approval comes from going along with them. (Incidentally, the unconscious reappears in the next chapter, where we consider the extent to which people may or may not be able to report on their own motivations and identities.)

Bourdieu: a different take on the same issues

As we have seen, Anthony Giddens's approach recognises that social norms and expectations are maintained and reproduced through everyday practices. His model tends to highlight the opportunities for flexibility and change, which is broadly optimistic and reassuring for progressively minded people (or, to put it another way, bad news for fundamentalists, of whatever persuasion). For example, we can see that a diverse array of factors over the past 30 or 40 years have led to a more accepting cultural climate for gay people in modern Western societies (although we have to recognise that these are still littered with considerable pockets of more traditional attitudes). These influential factors include changing government policies, pop songs, necessarily more open official communication about sexual practices in response to the AIDS crisis, high-profile celebrities and artists 'coming out', TV dramas, marriage and partnership laws, teen magazines, precedents set in legal rulings, political campaigns, and numerous other agents from family life, pop culture, lifestyle-related business, government and law. Everyone plays a part, from George Bush to George Michael, as well as your own relatives. Each particular instance is relatively unremarkable in itself – a pop star confirms that he is happy to be gay, or a law is changed to be slightly more liberal – but each of these occasions add up, over time, to a kind of slow-motion revolution in the cultural climate, because of the circuit of the micro (e.g. personal attitudes) and the macro (e.g. government policies) feeding one into the other. The everyday reflexivity about such lifestyle issues can lead, in Giddens's model, to fruitful changes.

A contrasting but related model is offered by French sociologist Pierre Bourdieu, whose work also seeks to connect up macro social structures with micro everyday practices. Bourdieu is noted within sociology for his concepts of *habitus* and *field*. Bourdieu does not accept that society is simply the collective term for a set of rational individual actors, nor that society is a set of structures existing 'above' and separate from individuals. The notion of *habitus* is intended to sit between these two poles, and to explain how a person becomes a product of their particular place in the social system and then is a kind of vehicle for its reproduction in others. The concept therefore connects macro-level social stratification with micro-level everyday life, but in a more fixed way than in Giddens, with little emphasis on the possibilities for change. Bourdieu offers more of an explanation – although not an *excuse* – for how the status quo is reproduced. He says – in characteristically dense prose – that the habitus is 'an acquired system of generative schemes objectively adjusted to the particular conditions in which it is constituted' (Bourdieu, 1977: 95). The word 'generative' here would be highlighted by Bourdieu fans who point out that the author emphasises people's *creative* responses to their circumstances; although stuck within a particular *field* – the inescapable boundaries in which we live – a person can find different ways to 'play the game' (Bourdieu and Wacquant, 1992: 98) – but not, usually, to get out of the game altogether.

There is room for manoeuvre for individuals, then; in various interviews and publications, Bourdieu emphasises that he in no way wants to portray people as the passive creations of a ready-made social order (see Bourdieu, 1990; Bourdieu and Wacquant 1992). The habitus is a subjective, internal construction, an experience of individual life, in a dialectical relationship with the wider world (the field). At the same time, though, Bourdieu seems to assign this social context such power that, as Richard Jenkins has put it, '[Bourdieu's] social universe ultimately remains one in which things happen to people, rather than a world in which they can intervene in their individual and collective destinies' (2002: 91). In the definition of habitus quoted above, for example, the 'generative schemes' – a phrase which could be taken to refer to people's individual and creative responses to the circumstances in which they find themselves – are actually said to be 'an *acquired* system' (my emphasis) and therefore cannot be very individual or creative; acquired behaviours are surely the kind of handed-down traditional responses which are the *opposite* of individual and creative action.

This casual determinism seems to infect all of Bourdieu's work even as he denies it. For example, in one interview in which the author dismisses those people who he says do not understand his work and accuse him of determinism, *on the same page* he suggests that his whole project could be summarised thus:

> [You could say] I am trying to develop a *genetic structuralism*: the analysis of objective structures – those of different *fields* – is inseparable from the analysis of the genesis, within biological individuals, of the mental structures which are to some extent the product of the incorporation of social structures; inseparable, too, from the analysis of the genesis of these social structures themselves: the social space, and the groups that occupy it, are the product of historical struggles (in which agents participate in accordance with their position in the social space and with the mental structures through which they apprehend this space).
>
> (Bourdieu, 1990: 14)

Although this makes a neat link between the social and the individual, a close reading soon gets the alarm bells ringing: the 'agents' don't seem to have any agency at all, as they merely 'participate in accordance with their position in the social space' and the corresponding set of 'mental structures' which they seem to have been given. Even the 'genetic' metaphor points directly to the notion that we are born with a certain set of codes which can determine our future in certain ways. Whilst saying that he cannot see why anyone would call him a determinist, then, Bourdieu paints a picture of people growing, like plants, according to a particular genetic plan. Part of Bourdieu's defence is that he is interested in how people adapt and live life in different circumstances – different fields – but he remains similar to the botanist, who is similarly interested in how plants adapt and live in different (literal) fields. It is not because of a misplaced sense of self-importance that people don't like to equated with vegetables. Individuals can face considerable financial and cultural constraints which contemporary sociology must always be aware of, but we need to assume that all individuals have more agency, and will produce more interesting solutions to their problems, than, say, potatoes would.

Richard Jenkins, who develops a thorough critique of Bourdieu whilst being careful to highlight ways in which the author offers fruitful concepts and is 'good to think with' (2002: 11), summarises the problem:

> Despite his apparent acknowledgement of, and enthusiasm for, resistance, it is difficult to find examples in his work of its efficacy or importance. The ongoing and successful reproduction of relationships of domination lies at the heart of Bourdieu's social theory ... Social change is peripheral to the model and difficult to account for.
>
> (Jenkins, 2002: 90–1)

This doesn't mean that Bourdieu is necessarily wrong, of course: maybe the most important point about modern society *is* that we are trapped in more-

or-less deterministic social structures which we may not even be aware of. And Bourdieu was not wheeled into this chapter just so that we could criticise him. Having briefly introduced his approach, I will now make use of his ideas in two ways; first, to give us a new perspective on the question – which I discussed in relation to Durkheim and Weber above – about the extent to which we should value the accounts provided by social actors themselves, and secondly to consider whether a hybrid model using ideas from both Bourdieu and Giddens may be feasible.

Can I ask you a question?

Earlier in this chapter we saw that Durkheim argued that sociologists could identify general 'social facts' by looking at macro-level information – such as official statistics, laws and prevalent religious doctrines – and therefore without needing to speak to individual social actors, whose personal views would not really contribute to the development of a broad sociological understanding. Weber, on the other hand, argued that a sociologist can't really make any sense of social activity without taking on board the explanations that people give for their own actions – and, indeed, that we cannot even classify some actions (such as an event in which a person dies) until we believe that we understand the personal interpretations of the actor(s) involved at the time (suicide, accident, manslaughter, murder?). Having briefly outlined the basic approaches of Giddens and Bourdieu, I can now consider what they would say about this question. Can we arrive at a useful understanding of social life or social experience by asking people themselves?

We saw above that Giddens acknowledges that much everyday social activity is routine and in general would not regularly be explored in 'discursive consciousness'. However he also credits people with knowledge about their circumstances which is not simply a handy kind of awareness, but is actually *constitutive* of social experience. 'Social life,' he says, 'is continually contingently reproduced by knowledgeable human agents – that's what gives it fixity and that's what also produces change' (Giddens, in Giddens and Pierson, 1998: 90). Whilst Bourdieu primarily seems to see people being born into, and then reproducing, established social categories, Giddens argues that contemporary societies are characterised by an expansion in 'people's everyday knowledgeability' (ibid: 92). He asserts:

> Reflexivity has two senses, one very general, and the other more directly relevant to modern social life. All human beings are reflective in the sense in which thinking about what one does is part of doing it, whether consciously or on the level of practical consciousness. Social reflexivity refers to a world increasingly constituted by information rather than pre-given codes of conduct. It is how we live after the retreat of tradition and nature, because

of having to take so many forward-oriented decisions. In that sense, we live in a much more reflexive way than previous generations have done.

(Ibid: 115)

In this model, individuals have access to more information than ever before about how people live their lives, and the 'lifestyle' theme of many newspaper supplements, TV shows, magazines and other media means that we are regularly presented with narratives and tools for thinking about everyday life. The decline of tradition means that people are having to consider and evaluate their choices in a more conscious and deliberative way. Therefore, although aspects of existence may remain largely unconsidered, it would certainly make sense to explore people's feelings, assumptions and stumbling-blocks about everyday life through qualitative research.

Bourdieu, however, takes a different view. Research interviews, he suggests, prompt people to explain and justify their behaviour, rather than to merely present a description of it:

> The explanation that agents may provide of their own practice, thanks to a quasi theoretical reflection on their practice, conceals, even from their own eyes, the true nature of their practical mastery, i.e. that it is *learned ignorance* (*docta ignorantia*), a mode of practical knowledge not comprising knowledge of its own principles. It follows that this learned ignorance can only give rise to the misleading discourse of a speaker himself misled, ignorant both of the objective truth about his practical mastery (which is that it is ignorant of its own truth) and of the true principle of the knowledge his practical mastery contains.
>
> (Bourdieu, 1977: 19)

Bourdieu is saying, in other words, that although a person may have 'practical mastery' over their everyday activities – they may be highly competent in their field – the researcher cannot actually ask them to reflect upon this, because people are ignorant of their own level of ignorance. Unaware of quite *how* unaware of their own motivations they are, they inevitably generate accounts which are of no use to the researcher. This stance is consistent with Bourdieu's view that people's agency is heavily prescribed by the social circumstances in which they find themselves, but is still a surprising illustration of the extent to which he has little time for other people's reflections on their existence. (Presumably Bourdieu considers that his own account, unlike that of other members of society, is uniquely pertinent.) Jenkins summarises Bourdieu's argument thus:

> The actors' own explanations of their practice are (a) no more than another practice, part of the world of empirical reality, and hence (b)

from a realist perspective, either insufficient or unreliable. They are, rather, something to be explained.

(Jenkins, 2002: 95)

Of course, this view includes a sensible methodological point. Rather than necessarily taking people's accounts to be perfect descriptions of their actual practices, we need to consider *why* they provide the kinds of accounts that they do. The problem, though, is that this sends us down the only alternative path, in which we assume that the explanation presented by an external 'expert' is superior to that produced by the actor themselves. Of course, this *can* happen: in psychoanalysis, for example, the therapist's explanation for why their client did something might *sometimes* seem incredibly insightful and accurate, even though the client would not have thought of it themselves. But this does not always happen, and we would usually only feel pleased with the 'revelation' if the client *themselves* thinks there's something in it. Bourdieu goes one step further, and doubts that it's ever worth asking people themselves. As Jenkins goes on directly to say:

> While the reality to be explained consists solely of individuals and things and the relations between them, 'what is really going on' ('real' reality) is more than or different to that empirical universe. As a result, despite his rejection of the epistemological arrogance of structuralism, where the social scientist (like mother) knows best, he eventually adopts a similar position. Actors may believe that they act, at least in part, by formulating goals, making decisions and putting them into effect. They may, what is more, explain this to the inquiring sociologist. Bourdieu, however, knows that this is an illusion; the true explanation of behaviour is to be found in the habitus.
>
> (Ibid)

In other words, the 'actual' reasons for people's behaviour lies in their social circumstances (their class and upbringing and cultural milieu), and not in the reasons which they would give if you asked them. The patronising dimension of this approach is played out in Bourdieu's most famous book, *Distinction* (1984). This work develops a complex and important set of ideas about how distinctions in cultural taste are used as a marker of social identity, and presents a theory in which struggles over the meaning of things are a significant dimension of class struggle. The book *does* present some people's accounts of their everyday lives and cultural tastes, quoted at some length in their own words from interviews, but Bourdieu keeps these at arm's length, boxed-out from the main text. Instead he prefers statistical data from a number of surveys about cultural tastes, which he can use to show the connections between education, class and taste; demonstrating how people use cultural signifiers to position themselves in class terms, seeking to appear superior to those 'below' them and typically aspiring, not always successfully, to be like those 'above' them on the ladder, with the educated wealthy and the uneducated poor typically being less anxious about all this than those in between.

On the one hand Bourdieu's analysis effectively shows how cultural value is both socially constructed, and is a manifestation of inequality. At the same time, though, his approach presents the working classes as basically ignorant (especially when contrasted with the high-culture privileges and agency which Bourdieu himself enjoys), and permanently stuck at the bottom of the heap with no particular story to tell, or cultural contribution to make, themselves.

A hybrid model?

In recent years some researchers have noted the useful aspects of the self-reflexivity thesis proposed by Giddens and his followers, and the notion of habitus developed by Bourdieu, and sought to develop a hybrid model which would combine the best elements of both. At first glance, this seems an optimistic task. Bourdieu's vision of people primarily constrained by social circumstances, and who would not be able to account for their motivations and lifestyles, is clearly different to Giddens's picture of self-reflexive actors constructing their own identities in a social world in which traditional social constraints are on the decline. Bourdieu's argument problematises models which assume that people are rational and self-aware, and as Paul Sweetman says, 'indeed, this is partly the point' (2003: 536). Sweetman notes that for Bourdieu, reflexivity only springs up in times of crisis, when there is a temporary disjunction between the habitus and the field. However, proposing a model which employs elements of Giddens and Bourdieu, Sweetman suggests that:

> In conditions of late-, high-, or reflexive-modernity, endemic crises … can lead to a more or less permanent disruption of social position, or a more or less constant disjunction between habitus and field. In this context reflexivity ceases to reflect a temporary lack of fit between habitus and field but itself becomes habitual, and is thus incorporated into the habitus in the form of the flexible or *reflexive* habitus.
>
> (Sweetman, 2003: 541)

It is not clear whether putting the notion of self-reflexivity (which highlights agency) within the frame of the habitus (which is mostly an outline of constraint) can really work. The habitus *can* be seen as a space within which individuals invent and improvise, and 'play the game' of adapting to their given social situation (and Sweetman provides a spirited defence of this view, pp. 534–5), but – as I noted above – Bourdieu's more deterministic statements tend to override this interpretation and make the 'play' seem unimportant or even desperately pointless. And the notions of habitus and self-reflexivity *both* end up seeming weaker if we say that self-reflexivity has become merely a routine part of the habitus we're stuck in.

Matthew Adams (2006) has surveyed other attempts to combine the two different models. One strand seeks to 'keep' the recognition of people's reflexive subjectivity whilst using Bourdieu to 'dampen' the celebratory tone of self-fulfilment which the Giddens approach can suggest. Another less optimistic view draws upon the literature about self-reflexivity, but sees this discourse as a kind of conspiracy to avoid talking about real social differences. Overall he finds that:

> What does emerge from [this work] is a more complex portrayal of an embedded, embodied and contradictory reflexivity which is not naively envisaged as either some kind of internalised meta-reflection or simplistic liberatory potential against a backdrop of retreating social structure. A notion of habitus tempered by an ambiguous, complex, contradictory reflexivity suggests how social characterisations can be reproduced but also challenged, overturned in uneven, 'piecemeal' ways.
>
> (Adams, 2006: 521)

Some of these 'hybrid' theoretical models would appear to work better than others. But in the end, the question of the extent to which people take a reflexive attitude to their lives and are able to actually change their own circumstances (or not) is an empirical one, and we therefore may now benefit most from studies which seek to explore these questions in the real world. Therefore in the next chapter I turn back to science, mixed in with some philosophy, to consider what consciousness *actually means*. And then I'll move on, in the rest of the book, to explore new ways of capturing people's expressive reflections on their own lived existence, and to see if these can meaningfully contribute to social understanding.

Chapter 5

Inside the brain

Books about social research or research methods do not usually talk much about how the brain works in general, or the nature of conscious and unconscious thought in particular. Indeed, these things might not even appear to be relevant. In the social sciences it often seems to be assumed that people have a set of attitudes or opinions, as well as actual behaviours, which we can ask them about and which they will hopefully tell us. I say 'hopefully' here, because it is commonly acknowledged that there are difficulties in getting people to report on these things: some people are shy, prefer to be private, or may not want to admit to thoughts or behaviours which are frowned upon socially.

The assumption, nevertheless, is that these things already reside inside a person's brain – as if there is a written-down list of 'my attitudes', and another one of 'things I have done' – so that a researcher can come along and, as it were, collect a printout of this information (i.e. ask questions, get answers). So the standard problem recognised by researchers is that some people may not be willing to show you their list. There is also a concern that some respondents might *lie* about what is *actually* on their list.

This is straightforward stuff, though. Researchers can work out ways to make their subjects comfortable, so that they may be more willing to speak openly, and can devise strategies to avoid, or detect, the likelihood of people telling fibs. So you may be asking the question:

Why are we interested in the conscious and the unconscious?

Social researchers may be trying hard to access those internal lists of attitudes and behaviours, but this rests on a surprisingly naïve view of how their participants' brains might work. Maybe it's not really a 'view' – it's more a status quo attitude, where if you try to get at what someone 'really thinks' about something then you've obviously done your best to peek at their internal list. I think we really face a deeper problem, though: *what if there is no list?*

The traditional 'authentic self' model would assume that you can ask me my opinion on a particular issue, and I will be able to consult my internal list (or just instinctively 'know'), and therefore tell you what my opinion is. But if there is no list, or no instinctive knowing, then we have to consider a different model – let's call it the 'dynamically generated presentation of self' model. In this case, when you ask me my opinion on a particular issue, I work out what to say based on:

- a general matrix of feelings and memories which lead us towards what my answer would probably be on this particular question;
- my memory of what I have said about this issue before;
- my memory of what I have said to *you* before, about this and related issues;
- my desire to be consistent (or not);
- my willingness to admit to what I have previously said or thought about this issue;
- your possible response, and whether something positive or negative might follow on from different responses I might give (which may be a good or bad impression, or a prize, or a punishment);
- whether I can be bothered, or think it would be best, to respond seriously, or humorously;

and some other factors. This is not all consciously worked out, bit by bit, before I give you an answer, but the brain can make quick (though not necessarily brilliant) unconscious judgements on all this in a flash.

I don't know about you, but this model seems to fit with everyday experience. It's not great to admit to – it would seem better to be able to say 'I know my own mind' about a wide range of political, ethical, psychological and domestic issues. And of course, we are not usually 'all at sea'. On some – or perhaps many – issues we may well have a clear set of 'opinions'. Even here, though, it's not a ready-made 'list'. Having a clear set of opinions means, I am suggesting, that we have a good memory of what we usually say about these matters, and that we are happy about – maybe even proud of – the response which we typically generate on these questions. These opinions connect well with our sense of ourselves – the set of well-established thoughts (or memories of thoughts) which make up our 'identity' – and integrate well with our general identity-story. In these cases, we can generate an account of our firm opinion, and perhaps gain pleasure from the telling. Note that a *new* account is generated, though, and is bound to be nuanced somewhat according to the context – it's not the simple 'printout' of an established opinion.

On other matters, opinions are far from being ready-made. What do I think of the new Minister for Work and Pensions? Well, I hadn't really thought about it, but since you ask, I can generate a reasonably confident-seeming view based on the bits of information I can recall, plus my general feelings about that political party, plus what I usually *say* about that party, plus a desire to look well-informed. Similarly: what do I think of Microsoft? Courgettes? Iran? Polyester? Globalisation? Skimmed milk? The Pope? Nuclear power? I have some ideas, but if you want a few sentences on each of these then I'll have to generate them. What do I think about our quiet colleague Janet? Well, she's quiet; beyond that, I'll have to start generating again.

This 'dynamically generated presentation of self' model might appear to link with the work of Erving Goffman, whose influential *The Presentation of Self in Everyday Life* (1959) suggested that people create performances for the 'audience' of the people they are interacting with, in order – it is implied – to get along comfortably with them. The problem with Goffman is that it's never clear 'who' is directing the presentation – or why. Goffman's discussion stays at the level of the actor's on-stage performance; there seems to be a backstage agent – otherwise the stage would not be a stage – but this more authentic personality remains unexamined.

In the model which I have started to sketch here, I think we *do* want to know about the agent which is putting the 'presentation of self' together. How does this actually *work*? The agent is clearly your brain. So how does your brain work? As is well known, this is perhaps the most difficult question we could stumble into.

The idea of the unconscious

Let's begin with the basics. Conscious thought may seem mysterious, even miraculous, but we can agree that it happens. We'll come back to what consciousness actually is, shortly. What about the unconscious, though – does the unconscious even exist? Readers with a background knowledge of, say, Freud and Jung may think that this question is controversial in scientific circles – as I did, before throwing myself into the contemporary neuroscientific literature on consciousness. Not so. The arguments made by psychoanalysts *about* the unconscious remain highly controversial, but the *existence* of unconscious processing is widely accepted. This is a relief, because the common-sense notion of asking questions and receiving answers, which I was discussing above, seems to require it, because the brain simply doesn't have time to *consciously* run through a selection of possible presentational scenarios at every step. In some relaxed conversations we might 'work out' what we think about an issue by talking about it, but in other situations, such as a job interview, we have to generate confident speech and get it 'right first time'. In either of these cases, *something inside* is causing the words to come out of the mouth, with no 'breathing space' for much conscious composition of possible alternatives before that happens.

In fact, the idea that the brain is working on material above and beyond (or beneath and before) the conscious stream of thought has been around for centuries. In Guy Claxton's history of the unconscious, *The Wayward Mind*

(2006), he shows that 4,000 years ago, the ancient Egyptians believed in the subterranean ocean of Nun, which they would slip into when asleep, where mingled mythic elements representing the conscious and unconscious, including dark and powerful forces which could never be allowed into the daylight of consciousness (pp. 27–30). Although they did not have a word for what the Greeks would call the *psyche*, they divided their inner life into *Ba* and *Ka*:

> *Ba* is the principle of consciousness. When unconscious, through fainting or in sleep, it is *Ba* that has temporarily gone AWOL. And *Ka* is the fundamental source of life energy. It is the 'mains' into which we are still plugged while asleep. It is life-giving, and full of life – but not conscious. *Ka* is the unconscious life-support system that makes consciousness possible.
>
> (Claxton, 2006: 58)

A thousand years later, the classical Greek use of the word *psyche* also described an invisible life-force, but the unconscious sensor which would receive messages from the gods was in the *phrenes* (somewhere in the heart or chest). Claxton notes that Homer's writings about this make him 'one of the remote grandfathers of psychology, because he did address the question of what it was, inside people, that resonated to the wishes of Zeus and Athena' (p. 61) – wishes which were not the product of a person's own consciousness. Fast-forward from here to the eighteenth and nineteenth centuries, when language to describe unconscious events started to appear, alongside a range of ways of thinking about the mind. Claxton notes, perhaps exaggerating slightly:

> The unconscious was all the rage in the fashionable salons of mid-nineteenth century London and Paris. Repression and the archetypes were topics of widespread discussion long before Freud and Jung's successful rebranding of them. But speculations were wild and confused.
>
> (Claxton, 2006: 23)

This prehistory of what we call 'the unconscious' today has been explored in a range of historical studies, such as *The Unconscious Before Freud* (Whyte, 1979) and *The Discovery of the Unconscious* (Ellenberger, 1970). Let's pick up the story with Freud, though. If not the first, he was the most significant theorist of the unconscious mind that the world had then known.

Freud and the repressed unconscious

Sigmund Freud's model of the influence of the unconscious in everyday life, and its significance in explaining human behaviour, was to have a massive impact on twentieth-century thought. His ideas have infected the everyday 'explanations' which we are likely to think of when seeking to explain the motivations of artists, writers and murderers, as well as our friends and relations. Here is a typical Freud defence of the unconscious:

> It is both *necessary* and *legitimate* to postulate the unconscious, and … we have a great deal of *evidence* for its existence. It is necessary because the information provided by consciousness is riddled with gaps; in healthy and sick people alike, psychic acts frequently take place that we can explain only by presupposing other acts that are not registered by consciousness. These include not only 'slips' and dreams … but also in our most personal daily experience we encounter ideas of unknown origin and the results of thought processes whose workings remain hidden from us.
>
> (Freud, [1915] 2005: 50)

In fact, as indicated above, this much was not especially controversial and was a common part of nineteenth-century thought (Cousins, 2005: p. ix). It was Freud's development of these foundations – in particular the idea that the unconscious was the home of drives, desires and memories which were the *cause* of conscious thoughts and behaviours – which was especially groundbreaking, and successfully popularised by Freud and his followers. We do not need to go into great detail on Freud here, but it is worth noting his foresight, such as in this analogy:

> In psychoanalysis we have no choice but to insist that psychic processes are in themselves unconscious, and the way they are perceived by consciousness is comparable to the way the outside world is perceived by the sense organs.
>
> (Freud, [1915] 2005: 54)

Here Freud proposed a view which would emerge out of neuroscientific research many decades later: all brain activity is going on anyway – not just dealing with routines of bodily coordination and perception, but actually processing all the stuff of life – and we are not conscious of that work; consciousness merely offers a window on that activity. The metaphor used by Claxton is that the brain does all its hard work under the bonnet, like the engine in a car, and 'you', the conscious agent, simply get to look at the dashboard (2006: 341). I'll come back to this idea shortly.

Freud took this model of conscious and unconscious brain activity and moved with it in a particular direction, oriented towards solving the problems of his neurotic patients. His more detailed ideas about the unconscious were correspondingly concerned with *repression* – the ways in which potentially disturbing psychological matter was repressed, and subsequently had detrimental effects on everyday psychological life. The usefulness of these particular insights has been hotly debated ever since; more importantly for us, this approach lent a particular emphasis to Freud's general theory of the unconscious. 'Perhaps unwisely,' as Claxton delicately puts it, Freud subsequently 'tried to install *this* model of the unconscious – one designed to account for some of the odder oddities of the mind's operation – right at the centre of his view of the mind as a whole' (2006: 191). Freud made a very important contribution to twentieth-century thought by popularising and developing the view of the unconscious as vitally important to both everyday life and long-term personality and identity formation. However, some felt that his view of its effects was unnecessarily negative.

Jung and the creative unconscious

Carl Jung was strongly influenced by Freud, but after seven years of correspondence and friendship (1906–13), he came to reject Freud's particular version of psychoanalysis. As we have seen, Freud tended to focus on the negative impact of the unconscious, which was primarily seen as a dark pit into which unacceptable sexual and taboo thoughts were repressed. Nasty gases from this buried matter would come wafting up and cause unwanted effects in conscious life. Freudian psychoanalysis, therefore, was a matter of digging down into this dungeon to unearth, and thus neutralise, the toxic material – the corpses under the patio. Jung, on the other hand, saw the unconscious as a potentially much more positive and fruitful force, concerned with the present and future, and representing a necessary dimension which should be embraced, alongside consciousness, to appreciate the whole personality.

In particular, Jung saw the unconscious as the home of important creative and emotional feelings. He noted that Western culture has a tendency to value thinking over emotionalism, bolstered by its successes in industry and technology, which could lead individuals to become detached from their emotional selves. We learn to value a practical, logical kind of consciousness; but emotions and complexity are part of the whole self, and we see them manifested in anxieties and psychological 'problems', as well as dreams, and everyday reactions to events. Emotional responses are not 'composed' in consciousness, Jung observed, but appear anyway:

> The autonomy of the unconscious therefore begins where emotions are generated. Emotions are instinctive, involuntary reactions which upset the rational order of consciousness by their elemental outbursts.
>
> (Jung, [1939] 1998: 215)

Freud had arguably lost sight of the idea the consciousness was a small window onto the much broader spread of unconscious processing; as noted above, he came to view the unconscious primarily in terms of repression, as a kind of dustbin for stuff we are unwilling or unable to deal with. Jung suggested that Freud saw unconscious material as content which could potentially have been conscious, but which happened to have been repressed; whereas his own view was that unconscious content is 'utterly different' from that in consciousness, and evades understanding (ibid: 214). Nevertheless it is the motor which drives many of our finest achievements.

Jung therefore took a view that has more in common with today's thinking: 'Consciousness grows out of an autonomous psyche which is older than it, and which goes on functioning together with it or even in spite of it' (ibid: 218). If our authentic self lies in consciousness, then we would expect this consciousness to be the 'king' of our brainworld, exerting all the power and influence. However, Jung says, this is not the case:

> Unfortunately, the facts show the exact opposite: consciousness succumbs all too easily to unconscious influences, and these are often truer and wiser than our conscious thinking ... Normally the unconscious collaborates with the conscious without friction or disturbance, so that one is not even aware of its existence. But when an individual or a social group deviates too far from their instinctual foundations, they then experience the full impact of unconscious forces.
>
> (Ibid, pp. 218–19)

The unconscious here is a powerful guiding hand, 'intelligent and purposive', seeking 'balance' (ibid). Such ideas can appear quasi-mystical – seeming like a sentimental Hollywood message about the magic power of being 'true' to yourself and 'following your heart' – but Jung is only saying that your brain will ultimately want to look after itself, an idea which can be seen as being at the pragmatic and Darwinian end of a spectrum which has romantic and spiritual ideas at the *opposite* end. Since your brain, as a whole system, embodies both the conscious and unconscious, it is only right that the unconscious should provide a wise kind of 'correcting' function for the sometimes inappropriate or overambitious schemes cooked up in consciousness.

For example, a young man might put aside his ambition to be a fashion designer and instead embark upon a career in banking because it seemed to be a 'logical' choice (he always did quite well at maths in school, his father was a bank manager, and his family and peers thought it sounded like a good and respectable career). He might do moderately well at this work, whilst also being aware that he did not love the job. Meanwhile he might sleep badly, become ill often, and snap irritably at people, whilst not being quite sure why; and one day would simply be unable to go to work. These negative phenomena would be the unconscious asserting itself and seeking to pull the self onto a more appropriate path.

Jung therefore sought to capture insights from the unconscious realm within his therapeutic techniques, so that they could be used to better understand the self. He discovered that art-making and creative play could lead to an uninhibited state during which meaningful material would surface. Indeed, this discovery stemmed from his own experience: after his break with Freud, Jung went through 'a period of inner uncertainty' (Jung, [1961] 1997: 21), which only began to be resolved when he decided to reconnect with his childhood by building a little village, as he had done as a child, using stones by the lakeside. He continued this building game daily, possessed by 'the inner certainty that I was on the way to discovering my own myth' (ibid: 22), and it 'released a stream of fantasies' which he was able to subsequently analyse.

> This sort of thing has been consistent with me, and at any time in my later life when I came up against a blank wall, I painted a picture or hewed stone. Each such experience proved to be a *rite d'entrée* for the ideas and works that followed hard upon it.
>
> (ibid: 24)

Jung extrapolated from his own experience and began to use artistic techniques with his clients – emphatically *not* as an artistic exercise, but in order to bring to light inner feelings and to allow the meaning within a person's life to emerge. The *process* of artistic engagement is crucially important – 'the living effect upon the patient himself' (Jung, [1931] 1997: 93). Working on a painting for many hours might seem to be time-consuming and perhaps less valuable than *talking* through psychological problems with a therapist. But this is not so, Jung says:

> Because his fantasy does not strike him as entirely senseless, his busying himself with it only increases its effect on him. Moreover, the concrete shaping of the image enforces a continuous study of it in all its parts, so that it can develop its effects to the full.
>
> (Ibid)

The absorption in creating an artefact, and giving it meaning – in particular, the process of modifying and changing the work until it feels 'right' – can be very powerful. The 'meaning' may not be deliberately put in at the start, but may emerge from free artistic play. The Jungian therapist Joan Chodorow notes:

> Sometimes an image or idea appears first in the mind's eye, but it may or may not want to come out. More often than not, images arise in a completely spontaneous way as we work with an expressive medium. Sooner or later, the imagination is given expressive form.
>
> (Chodorow, 1997: 8)

Jung's ideas are, of course, much more complex than I have space to discuss here. They have been celebrated and criticised, perhaps in equal measure.

What is important for now is his prescient view of the relationship between the conscious and unconscious – with the unconscious being the broader ocean of brain activity, and consciousness a mere porthole onto that sea – and his view that spending time with attention focused on creative activities gives us an opportunity to reach down into that ocean and bring up some significant truths, a point which obviously supports one of the main contentions of this book.

The brain today

Today, the debates about consciousness take place at the intersection of neuroscience, philosophy and psychology. Different perspectives are in play, all on the same field but with a surprisingly broad range of disagreement even within those theories which look broadly credible and consistent with the best available science. I do not intend to discuss all of the theories here, but useful introductions include Blackmore (2003) and Rose (2006).

One of the main debates today regarding consciousness is about whether consciousness lies somehow 'beyond' brain processes. When all of the brain's operations are identified and explained, will there still be something else – consciousness itself – which has been left out? David Chalmers has characterised this dilemma as the 'easy problem' of how parts of the brain work, versus the 'hard problem' of how subjective experience arises in an objective world:

> I think there are reasons ... for saying that subjective experience can't be reduced to a brain process. No explanation solely in terms of brain processes will be such that we can deduce the existence of consciousness from it.
>
> (Chalmers, 2005: 42)

Chalmers suggests that consciousness might be a *fundamental*, irreducible aspect of the universe – like space, time or mass – and that science should proceed to work out the nature of the connection between consciousness and brain processes. A number of leading scientists and philosophers of consciousness, including John Searle and Roger Penrose, agree with this kind of view, that consciousness must be somehow 'more' than mere brain operations.

Others, however, argue that this approach is rather strange because it relies on an intangible, almost 'magic', dimension. It is able to generate mystic celebrations of 'qualia' – the unique subjective qualities of any experience, such as the redness of a flower, or the smell of a favourite meal, or feelings of love – but not explain them, because their unexplainability is exactly the point. *Other* leading scientists and philosophers of consciousness – including Patricia Churchland, Paul Churchland, Francis Crick, Kevin O'Regan and

Daniel Dennett – would argue (in their own varying ways) that these qualia are just mixtures of perceptions and thoughts and can be explained, like all of consciousness, as things produced in the brain.

In the following sections I will be building on the latter perspective, and outlining the ideas of Daniel Dennett and his followers, who offer an explanation which I consider to be convincing, and which – as it turns out – includes an idea about the brain as a narrative-producing engine which will be of significance in later chapters on the production of identity.

Where is my mind?: Dennett vs Descartes

In *Consciousness Explained*, Daniel Dennett (1991) sets out to show how consciousness really works, as something that takes place in the brain – the actual kind of brain that we know humans to have. His model is in direct opposition to the mind/body dualism established by seventeenth-century philosopher René Descartes – which itself was an elaboration of previous philosophical discussion dating back to Plato, and which today remains the common way of thinking about the 'mind' as distinct from the physical matter of the brain. In Descartes's model, established in *Meditationes de prima philosophia* (1641), the body exists in the world, and its brain does functional work – the calculations of everyday life, if you like – but this body interacts with the mind, which is a non-physical kind of selfhood, where consciousness and self-awareness are to be found. This is the 'me' that I am aware of, talking away inside my head, making judgements, observations, ideas and having emotional feelings. This 'me', Descartes noted, can wonder if my body really exists at all, but cannot question its own existence – and this is a primary piece of evidence that there is a separation between the 'me' of my mind, and the 'me' which is my worldly body.

This model supposes that there is a particular place within the brain, which Dennett calls the 'Cartesian theatre', 'where "it all comes together" and consciousness happens' (1991: 39). This is the show which 'I' am the audience of, and comment on and react to. Material comes onto the stage – 'enters consciousness' – and this stage is the place where 'I' deal with it. Dennett notes that although 'materialism' has become widely accepted – materialism in this context meaning the recognition that the mind/brain is just physical material with no other non-physical dimension – the idea of a central 'place' for consciousness remains quietly popular. Dennett calls this Cartesian materialism:

> Cartesian materialism is the view that there is a crucial finish line or boundary somewhere in the brain, marking a place where the order of arrival equals the order of 'presentation' in experience because *what happens there* is what you are conscious of.
>
> (Dennett, 1991: 107)

He notes that a number of theorists of consciousness retain something like this model, which is revealed when it is said that something 'enters consciousness' or that our brain 'tells us' something. *Where* has this information entered, Dennett would ask, or *who* has it been told to? As he remarked in a recent interview, 'You won't have a theory of consciousness if you still have the first person in there, because that was what it was your job to explain' (Dennett, 2005b: 87).

There are certain empirical prompts for questioning the authority of the Cartesian theatre as a kind of central HQ. For example, some widely discussed experiments by Ben Libet (1985) asked subjects to wiggle a finger whenever they chose to, and to state soon afterwards the moment when they had decided to do so (by reporting the position of a spot of light that was moving in a circle). It was found that electrodes connected to the subjects' heads indicated 'readiness potentials' – neural activity indicating that the action was about to happen – up to half a second *before* the moment when the subjects reported that their decision had been made. As Dennett says,

> This seems to show that your consciousness lags behind the brain processes that actually control your body. Many find this an unsettling and even depressing prospect, for it seems to rule out a real (as opposed to illusory) 'executive role' for 'the conscious self'.
>
> (Dennett, 1991: 163)

Dennett does not refer to the Libet studies because he wants to show that consciousness is not in 'control' of what we do – that is not his intention. Indeed, he is critical of Libet's attempts to pin down a single instant when a decision is made, because that again reminds us of the Cartesian theatre, where a little guy sits inside your brain making the executive decisions and sending out orders. Dennett's view is rather more radical: consciousness does not appear in one central place, but happens across the brain, and is not a linear sequence of thought-events, but is a lot of parallel processing happening at once. We are not necessarily 'aware' of – focusing attention on – all this stuff all the time, and we can probably reserve a place for the 'headline' zone which is the primary string of stuff that I would call 'what I'm currently thinking'.

A neat (and scientifically uncontroversial) analogy is with visual perception: it is a matter of fact that the image on your retina swims all over the place, and your eyes dart around grabbing information from around five points every second, but this is edited and steadied early in the processing so that the interpretation that we 'see' has been cleaned up tremendously (Dennett, 1991: 111). It is as if the technically inept home movie being recorded by your eyes is being continuously remade, to the most glossy Hollywood standards, by your brain. Dennett's model suggests that the brain is working on *stuff generally* – not just visual perception, but everything – in much the same way.

We can selectively attend to parts of these workings, or just let it carry on. (This 'attention', I see you asking – is this the reappearance of the Cartesian theatre? Probably not, because not everything has to pass through it – it's not running the show, and may be indifferent to much of it; but this is a question we will return to shortly.)

Can this be right?

There are some clues from everyday experience which suggest that this, although rather uncomfortable, is probably what is happening in our heads. For example, consider decision-making. Dennett suggests that 'We do not witness [a decision] being *made*; we witness its *arrival*' (Dennett, 1984: 78). This is counter-intuitive, of course, and surprisingly seems to show up most clearly in the case of big decisions – ones you would expect we would want to apply our thoughtful consciousness to most carefully. Dennett gives the example of deciding whether or not to accept a job offer. Rather than actively applying 'thought' to this big decision, a person might 'leave it for now', but within a day or so would know what their response was. I don't know about you – indeed, the fact that I *cannot* know about you is one of the stumbling-blocks for consciousness studies – but a lot of my decisions seem to happen like that. This is, perhaps, the default way in which decisions are made, and because it doesn't seem at all thorough (in terms of conscious thinking-through), there is a market for popular psychology books, such as the *Six Thinking Hats* of Edward de Bono (2000), or strategic planning techniques such as SWOT analysis (Strengths, Weaknesses, Opportunities and Threats), that offer us systematic ways to go through decisions consciously, weighing up all the angles. But the fact that we might need a *book* to tell us how to make decisions carefully and consciously only seems to highlight the fact that decisions are often not the product of rigorous conscious thought. Dennett brings us back to that example of the job offer:

> 'I have decided to take the job,' one says. And one very clearly takes oneself to be reporting on something one has done recently, but reminiscence shows only that yesterday one was undecided, and today one is no longer undecided; at some moment in the interval the decision *must have happened*, without fanfare.
>
> (Dennett, 1984: 80)

This means that key turning-points in your life can be things which you appear to hear about afterwards. It is as if the brain has worked out the best suggestion, so that it becomes a decision which we are conscious of. Or as Dennett puts it, as individuals 'we are building a psychological theory of "decision" by idealising and extending our actual practice, by inserting decisions where theory demands them, not where we have any first-hand experience of them' (ibid).

To be honest, this idea of how decisions happen made me feel slightly sick when I first read it, because it seemed to match with my experiences, and yet I like to think that there is a conscious 'me' who is in charge of what I do. Who's making those decisions if it is *not* 'me'?! Dennett doesn't help by asking 'Are decisions voluntary? Or are they things that happen to us?' (p. 78). This can seem rather terrifying. The good news, I think, is that our decisions *are*, of course, generated by our own brains, and so don't 'happen to us' in a wholly alien way. A decision will be selected and become something I'm conscious of, because my brain has found that it integrates well with other decisions, orientations and behaviour – it 'feels right', as one might say – which means, thankfully, that it is consistent with my values.

Therefore, it does not follow from this that self-identity is a complete fake and that your body is actually being operated by external forces. Comfortingly, your brain may be doing work which 'you' are not conscious of, but it's still your brain: it is *you*. As Dennett put it in a later book, 'You are not out of the loop; you *are* the loop' (2004: 242). This model is not meant to suggest that the conscious part of decision-making is irrelevant – on the contrary, if we bother to apply consciousness to a topic then that is bound to have an impact. But again, the mildness of this statement seems shocking – rigorous conscious thought is at best like 'a helpful bonus' in the decision-making process?! I suppose that the main difficulty here is that one doesn't like to think that one's consciousness is the equivalent of the minister in the classic TV satire *Yes Minister*, who is encouraged by his civil servants to believe that he is in charge, even though all of the important decisions are actually being made somewhere else.

What does it all mean?

To make things clearer, let's recap on key points from this section. You may wish to insert the word 'arguably' before each of these points:

- there is not a central place in the brain, the Cartesian theatre, where 'I' observe the show and provide directions;
- thoughts do not occur in a linear stream; rather, consciousness happens continuously across the brain, although some material is headlined whilst other stuff is going on;
- decisions may be arrived at over time, and we realise they are 'made' after we have settled on them, although the actual point of 'having made a decision' may be a post-hoc construction.

Perhaps the baffling thing now, then, is what and where are the 'thoughts' that I am having? I am, at this moment, having thoughts, and I expect you are too.

I can see a particular scene before me – desk, books, computer, window – and I have thoughts in my head, as well, not connected with my visual perception, but happening in a pretty linear string, mostly to do with what I am going to write next, because I am writing this book, but also cross-cut with thoughts about what to eat for tea, what my wife might be doing now, and a kind of desire to go outside and probably go to a shop. Is Dennett telling me that all of this is some kind of illusion, not really what the brain is up to at all? And – importantly for this book – does that mean that the broader thoughts I have about myself, my identity, are an illusion too?

The answer, of course, is 'no' to both of these. Consciousness is a manifestation of what is actually going on in the brain – a continually updated set of headlines – and we can twist attention to point at different things. Bernard Baars, a cognitive neuroscientist, uses the metaphor of a spotlight shining on a stage. Whatever is in the light spot, is conscious, and everything else – which includes an audience and a production team – is unconscious. The spotlight is not stuck on one point – it can shine all over the place – and so different material can flip in and out of consciousness very quickly (Baars, 2005: 14–16). Confusingly, then, it's a theatre metaphor, but it's different to the one derided by Dennett; it's probably better to think of this one as the spotlight metaphor. The 'headlines' metaphor, which I brought in above, would have headlines about different things being generated all the time, and different subjects would be available to be pulled up, although some may be less likely to be accessed than others. Similarly, my sense of my identity is basically headlines based on memories of things that seem important to me. These headlines are tentative, though – subject to revision. And that's where Dennett's Multiple Drafts Model may be useful. This model is Dennett's proposed alternative to the Cartesian theatre model.

The Multiple Drafts Model

Daniel Dennett's Multiple Drafts Model is outlined most fully in *Consciousness Explained* (1991). We have already seen that Dennett argues that the brain is continuously processing sensory inputs, as well as all other thoughts, in parallel and on multiple tracks. You will recall the point, mentioned above, that in visual perception, the brain re-edits the rubbishy home movies presented by our eyes and turns them into the steady and clear vision that we (most people) experience; and the implication that consciousness is like that, on a grand scale, dynamically producing the 'movie version' of the messy brain contents which consciousness can't deal with all at once.

It is not unusual for this claim to be made about perception – indeed, Dennett says that 'virtually all theories of perception' agree that various parts of the brain work in unison to edit together our 'experience' of the world:

These editorial processes occur over large fractions of a second, during which time various additions, incorporations, emendations, and overwritings of content can occur, in various orders. We don't directly experience what happens on our retinas, in our ears, on the surface of our skin. What we actually experience is a product of many processes of interpretation – editorial processes, in effect.

(Dennett, 1991: 112)

Unlike some other theorists, however, Dennett says that observations (by any of the senses) only have to be made once, and are not re-presented in a Cartesian theatre. We don't experience a constant, chaotic clamour of perceptions coming in, though; the brain is doing more processing to make sense of it all. This is how Dennett explains what happens:

These spatially and temporally distributed content-fixations [observations or perceptions] in the brain are precisely locatable in both space and time, but their onsets do *not* mark the onset of consciousness of their content. It is always an open question whether any particular content thus discriminated will eventually appear as an element in conscious experience, and it is a confusion ... to ask *when it becomes conscious.* These distributed content-discriminations yield, over the course of time, something *rather like* a narrative stream or sequence, which can be thought of as subject to continual editing by many processes distributed around in the brain, and continuing indefinitely into the future.

(Dennett, 1991: 113; emphases in original)

We might wonder here whether this is not the return of the Cartesian theatre, a stage across which this narrative is played. But I think Dennett is trying to explain why it can *seem like* a single coherent narrative is playing in the theatre, even though there is no director, no audience and the stuff on stage is being bashed about, re-edited, having bits put in and bits taken away, in all dimensions and all the time; more like a war in an editing suite than a comfortable night at the opera. He goes directly on to say:

This stream of contents is only rather like a narrative because of its multiplicity; at any point in time there are multiple 'drafts' of narrative fragments at various stages of editing in various places in the brain ... Most important, the Multiple Drafts model avoids the tempting mistake of supposing that there must be a single narrative (the 'final' or 'published' draft, you might say) that is canonical – that is the *actual* stream of consciousness of the subject, whether or not the experimenter (or even the subject) can gain access to it.

(Ibid: emphases in original)

Occasionally we catch a glimpse of this happening when we become aware of a momentary visual-processing mistake. For example, as I came downstairs this morning I thought – for a fraction of a second – that the cat was waiting for me at the bottom, before I realised that it was actually shoes in an odd position. This wasn't a detailed thought or mental picture, just that it entered my awareness that my brain had gone 'Cat!' half a second before it said 'Oh, shoes!' The first draft had barely become formed before being boshed aside by the second (more correct) draft. That the first draft had entered consciousness at all is relatively unusual – presumably the brain is doing this kind of thing all the time. Perhaps my alertness to the cat possibility (because it would be nice to see the cat) meant that it entered consciousness – despite this actually being a mistake – whereas if, say, the shoes were initially interpreted as a jumper or general 'household stuff' then this wouldn't even become something I was aware of, until at some point the correct 'shoes' observation would be noted.

Fame in the brain

Now, this discussion is about our moment-to-moment perception of the immediate environment, and you might be thinking that we need to be considering a bigger picture of consciousness, as a whole view of life and the world. I'll come to that in a moment. Before I do, there seems to be an unresolved question about what Dennett means when he admits that it is 'an open question' whether something 'will eventually appear as an element in conscious experience' (as quoted above). How does the brain decide what appears in consciousness and what does not? Perhaps Dennett would admit that this is not yet empirically known, but more recently, he has 'recast' the Multiple Drafts Model as the 'fame in the brain' model. This is not a change of direction, but is intended to clarify this issue of how we come to be conscious of something:

> The basic idea is that consciousness is more like fame than television; it is not a special 'medium of representation' in the brain into which content-bearing events must be 'transduced' in order to become conscious. It is rather a matter of content-bearing events in the brain achieving something a bit like fame in competition with other fame-seeking (or at any rate potentially fame-finding) events.
>
> (Dennett, 2005a: 160)

Dennett says that this newer metaphor is an attempt to find 'a sufficiently vivid and imagination-friendly antidote to the Cartesian imagery we have all grown up with' (ibid: 136). It doesn't seem to be *quite* work – Dennett himself is quick to admit that 'fame' may not be exactly the right notion, not least of all because we begin to wonder *in whose eyes* these mental 'events' gain their 'fame'. He suggests an alternative: 'Consciousness is not so much fame, then, as political influence – a good slang term is *clout*' (ibid: 137). Certain mental events have sufficient *clout*, or *influence*, to grab attention and become part of consciousness. Importantly, attention is not turned *towards* these events by a knowing consciousness – since Dennett does not allow for a separate 'observer' within consciousness making judgements like that – but rather that they bump their way into consciousness by virtue of their fame, power or clout.

The longer-term self

As noted above, though, this is a rather momentary model of consciousness, about millisecond discriminations of things perceived. That is because, of course, Dennett would say that consciousness is nothing other than multiple processes happening at any particular moment. But my general awareness of the world, and my thoughts about who I am, what I have done, and what I might do in the future ... where does all this fit in? Logically enough, this is where *memory* comes in. My thoughts about my past life (whether a decade ago, last week, or five minutes ago) are, of course, all based on memory – not only (my version of) 'what happened', but also my thoughts and emotions connected with it. And indeed my plans and ideas for the future are all stored in memory too – so memory can be connected with the future as well as the past. (I say my future plans are 'all stored' – but of course, the ones I have forgotten about are not handily stored there, and must be irrelevant anyway if I have forgotten them. Except that – to make things more complicated – memory seems to have different layers, with some material being readily accessible, whilst other things seem to be forgotten until 'something reminds me' that I have actually had a particular idea before. But in any case, memory is the storehouse where – although they may not be instantly accessible – all our records of experiences, ideas and plans are kept.)

Dennett's model assumes that memory is centrally important, as it's where you may (or may not) keep the reasonably 'settled' draft of anything that happened (or was thought) more than half a second ago:

> The Multiple Drafts model makes 'writing it down' in memory criterial for consciousness: that is *what it is* for the 'given' to be 'taken' – to be taken one way rather than another.
>
> (Dennett, 1991: 132)

This is part of the reason why the movie *Memento* (Nolan, 2000) is so compelling, as its central character, Leonard, has anterograde amnesia and is unable to 'write down' things in memory. He therefore continually faces the question of what he is doing in any given situation, what has just happened, and what his own intentions might be. Sometimes he is able to *literally* write things down in order to orient himself; in particular he writes notes on a stack of Polaroids that he carries with him, and has especially important information tattooed onto his body, so that he can't miss it. Characters trick him by feeding him misinformation about what recently happened, or by enticing him to make misleading notes to himself, effectively adding elements to his sense of identity which he didn't actually put there himself.

An extreme real-life case is that of Clive Wearing, formerly a successful conductor and BBC producer, who in 1985, at the age of 47, contracted a viral infection which damaged his brain. Wearing lives entirely in the moment and can speak in sentences, but is not aware of what his previous sentence was. He remembers that he loves his wife, Deborah Wearing – who has written their story in her moving book *Forever Today* (2005) – but cannot remember their wedding. Indeed, he cannot remember if he last saw her one minute or one decade ago. He continually 'wakes up', not simply thinking that he has awoken *today*, but actually believing that he has become conscious *for the first time* since becoming ill. He writes in a diary, repeatedly noting that he had become fully awake for the first time; but he also feels it necessary to cross out notes made minutes earlier, which say that he was awake, which *now* he regards as obviously mistaken. Although lacking almost all knowledge about himself, what he has done, or where he is, Clive retains the wit, intelligence and personality which he had before – although he is not able to apply it to anything, except within a single moment. Deborah, still adoring him, writes that Clive 'was living evidence that you could lose almost everything you ever knew *about* yourself and still *be* yourself' (Wearing, 2005: 272). In an interview for a television documentary, reflecting on his experience, Clive argued that he lacks not simply memory, but consciousness itself: '"I" [am not] conscious, "I have" no knowledge of it at all! Consciousness has to involve "me"!' (ibid: 247). His wife observes, 'Without memory, without something inside oneself available to conscious inspection, there is no evidence of consciousness' (ibid).

Oliver Sacks has considered a similar case in 'The Lost Mariner', a chapter in his book of psychiatric case studies, *The Man who Mistook his Wife for a Hat* (1985). Sacks is led to wonder, 'What sort of a life (if any), what sort of a world, what sort of a self, can be preserved in a man who has lost the greater part of his memory and, with this, his past, and his moorings in time?' (p. 22). Sacks attempts an optimistic answer, finding that his patient is still able to find moment-to-moment richness in the world – contemplating nature, music, art, or engaged in routines in the garden or chapel – but the man has no long-term developing 'self' or sense of continuing 'identity', because he is unable to create the memories which would constitute it, give it coherence, and enable him to give some kind of account of it.

These examples highlight the importance of memory for identity. If you can't 'write it down' then experience becomes wholly transitory and, therefore, irrelevant beyond the moment in which it is happening. All your plans and ideas about your life are in exactly the same boat – completely pointless unless 'written down' in memory. Thus – as Giddens highlighted in the previous chapter, although he came to it from a sociological rather than neuroscientific route – *the stories we tell about ourselves* are crucially important to identity. It doesn't matter if these stories are 'told' to others, or just to ourselves (although social acceptability is compromised if we tell an incoherent set of stories to others), but in either case the stories (or selection of story elements) have to be laid down in memory first.

Dennett argues that a (relatively recent) product of evolution is this necessary human ability to create narratives about ourselves. Just as ants, beavers and many other animals build environments for themselves to live in, without really having to *decide* whether or not to do this, human environments are made, in important ways, from the words we generate about them.

> These words are potent elements of our environment that we readily incorporate, ingesting and extruding them, weaving them like spiderwebs into self-protective strings of *narrative* ... Our fundamental tactic of self-preservation, self-control, and self-definition is not spinning webs or building dams, but telling stories, and more particularly concocting and controlling the story we tell others – and ourselves – about who we are.
>
> (Dennett, 1991: 417–18)

Dennett casts the idea of the 'self' as 'the centre of narrative gravity'. As he points out, an object's centre of gravity is not an actual *thing* in the world, but it is still something that exists and has real consequences. The self is like that too, 'real' enough to have meaningful implications, even if it is just a metaphorical hub around which we spin stories. The corollary of this is that our self only really continues to exist if we continue to generate narratives.

Dennett notes that this conception of the narrative-spinning self fits happily with other work in neuroscience, such as that of William Calvin (1989) and others, as well as with work in cultural and literary studies influenced by Jacques Derrida, which sees the self as a produced text. These themes of narrative and storytelling will reappear in this book in Chapter 9, as we see people spinning stories about themselves within creative research methods.

Critics and miracles

Dennett's arguments, although counter-intuitive, seem to be winning. He has prominent critics, such as John Searle, a professor of philosophy at Berkeley, with whom he had a somewhat furious row in the pages of the *New York Review of Books* in the mid-1990s. That discussion is reproduced in Searle (1997) – including Dennett's robust replies – and it is surprising that Searle would include it in his own book, since his mode of attack seems to be to merely cite Dennett's arguments in a tone of astonishment – like a child repeating what you've just said in a silly voice. Searle's critique remains at the level of someone who thinks it is bizarre, and obviously wrong, to be told that the brain cannot contain magical stuff above and beyond what the biological brain could actually do. His argument is therefore, ironically, just like the Sidney Harris cartoon on p. 38 of *Consciousness Explained*, where a scientist has written on his blackboard a string of complex equations, with a bit in the middle which says 'And then a miracle occurs', followed by more complex equations. In the cartoon a colleague is pointing at the 'miracle' bit and observing, 'I think you should be more explicit here in step two'. Searle is distressed to have his miracle taken away, but cannot propose anything to fill the gap.

Opponents of Dennett's perspective like to use the notion of qualia to 'show' that the brain cannot be the incredibly complex biological *computer* that his view suggests that it is. A computer, the reasoning goes, would simply not produce the unique subjective senses that we get from a vibrant flower or lovely meal. However, we need to use some imagination here. If we're talking not just about a computer like your PC at home, but an *incredibly complex biological* computer, then it seems conceivable that it could experience these sensations. And, the confident Dennett would say, we know from our own experience that it does.

And so the implications for social research methods are …

We have taken this detour into the science of the brain, and the philosophy of the mind, because it has implications for how social researchers go about doing research. To summarise, those implications are:

- most brain activity is unconscious; consciousness is just the icing on the cake or the dashboard on which we can monitor the brain's 'highlights';
- asking people questions about their brain contents is, then, one method open to researchers, but I can only tell you what I can see on my dashboard at the moment, not what's actually happening in the middle of the machine;
- human brains have evolved to be narrative-producing engines, and the most important stories are those we tell about ourselves;
- approaches which invite people to reach down into the 'engine' and pull up a narrative in a different way might, then, reveal different kinds of account and give us a fuller understanding of those subjectivities.

Incidentally, this does not all mean that strong feelings such as *love* are just an illusion. Perhaps love happens when two brains fizz together especially well, have an interest in similar narratives and concerns, and find pleasure in each others' workings. Certainly Clive Wearing, the 'man with the seven second memory', remained very much in love with his wife Deborah, and she with him, in spite of his very limited chronological awareness, suggesting that strong love can have a 'sealed in' quality, as Deborah puts it (Brown, 2005), remaining even when everyday calculations or memories are no longer possible. (Non-sentimentalists will say it's just that Clive's virus happened, by chance, not to destroy the bit of long-term memory with Deborah in it; but on the other hand, it destroyed almost everything else … .)

Having established a model which has the brain doing all kinds of work, only some of which we're conscious of, and rolling out draft narratives all the time, we will move on, in the following chapters, to look in more detail at how research methods can use visual, creative, metaphorical and storytelling techniques to explore the experiences and self-identities which these kinds of brains produce.

Chapter 6

Using visual and creative methods

In Chapter 2, I noted that everyone *does have* a sense of having an 'identity', and considered the historically well-established human desire to express something about ourselves through creative and artistic acts. In Chapter 3, I considered the ability of qualitative social research to generate new knowledge about the world, through a discussion of the philosophy of science. In Chapter 4, I looked at sociological discussion of the relative importance of people's own understandings of social experiences, and then in Chapter 5, I considered what consciousness and identity might really mean, and how they might work, making use of insights from psychology, cognitive science and neuroscience. All of these discussions have been necessary background material to the main purpose of this book, which is to introduce 'new creative research methods' – research processes in which people are asked to *make* things, and then reflect on them, rather than having to speak instant reports, or 'reveal' themselves in verbal discussion. So I hope the motives for the previous chapters have been reasonably clear:

- I had to establish that people have a sense of 'identity' themselves, because that's what I want to explore. Although social researchers may reserve the right to observe and label phenomena that individuals themselves may not be aware of, it certainly helps our discussion of self-identity if this is something which people themselves recognise as having meaning.
- It was valuable to note that humans had an interest in producing visual and artistic expressions of the self and their existence, stretching back over thousands of years, to show that these research methods are not 'alternative' in a random, illogical or pointlessly 'novel' way, but rather that they connect with a deep pool of long-existing human expressive practice.
- As knowledge is produced through science – in its broadest sense, including social science – it was important to consider the philosophical debates about what science is able to do and show, so that we can formulate a positive answer to the question of whether these new methods can be regarded as legitimate.

• Since these methods often involve explorations of personal identity, I considered sociological approaches to personal experience, and how this can be researched; and then looked at what neuroscience can tell us about the conscious and unconscious brain processes which constitute the empirical experience of 'self' and 'identity'.

In this chapter, then, I will begin to consider studies where people have made things and worked with visual material. I'll begin with my own studies; this is the route by which I got into this work, so I hope it makes a sensible entry point into the story.

The 'Video Critical' study

As explained in Chapter 1, I began to explore creative research methods as a response to the hopeless legacy of media 'effects' studies, which seemed to be designed to trap participants into giving just one or two pre-set responses, rather than allowing them to communicate their own experiences or engage in a meaningful way with researchers. The research question of my particular study was whether the greater amount of discussion of environmental issues on television in the early 1990s had led children to be more aware of, and concerned about, environmental issues. My research showed that there definitely *had* been much more material about environmental matters in television programmes watched by children, including drama serials, cartoons, magazine and current affairs shows, as well as dedicated pro-environmental children's programmes. And the children who took part in my study, aged 7 to 11 across a range of backgrounds – many from deprived inner-city schools in Leeds, UK – had seen several of these programmes, and were excited about 'the environment' as a topic. I worked with 53 children across seven groups (from seven different schools), and saw them for afternoon sessions for five or six weeks (see Gauntlett, 1997, for full details; online version available at www.artlab.org.uk/videocritical). As mentioned in Chapter 1, when I met each group for the first time, I conducted a group interview discussion, in the style of a focus group, to establish what the children had to say about the topic. Their responses reflected a broad general concern for the environment, as well as awareness of the detail of particular matters such as recycling and acid rain. Each of these first-week sessions seemed fine and informative, and I could have conducted a number of focus groups like this, and come away with a reliable-looking body of 'knowledge' about children's environmental enthusiasms and interests.

However, of course, the study was not just a series of focus groups. The group interview was merely a starting point, to see what the participants *said*, before they were given the opportunity to make a video, in the following weeks, which represented a much more worked-on and thought-through expression of their feelings about the environment. Video was a powerful tool

Figure 6.1 Scenes from the 'Video Critical' videos

to use. The children were delighted to be able to see themselves on TV (and incorporated clever, ironic parodies of television presenting styles in some of their performances). They found that they could film things after the most basic of instructions – I simply showed them how to start and stop recording, and how to zoom, and tried to suggest (sometimes in vain) that the results would look better if they did not whoosh the lens all over the place. This immediacy and easiness was, I felt, important. The use of a tripod and the camera's auto-focus feature meant that almost all of the material was fine to look at – steady and in focus. Other video projects have given young people much more substantial 'training' before allowing them to really get started, and some visual sociologists have suggested that this is essential in order to achieve satisfactory-looking material. I would disagree. Setting standards of 'professionalism' spoils the instant, straightforward nature of video-making which make it so valuable and 'democratic'. Although a few of their earliest recordings were a bit too hectic to be very watchable, the children quickly learned from experience, and the act of filming was seen as so simple and transparent that there were actually no arguments or claims about who was 'better' at filming. Their videos were made with a 'point and shoot' aesthetic; they were not worried about setups or lighting, although they were excited to get certain things in shot, such as a passing train, a particular flower, or anything which tarnished the environment.

The immediacy of video was recognised by Tony Dowmunt as early as the late 1970s; his work with young people and Sony Portapaks led to a belief that the immediacy of video production 'is particularly valuable when working with less confident young people, whose other experiences of learning may have led to them being labelled, or feeling themselves to be, failures' (1980: 4). The video camera certainly seemed to be an 'enabling' technology in my study, as participants who were not strong on traditional school tasks proved themselves to be effective audio-visual communicators. The even grander idea that video projects such as this are 'empowering' remains questionable; critics such as Buckingham and Sefton-Green (1994: 209) have argued that this is just a discourse which cheers up well-educated do-gooders but may not mean much to the actual people in whose name it is celebrated. Nevertheless, evidence does suggest that video-making can help to increase young people's communicative confidence. Robin Bower, who ran a video project at his school in the Peak District, commented that 'asking pupils to articulate their views is a vital step to their own understanding of issues and of their position, and giving them the means to communicate those views is a liberating process which will hopefully empower them to influence others' (1992: 317). Furthermore, the prominent cultural theorist Stuart Hall has argued that 'it is important to get people into producing their own images because ... they can then contrast the images they produce of themselves against the dominant images which they are offered, and so they know that social communication is a matter of conflict between alternative readings of society' (quoted in Grahame, 1991: 149). In the 'Video Critical' project it was especially apparent that the ethnic minority participants – of whom there were several, at the inner-city schools in particular – were able to see more minority faces in their *own* videos than they usually would on TV; and they were able to speak in their own voices, make their own points, in a way that was very pleasing for them, and lifted their spirits temporarily, even if we could not definitely say that it was 'empowering' in some long-term, permanent sense.

The video-making method as a kind of ethnography

The method, then, gave children an opportunity, which was unusual for them, to quickly gather a set of moving pictures about things they wanted to show, and to talk about them to camera as amateur first-person documentary makers. It was also distinctive for other reasons, as I explained at the time:

> The use of the video equipment in this new method means that mediated perceptions of contemporary society can be explored with the media tools of that culture. The researcher spends time with the subjects, in the manner of ethnography, but the video camera provides a structure

and a focus for the use of that time. The subjects themselves are able to make a statement about society or experience through the video material they produce. This will not be 'pure' in the sense that they cannot record the image of their dreams or hopes, and because it is likely to be affected by their experience of television, the popular version of the medium. Nevertheless, these factors add further layers of interest, and the method's open invitation to creative response has the benefit of allowing the researcher to collect complex and mediated responses which it is impossible to obtain with the rigid and formal procedures of experimental and questionnaire survey research, these being methods which define the responses which they are looking for *in advance*.

(Gauntlett, 1997: 80)

The study was a kind of activity-based ethnography, then, or could be called ethnographic action research: the participants were given something to *do*, and were observed in the process of doing it; but also it was a visual sociology study, in which participants were asked to produce images (and soundtrack) to articulate what they wanted to say. The researcher's role was a kind of participant observation; I was not one of the film-making group, as such, but followed and helped each group – as well as taking the 'teacher' role of keeping them together, making sure they didn't get lost or run over, etc. – whilst also inconspicuously recording the process and discussions (some of which, conveniently, could be filmed along the way).

To justify this mix of ethnographic-ish methods, I referred to arguments made by Anthony Giddens in *New Rules of Sociological Method* (1976), in which he pointed out that seeking to understand the meaning which others give to their actions is something that people do all the time, as part of everyday social life, and is not just a pursuit of sociologists. This means that sociologists are engaged in the same process, and using the same resources – although perhaps articulated differently – as people in everyday life. The corollary of this is that 'the "practical theorising" of laymen cannot merely be dismissed by the observer as an obstacle to the "scientific" understanding of social conduct, but is a vital element whereby that conduct is constituted or "made to happen" by social actors' (Giddens, 1976: 52–3). The sociologist's concepts therefore depend on and incorporate a prior understanding of those used by the 'lay' person, which themselves rest on a stock of taken-for-granted, implicit knowledge about the social world. Since the video project gives participants an opportunity to produce a mediated account of their own perceptions of the social world, it represents an adequately authentic way of gathering the knowledge of social actors. Since the videos were made by groups, the recorded material is (more or less) the product of group consensus, but that in itself has parallels with how we come to form understandings in everyday life, through interactions with peers. This is not wholly a blessing: we have to admit that it is problematic that each video was produced by a group, as this means that each video will not show any one individual's feelings about the environment. Nevertheless, on a different level, it may be an authentic reflection of how groups achieve consensus on social issues.

A particular benefit of the video-making process was that it was able to 'make implicit knowledge explicit', as Gemma Moss put it (1993: 179), as it led children to produce accounts of their perceptions of anti-environmental factors, and the workings of certain social institutions (notably 'the Council'). It also helped to develop understandings of how media texts contribute to the structuring of social relations, as we will see in a moment.

Making videos is not a quick and convenient research method, but this is to its advantage. As with many projects discussed in this book, *spending time* is significant, both in the sense of the time spent on the production project itself, working through the ideas and story of each video, and also in the time spent between the researcher and participants working together on a project.

> On a more basic level, through spending time with those media consumers being studied, the researcher gains an understanding of the way in which their views of the media are 'truthful' for them, as well as the detail and texture of the meanings which they develop from media texts, and the 'lifeworld' which informs them.
>
> (Gauntlett, 1997: 82–3)

Through spending time together to make a video, the researcher and participants would at various times be engaged in casual chat about a range of unrelated issues, from the mundane logistics of carrying the camera equipment, to favourite pastimes, likes and dislikes, school, boredom, friendships and community. The project therefore was able to access some of the 'back stage' talk which Peter Dahlgren (1988) has noted was unlikely to be collected in the relatively formal contexts of an interview or focus group, where there is a tendency to 'artificial' kinds of talk about television. At the same time the study enabled children to engage in a 'concrete', applied way with the environment, by being in it and making a film about it.

> The method allows children to demonstrate their knowledge of *environmental discourses*. These would not come naturally to the fore in questionnaire responses, and *might* surface in interviews, but most likely not in circumstances where children could apply and connect them directly to concrete aspects of everyday life. The video project, over a number of weeks, gives children both the leisure and the opportunity to reveal their actual knowledge of environmental concerns, and ability to connect this – where available – to relevant parts of their lives.
>
> (Gauntlett, 1997: 83–4)

When I did this study in the mid-1990s, some scholars – such as my PhD external examiner, David Buckingham – expressed concern that I had 'skipped a stage' in a procession which would lead from (1) the media itself, through (2) children's interpretations of the media, to (3) children's own media productions. On the one hand I had clearly covered (1), through analysis of the media itself and interviews with the producers of children's shows which included environmental material, such as *Blue Peter* (a factual magazine programme), *Newsround* (news) and *The Animals of Farthing Wood* (a cartoon drama). I had also done (3), by working with children to produce videos. But, I was asked, why had I jumped from (1) to (3), without doing (2), which would have to involve talking with children about (1) – what they made of the media messages in question.

My answer was, of course, that the children were doing (2) – providing the researcher with information about their understandings of media material about the environment – by doing (3), making the video. So (2) is achieved through a production process, rather than via the conventional route of focus groups or interviews; but of course it should be noted that those verbal exercises themselves involve production of a kind – the production of talk about the media, in a formal and unusual interaction with a researcher.

An extract from the process

Although I shouldn't fill up my new book with chunks of an old book, it seems worthwhile quoting one extract from the accounts of video production in *Video Critical*. This is from the making of the video at Little London Primary School, where over a six-week period I worked with the youngest group of six children, aged 7 to 8, making a video about the environment. Despite – or perhaps because of – being so young, these children had no qualms about talking at some length to camera. They also demonstrably grasped the idea that material could be filmed out of sequence and then edited into a more narratively suitable order later – even though the psychological literature I had read suggested that this would be beyond such young children. This extract picks up at week three:

> In the remaining four weeks, whilst the appeal of running around and in particular, for this group, dancing (including some imitation of rather thrusting dances from *Top of the Pops*) remained strong, the children kept to an environment-related agenda with little need for reminders. Indeed, they produced more unprompted surprises than most groups, as seen in Deneika's enthusiasm for Africa, coupled with an awareness of racism in Britain, and Vicky and Mariam's ability to talk about almost anything at some length. Significantly, without being told to, the children performed for the camera in a way which anticipated an audience of others, asking the 'viewers' rhetorical questions, wishing them well, and signposting

their presentations (almost all of which were prefaced with 'Hello, my name is … and I am going to be talking about …', and closed with 'And that is the end of my story'). They also captured interesting visual material on tape, such as a broad range of scenery, movement, stepping into shot, their ubiquitous dancing, and minor gymnastics. The children also seemed aware of the opportunity for individual expression, so that, for example, when one child was suggesting words to Josiah, Celie hissed 'Don't *tell* him what to say' – not to deny Josiah assistance, but in favour of letting him express things *himself*.

The following exchange, from the final week where the children interviewed each other on camera, shows how the children had – on the *whole* – remained focused upon the aims of the project:

Celie: What have you been doing in this project?
Vicky: I have been talking about the environment, and talking about litter, and talking about rubbish, and talking about grass, and everything.
Celie: Did you enjoy filming?
Vicky: Yes I did actually, I enjoyed filming and I enjoyed doing the talking and that.
Celie: Did you enjoy talking about the environment?
Vicky: Yeah I did. But I still wanted to talk about dancing.

Mariam, a working-class Black girl aged seven, was able to speak at particular length to the camera, and rather than being repetitive or with little point, her utterances were often surprisingly complex. In the following example, Mariam speaks of the excitement and variety of environmental video work with an enthusiasm and scope which threatens to reach beyond her basic language ability, and which was accompanied by many expressive gestures:

Amanda: Which bits did you find interesting?
Mariam: The interesting thing of filming is you can talk about something, and talk about flowers, and roads, and playground, and slide, and some environment work, about trees: we talk about loads of things. Maybe you could, if you have camera, you could film, your friend could film you or you could film yourself; it is very lovely, and I *mean* it is very lovely, because if you look out for anyplace or playground, you see loads of things you could do with environment work. Everywhere you go you can see something that you do about the environment. And I *really* mean it. Because if you see out the schools, or you go to buy something, the environment is *there*. That's the end of my story.

The ideas about the 'everywhereness' of the environment at the heart of this speech are ones which Mariam has thought of and developed herself, as far as can be gathered, and they are expressed in her own terms. Whilst not conforming to the highest adult standards of clear presentation, her speech reflects an environmental awareness and enthusiasm which was not so evident in most of the other, older children in this study.

(Gauntlett, 1997: 102–3)

The video production method was, then, a powerful way of enabling these young children to communicate their connections with the environment, and environmental issues. My observation of them making a video over a number of weeks provided a rich seam of information which would otherwise have been inaccessible to a researcher.

Some inevitable limitations

Of course, every method and research process has its drawbacks. Some of the imperfections of this one are pretty obvious; in my view they are outweighed by the advantages. But it's worth acknowledging them.

First of all, the process is an *intervention*, and a pretty obvious one. Whilst a focus group can perhaps be disguised – not very convincingly – as someone stopping by for a chat, the video production process, which requires creative work with technical equipment over a number of days, is not something you could slip under a participants' radar. (Having said that, it would not necessarily be clear to schoolchildren that they are taking part in 'research', because it is not uncommon for external guests to work with pupils on particular projects, which are done for the sake of education rather than research. In my own case, I did tell the children that I was conducting research and wanted to see 'what they think' about the environment.) Therefore, of course, participants are aware that they are taking part in a research project, and may 'perform' accordingly. In the case of my video study, then, there is obviously a possibility that the children would know that I was looking for their connection with, or concern about, the environment, and therefore would generate performances of these connections and concerns for my benefit. We should note, too, that this is consistent with general school experience, where a teacher says, for example, that you're going to write a poem about fireworks, and so you write a poem about fireworks – and there is not normally an option to say that you have no interest in fireworks.

So, we have to admit this is a potential problem – a kind of interference or distortion created by participants' well-meaning tendency to fill the time by doing what they think is expected. But on the other hand:

- you could say the same about most other methods; and
- the longer-term nature of this kind of study means that, over time, a more honest and realistic picture is likely to emerge.

Therefore, for example, a focus group is just as likely to be distorted by the participants' tendency to say any old thing to pass the time and maybe give the researcher what they want; and because a focus group is typically a one-off event, the inaccurate impressions created will not be subsequently modified. In the video production method, on the other hand, a more honest equilibrium can be arrived at over time. Furthermore, the more lengthy and drawn-out process of making a film about something is likely, I would suggest, to lead to more authentic responses; having to record pictures and produce a narrative about something is likely to focus the mind and lead to more carefully crafted statements. Having said that, it remains the case, of course, that a research participant in any sociological study can create false or misleading impressions if they want to.

Another potential problem is more specific to studies which use the medium of video (or film) in particular. Here the distortion can arise from the possibility that the method can include an imperative to film *things*; and therefore that only filmable things are included or discussed. In the case of a study about the environment, for example, this might mean that participants are more likely to focus on things that they can capture on camera (such as rubbish on the street) and less likely to include things which are more difficult to film (such as global warming). In my study the children did find ways around this, such as by using a classroom globe as a visual aid whilst talking about global issues; but there was probably a bias towards the local and filmable, rather than the distant and abstract. Video representation *can*, of course, be symbolic and metaphorical, but inexperienced video-makers are likely to go for a simple point-and-shoot process which would favour convenient filmable objects rather than non-literal imagery. (This problem points us towards the idea of a wholly metaphorical approach – such as the Lego Serious Play method discussed in Chapters 8 and 9.)

The videos in my project were made in groups, and so represented a kind of group consensus rather than a set of individual views. As I noted above, this can be seen as having value in the sense that it mirrors the way in which opinions are shaped by interactions with peers, but also of course it is disappointing that individual perspectives may be smoothed out or stifled. Video projects could, in fact, be made on an individual basis, but it would be much more time-consuming if the researcher was to observe the process for each individual – and, crucially, there would be much less *interaction* to observe. The group nature of the task is defensible as a simulation of how social knowledge is constructed, and as an activity which deliberately provokes relevant discursive interactions which the researcher can observe and learn from.

Findings of the study

The actual findings of the *Video Critical* study are perhaps unimportant here, as this discussion is primarily about research methods. However, some consideration of the findings enables us to see how the data were treated, and what a study of this kind was *able* to show.

Having gathered extensive ethnographic observational notes, interviews and recordings of discussions from throughout the process of the video-making activities, as well as the actual finished videos themselves, I used this data in three ways. First, various aspects of the project experience were discussed in a collection of notes covering children's relationship to the environment, their 'reading' of broadcast television texts, the 'writing' of video texts, and issues of race and gender. This allowed for some general discussion of, for example, the children's production styles (mostly naturalistic and presented in an information-giving manner, but with sprinklings of playfulness and experimentation across the board), and the ways in which the project gave a voice to the more marginalised children. This kind of discussion was in a 'common-sense' observational mode rather than being a systematic and prescribed analysis technique, but captured important detail which might have been filtered out by a more mechanical analysis.

The second and third kinds of analysis were of the more formal kind. I remain pleased that, although I was a PhD student at the time – impressionable and wanting to jump through the correct academic hoops – I was able to determine that 'discourse analysis' is a relatively meaningless phrase, applied to a wide range of interpretive strategies from the quantitative and formulaic to more general and unsystematic discussion of data. I could not see what it meant to 'do' discourse analysis, or what benefits one could confidently say that 'discourse analysis' would bring. In the intervening years I have concluded that this hunch was correct.

My second approach, then, was a *theme analysis* of the videos, a straightforward but revealing process used to identify elements and conflicts common to all of the productions. This found ten elements which appeared, in some way or other, in each of the videos. These were: appreciation of the locality; environmental responsibility; the City Council's responsibility; litter and pollution; traffic; parks, and the city; trees; community; play; and audience-oriented performance and entertainment. It was especially interesting that a number of these themes reflect a dialogue about *responsibilities*; the kind of complex and sometimes contradictory set of judgements and negotiations which do not come through in a focus group but are revealed in a more time-intensive process of creative decision-making and discussion such as this.

Interestingly, the process also revealed two central conflicts which appeared in all of the videos. The first of these was 'Being environmentally responsible' versus 'Having an easy time' – the children generally wanted to do both of these, and often found them to be not easily compatible. They also felt that, as children, they should be able to play and not carry such serious burdens, whilst at the same time they positioned themselves as the wise group who might be able to prevent adults from making so many stupid environmental mistakes. This connects with the second of the two key conflicts, which was

'Children's own responsibility to change things and improve the environment' versus '*Adults*' responsibility to change things and improve the environment'. On the one hand, children thought of themselves as key stakeholders in the planet's future, and potentially its best defenders, but on the other hand they had a (realistic) sense of powerlessness in the face of big grown-up problems.

Finally, a *narrative analysis* examined the videos in terms of the stories or arguments about the environment which the children constructed, as well as considering the environmental themes and perspectives which the children did not include. This process built on the point made by James Deese (1983: p. xiii) that narratives are 'accounts of events from a very human point of view', and that 'every narrative is realised in only one particular way out of the countless ways it might have been realised'. Similarly, Hayes and Flower (1983) had argued that the act of creating narratives – through writing or, I might suggest, making a video – is goal-directed, providing logic and coherence to the process of narrative production 'even when writers perceive their own experience as chaotic and unpredictable' (p. 210). It was also noted that, as well as the manifest content, narratives 'also convey the subjective reactions of the narrator towards the tale as well as his or her feelings and attitudes about the persons to whom the narrative is addressed' (Deese, 1983: xv). We can learn a lot, then, from the stories that are told and the *way* that they are told.

It was found that all of the videos were versions of one central narrative, 'This is our environment', in which the children told the video audience about positive and negative aspects of the area in which they lived and worked. Within this broad field were four subnarratives: 'This is our environment – a critical tour'; 'This is our environment – all around us'; 'This is our environment – a comparison of two areas'; and 'This is our environment – and how we would improve it'. These were not mutually exclusive: indeed, all of the videos included some aspects of the critical tour, noted that the environment is all around us, compared parts with other parts and suggested improvements.

With the narratives considered more in terms of *how the story was told*, two dominant narrative themes were identified: 'The world is in a bad state → we must try to improve it', and 'Other people are spoiling the environment → they must stop'. The tone, authorial voice, and implied audience, of the narratives were also discussed. Importantly, *silences* in the videos were also considered: stories that were *not* told. The typical narratives, discussing good and bad points of the local environment, contrasted sharply with two basic narratives *not* featured in the videos: 'This is our global environment – and its problems', and 'This is our environment – polluted and ruined by industry'. Similarly, it was noted that the narrative theme 'The world is in a bad state' led to the solution 'we must try to improve it' rather than 'government and industry must try to improve it'; and that 'Other people are spoiling the environment' led to 'they must stop' rather than 'they must be stopped'. In other words, the narrative analysis showed that the stories about the environment, including the identified problems and projected solutions, were on the level of the local and the individual, not on the level of the global and the communal or corporate.

The study, then, found that children saw environmental problems as the result of careless and apathetic individual behaviour – of adults or children – rather than being a consequence of organised adult industrial or governmental activity. The analysis of environmental television programmes watched by children showed that this was also the perspective most commonly suggested on screen – problems were caused by forgetful or ill-advised adults, and could be solved by reforms and through the enlightened behaviour of individuals. Building theoretically upon the findings of the analyses, *Video Critical* concluded that the interpretation of environmental problems had been subject to 'hegemonic bending', so that the taken-for-granted understanding of these issues had been 'bent' in a particular way, highlighting some explanations at the expense of others. The children's awareness of both problems and solutions was therefore limited, and potentially rendered ineffective, whilst at the same time a notion of 'oppositional' action was incorporated into media discourses: children were encouraged to 'fight' for the planet, and led to believe that they were well-informed on the subject, whilst not being aware that these interpretations were, at least, partial and questionable. This was not a conspiracy theory, of course; rather just a consequence of the way in which television talks to children about certain issues – a result of the professional socialisation of producers in which they learn to be somewhat reassuring, not especially 'political', and to offer solutions that children can do themselves (Gauntlett, 1997: 149–50).

Conclusions such as these could perhaps have been reached by different routes. However, the video-making project enabled children to tell their own stories, setting an agenda and showing that they were considerably more media literate than contemporary psychological and education literature seemed to predict. The time spent going through a particular creative production process meant that the participants' more fundamental concerns were able to emerge from the jungle of potential and received opinions, and were expressed on their own terms.

Visual sociology

The *Video Critical* study, I can note with hindsight, was one of a number of more-or-less contemporaneous projects which were conducted in the 1990s, and which together laid the groundwork for the emergence of a kind of research which is increasingly recognised as 'visual sociology'. This is a reasonably new category within the domain of sociology, and includes elements which may previously have been thought of as being predominantly in the domains of anthropology, art history, photography studies or qualitative research methods.

Although visual sociology has only quite recently begun to be widely recognised as a legitimate and coherent domain within the discipline of sociology, the cause of visual sociology has been promoted – and indeed shaped – for a quarter of a century, through the activities, conferences and publications of the International Visual Sociology Association (IVSA). The association was established in 1981 by Leonard M. Henny, Douglas Harper, and a group of colleagues who wanted to extend the use of documentary photography, and photographs as documents, in the practice of sociology, and to foster a community of 'visually driven thinkers' (see Chaplin, 1994: 222–3). Harper's own account identifies the roots of visual sociology in the 1960s, when photographic studies of black ghetto life, drug culture, the civil rights movement and anti-war protests, amongst other topics, were produced by documentary photographers (1998: 28). These in turn were inspired by earlier projects such as Jacob Riis's study of the poverty of the urban immigrant, *How the Other Half Lives*, first published in 1890. Some of these photographic studies were relatively naïve in sociological terms, providing pictures of what social problems and movements *looked like*, but offering no particular frame in terms of ideology, representation or political context. The images were usually taken by the photographer/researcher themselves, and so tended to be socially concerned extensions of 'the art of photography', rather than authentic documents of lived experience – although we should note that in a number of cases the photographer spent time with their 'subjects' (sic) to acquire a rich, ethnographic understanding of their lives.

This kind of heritage informed the nascent IVSA, so that we can see in much IVSA work to date, and in its continuing heritage, an emphasis on rather literal imagery – photographs of things – and on the camera and photographic aesthetics. Jon Prosser's edited collection *Image-Based Research*, published in 1998, offers a valuable overview of the kind of work being done in the 1990s, and of IVSA members generally, a number of whom are represented in the book. It's a very useful collection, but there are some clear themes and tendencies: often the contributors slide from talking about the use of visual material in research to advising the researcher on how best to frame their photographs, so that the reader is hit with the realisation that, first of all, the talk of 'images' actually means 'photos', and that, secondly, it's the researcher holding the camera. (This continues to happen in visual sociology publications; for example, in a recent article by one of the IVSA old hands, John Grady (2004), the author immediately slips from a general statement about the value of the visual – 'the image is a unique form of data' – to saying that 'what you see is what the camera got' (p. 18), and on the next page, mention of 'working with images' slips straight into the statement that 'cameras have to be pointed at the right thing' (p. 19), revealing an old-fashioned faith in photography to which a footnote about the possibility of digital manipulation doesn't make much difference.)

It's clearly a nice idea that sociology should be more visual, and that sociologists can pursue this goal by taking photographs and sticking them into their publications. Harper, for example, says that 'Images allow us [as sociologists] to make statements which cannot be made by words, and the world we see is saturated with sociological meaning' (1998: 38). But since it's never entirely clear what a picture 'says', this remains somewhat problematic. (The solution, I think – as I have already indicated – comes when you get participants to both create images and to speak about their meaning.)

Most visual sociologists, of course, are not ignorant of possible problems with their approaches; Harper himself discusses the postmodern critique of documentary photography, noting that meaning is not 'fixed' in a photograph but is created by the viewer, and pointing out that documentary photography 'typically focuses on the specific and thus hides or mutes the critiques of the system; social problems are portrayed as personal stories and social ugliness is made beautiful or provocative' (ibid: 32). You still get the impression, though, that he doesn't want to hand over his camera.

Photo elicitation

As a kind of solution to the problems inherent in the relationship between photographer and subject, Harper outlines the photo-elicitation interview, which was first described by John Collier in *Visual Anthropology* (1967). In this process, the researcher shows the interviewee photographs – usually to do with their own social world – and asks questions about the pictures and their meanings. Harper notes that the traditional open-ended language interview 'rests on the assumption that the researcher will ask questions that are culturally meaningful to the subject' (1998: 35), which they may or may not be able to do. In contrast, the photo-elicitation technique is led by images, which are meant to provide a bridge to the interviewee's inner meaningful worlds. 'Typically these are photographs that the researcher has made of the subject's world,' says Harper (ibid), although recently it has become more common to use photographs made by participants themselves. In any case, Harper does not think that researchers who take the photographs themselves are necessarily the experts regarding the *meaning* of the images; on the contrary:

A shocking thing happens in this interview format; the photographer, who knows his or her photograph as its maker (often having slaved over its creation in the darkroom) suddenly confronts the realisation that he or she knows little or nothing about the cultural information contained in the image. As the individual pictured (or the individual from the pictured world) interprets the image, a dialogue is created in which the typical research roles are reversed. The researcher becomes a listener and one who encourages the dialogue to continue. The individual who describes the images must be convinced that their taken-for-granted understanding of the images is not shared by the researcher, often a startling realisation for the subject as well!

(Ibid: 35)

This, then, is a useful way of getting images into the heart of the research process, and (I would say) is especially valuable if the photographs have been taken by the interviewee themselves, or significant others in their cultural worlds, whether previously – for the family photo album, for example – or especially for the research project. The participants then get the opportunity to communicate their own *visual* voice, as well as being able to add thoughts (meanings and commentary) verbally about the images. In his 1998 chapter, Harper seems aware of this idea, referring to one Dutch study where 'the subjects direct the photography' (p. 36), but the approach seems to have been uncommon at that time. But, whoever has produced the image, photo elicitation is a good way to get a selection of interpretations pinned down. On the one hand, the researcher may have a set of pictures – each of which 'could speak a thousand words', but whose thousand words would it speak? Then on the other hand, to solve this conundrum, the researcher also collects the thoughts which a particular person did actually speak when confronted with the image. The picture and the words together form a meaningful package – a subjective response to the world, of course, but a rich one, which can be used alongside other such packages to help sociologists understand how participants see their worlds.

Using the visual in visual sociology

In Prosser's book there are some interesting cases where, indeed, the participants have been asked to create the visual data as well as commentary. For example, in a project by Schratz and Steiner-Löffler (1998), primary school children in Vienna were asked to take photographs of aspects of their school which they liked and disliked, and to discuss these photographs, as part of the formal process of school evaluation. The authors report that this gave children a rare opportunity to have a focused conversation about which spaces made them happy or unhappy around the school. The physical act of going around taking photographs is more 'hands on' than mere discussion, and enabled quieter or less assertive pupils to have their feelings represented in the study. Furthermore, the images and comments helped *teachers* to appreciate children's feelings about the school. The authors also suggest that the very fact that the photography project was taking place opened up a new level of reflection and self-evaluation within the school.

A study by Whetton and McWhirter (1998), meanwhile, showed how children's drawings could be used to explore their understanding (and misinterpretation) of health campaigns. Noreen Whetton had developed the 'Draw and Write Technique' in 1972, as part of a project which had established that although children aged 7 to 8 may not be able to communicate certain emotions through words (whether written or spoken), they could feel them, and understand them in others. This was revealed through the children's drawings, and their subsequent faltering speech about the emotions depicted in the drawings:

> It became apparent that the children experienced and empathised with a wide range of emotions including anger, frustration, despair, remorse, guilt, embarrassment and relief as well as delight, enjoyment, excitement. The children differed only from adults in that they did not have the vocabulary to express themselves.
>
> (Whetton and McWhirter, 1998: 273)

Since then, Whetton, with colleagues, has used children's drawings to explore various aspects of their world, such as a study looking at how they drew a story involving drug dealers (Williams, Whetton and Moon, 1989a), a study exploring how children picture the insides of their bodies (Williams, Whetton and Moon 1989b) and the study revealing children's interpretations of dental health campaigns (Whetton and McWhirter, 1998). The authors note children's ability to use simple images as a kind of communicative shorthand:

> It is important to note that children's images consist of a mixture of stereotypes and drawing conventions. Children know that women are not triangular ... and that all houses are not detached with chimneys that smoke, but they use these images as a short hand for the concept of woman or home.
>
> (Ibid: 269)

Through such drawings, children were able to show researchers that they understood health issues – which for the children, it was found, included mental and environmental health and well-being, as well as more obvious illnesses – much more fully than expected. Whetton's projects have enabled health educators to provide information and educational resources which are 'truthful, while respecting and being consistent with children's own logical construction of meaning' (p. 282). Studies like this have taken children's visual productions as a starting-point, and used these to begin to explore their meaningful worlds and experience.

The development of the visual sociology field can be tracked (in one way) through the books which have appeared. There are those which stem from a broadly anthropological tradition, such as the introductions by Marcus Banks (2001), Sarah Pink (2001), and Pink, Kürti and Afonso (2004), which highlight the importance of the previously somewhat neglected visual dimension in anthropological and social research. These works generally emphasise the need to examine the already-existing visual aspects of a culture, in order to more fully understand it – which, of course, no one would disagree with, although as always there can be problems with how researchers choose to 'interpret' other people's images. The collection *Picturing the Social Landscape* (2004), edited by Caroline Knowles and Paul Sweetman, has a more sociological orientation, and announces at the start that 'This collection attempts to do something a bit different'. Happily, the editors explain that they understand visual sociology to be not simply a sociology of the visual world (which can mean almost *everything*), but research which involves work with visuals within its own *process*:

> In talking about visual methods, then, we are referring to the use of visual material as an integral part of the research process, whether as a form of data, a means of generating further data, or a means of representing 'results'. Despite the conflation of these two aspects of visual sociology in certain introductory texts, our understanding of visual methods does not, in the main, extend to forms of analysis such as semiotics or content analysis, in which forms of already existing visual material is the focus of research or *object* of enquiry, but, except in so far as it is what is looked *at*, does not play an integral part in the research process itself.
>
> (Knowles and Sweetman, 2004: 5)

This is a valuable clarification, spelling out what is (or should be) an obvious bit of definition: visual sociology has got to be an approach which embraces visual practices, and not (just) the practice of writing about visual things. As well as helping to establish what visual sociology is in practical terms, Knowles and Sweetman are clear on its theoretical advantages too:

> The sociological imagination works particularly well through visual strategies, which capture the particular, the local, the personal and the familiar while suggesting a bigger landscape beyond and challenging us to draw the comparisons between the two ... Visual techniques ... are an analytically charged set of methodologies which incline researchers towards the tracing of connections between things of quite different social scope and scale.
>
> (Ibid: 8)

Their edited collection shows this thesis in action through studies which include Charles Suchar's study of the gentrification of areas of Chicago and Amsterdam, which used photography and ethnographic experience to connect micro- and macro-level changes in community life; Douglas Harper's photographic study of 'Wednesday-night bowling' among the rural working class in northern New York state; and Elizabeth Chaplin's more personal account of her own daily photographic visual diary. In these cases, put most simply, photographs are made by the sociologist as part of their practice of their sociology. In other cases, visual material is made by the participants and plays a different role, providing 'data' about social experience which sociological findings are then built on top of. For example, Alan Latham discusses his 'diary-photo diary-interview method (DPDIM)' in which everyday life is captured through sets of diaries and accompanying photographs which are discussed with the researcher. 'This bricolage of text, talk and photography opens up a wide range of possibilities for narrating people's life paths that simultaneously convey a sense of people's movement through time-space and something of the sensation, style *and productiveness* of that movement,' he notes (Latham, 2004: 126). The combination of these elements, plus time-geography diagrams which show movement from place to place, are not so much used for 'triangulation' (to improve reliability) but rather to provide different streams of information about the qualitative experience of an ordinary day in someone's life.

Ruth Holliday's chapter on the use of video diaries highlights other possibilities afforded by visual approaches. Her study aimed 'to examine the performative nature of queer identities' (2004: 49) through a study in which respondents were asked to consider different 'work, rest and play' aspects of their lives by dressing in the clothes which they would wear in different situations, and to speak about their 'self-presentation strategies'. She suggests that her research process does not involve the researcher 'taking' accounts or representations from the respondents; reflexivity is not 'captured'. Rather, the video diary-making process is just an extension of the *reflections* of self which individuals necessarily already produce. Such reflections take place outside the individuals' own self. In other words, although you can't capture actual bits of a person's self, you clearly *can* collect instances of self-expression. The video diary approach was clearly an invitation for respondents to produce a *representation* of themselves; they could 'stage', work on, rerecord or delete material before it was even seen by the researcher. Whilst some scholars might be concerned that this procedure would not produce sufficiently 'accurate' or 'authentic' results, Holliday argues that it is a positive feature, giving the participant 'greater "editorial control" over the material disclosed' (p. 51).

Holliday found that the video diaries were 'full of performances' – including 'dancing and singing, jokey telephone conversations, [and] mock debates between soft toys' (p. 52) – but when *alone* with the video camera, participants switched into a different mode and would confide intimate information. The diaries also captured significant but often unremarked aspects of everyday life, such as the rituals of personal healthcare and grooming. Holliday is critical of researchers who romanticise the 'empowering' potential of their research projects, but ultimately sees her own research process very positively as one in which participants can actively *share* their cultural worlds (pp. 60–1).

In this chapter I have outlined my own entrance into the world of visual sociology, and have introduced some aspects of this emerging field, its brief history, and some of its typical approaches. The next chapter goes on to look at a few more recent examples, and related areas.

Chapter 7

More visual sociologies

The previous chapter discussed the emergence of 'visual sociology', including an outline of my own video project, and other studies mostly from the 1990s. This chapter follows on directly, beginning with discussion of a few more selected recent studies. I then take a quick look at the related academic field of 'visual culture', and turn to projects which are similar to visual sociology but are conducted by artists, and/or take place in the public activities of art museums and galleries. Finally, I consider briefly what I learned from doing a study in which people were asked to produce drawings.

Other visual studies with young people

There are a number of other sociological studies which have used visual methods, of course – the International Visual Sociology Association has been publishing articles about such studies for 25 years – and there is not room to discuss them all here. However, it is worth briefly noting a few examples, to demonstrate the range of approaches and topics. It is not possible to present these studies in a linear chronological sequence, because some projects have been running concurrently and independently. In other words, different researchers in different parts of the world have been working on similar things at the same time, but will not have been aware of the other, related projects. For example, a few months after I had worked with groups of children to make videos for the *Video Critical* study – but before that book was published in 1997 – Gerry Bloustein, on the other side of the world, was conducting a study in which ten Australian girls were given a compact video camera and invited to make videos about their everyday lives. Bloustein's article about the project, '"It's Different to a Mirror 'cos it Talks to you": Teenage Girls, Video Cameras and Identity', was published in 1998. It is only in retrospect that we can see that we were doing (broadly) similar things at a similar time.

Bloustein felt that the video method enabled the researcher to examine 'the way each girl chose to interpret, negotiate, challenge and explore her developing sense of self, and her relationships with the various social institutions of which she was a part' (1998: 117). The camera became 'a tool for interpreting and redefining their worlds' and revealed 'the perceptual frames and boundaries the individuals placed upon themselves' (ibid). As in my own study, the researcher recognised that ethnographic observations of the *process* of video production were 'data' which were just as valuable as the video productions themselves. Bloustein placed a greater emphasis on the interesting dimension of the construction of identities – or *representations* of 'identities' at least – through the video-making process:

> There seemed to be an awareness by all the girls that the camera was an exciting way of simultaneously exploring and constructing themselves, discovering and constituting 'the real me' and emphasising difference. Hilary, for example, wanted to show how '*other* girls acted and behaved' and that 'not everyone is the same. We are all individuals.' She was aware of the power of media representation and was annoyed that, as she perceived it, teenagers were so often depicted in a negative light . . . In this way, then, she and some of the others saw the potential of the camera as a political tool, a vehicle for presenting alternative points of view to a wider audience.
>
> (Bloustein, 1998: 118)

In particular, Bloustein highlights the 'playful' nature of the identity-experimentation taking place in the video-making processes, although the play had a serious and sceptical orientation. The teenage participants did not believe that their videos would serve any external political purpose, but Bloustein is convinced that they played a valuable role in the inner reflective process of 'self-making'.

On a bigger and more formal scale was the European Commission-funded project, CHICAM – Children in Communication about Migration (see www.chicam.net) – probably the biggest sociological creative-production study to date. This international collaborative project, co-ordinated by David Buckingham, established 'media clubs' in six European countries (England, Italy, Sweden, Germany, the Netherlands and Greece) in which a researcher and a media educator worked with recently arrived refugee and migrant young people to make visual representations of their lives and experiences (De Block, Buckingham and Banaji, 2005). The material was shared and discussed between the groups, over the internet. The videos made by the children are perhaps the most striking, but in addition they used collage (with cut-up magazines), arrangements of photographs with music, and specific photo tasks (such as a photo essay on likes and dislikes, or on national symbols), all of which were shared and discussed internationally via an online platform. Peter Holzwarth and Björn Maurer, who worked on the project, wrote that:

> In an era when audio-visual media play an increasingly influential role in children's and adolescent's perceptions, it is important that researchers

not rely on verbal approaches alone, but also give young people the opportunity to express themselves in contemporary media forms . . . These works provide openings into the children's world which language barriers would otherwise render inaccessible.

(2003: 127, 136)

David Buckingham's previous work on children's media literacy in the 1990s was undoubtedly an influence upon this emerging sphere (e.g. Buckingham, 1993b; Buckingham and Sefton-Green, 1994). More recently, Buckingham and Bragg's study of young people's responses to media portrayals of sex and personal relationships (2004) gave teenage participants a blank notebook and asked them to keep a 'diary' or 'scrapbook', containing personal reflections upon such material seen in the media. This enabled the researchers to show that children frequently encountered material about sex and relationships in the media, but sometimes found it difficult to identify the 'messages' within this material, and that the messages were mixed. The research methods helped to reveal that the children were '"literate", and often highly critical' consumers (p. 238) who asserted their own agendas, were often surprisingly moralistic, and who – in the younger cases – would (occasionally) admit to not understanding some sexual references.

Visual studies of homelessness

A recent study by Alan Radley, Darrin Hodgetts and Andrea Cullen (2005) sought to contribute to our understanding of homelessness, by giving disposable cameras to 12 homeless individuals in London. The study set out to explore 'how homeless people "make their home" in the city as a material expression of their way of life' (p. 275) and sought to flesh out the activity that took place in their lives 'in spite of being dispossessed of numerous advantages' (p. 274). Clearly there is more to being homeless than is suggested by the negative definition of not having a permanent home. Participants were interviewed before they took their photographs, and afterwards as they discussed the photographs with the interviewer. They were also asked to pick out, from the complete set, the photographs which best captured their experience of homelessness. The researchers explain that their aim was not to understand the pictures *per se*, but to arrive at 'an understanding *with* the photographs about the lives of the respondents concerned' (p. 278) – which is, I believe, the best approach.

Like other visual studies, this project helped to create a more authentic picture of lived experience than more traditional studies might do. For instance, the very idea of showing 'how homeless people "make their home" in the city' might seem oddly romantic, given the general perception that homelessness would be an experience with few positive aspects. However, the study was able to show the pride which these individuals took in their street knowledge and imaginative survival skills, as well as the diversity of experiences amongst those who happened to be bracketed together within the 'homeless' category.

Disposable cameras, as well as other visual methods, were used in a study of street children in Kampala, Uganda, by Lorraine Young and Hazel Barrett (2001). As academics in the field of geography, these researchers used four different 'visual "action" methods' to gather information from street children 'about their interactions with the socio-spatial environment' (p. 141). Fifteen children were asked to produce a 'photo diary', taking pictures of activities and places they visited over a 24-hour period. After processing, these images were discussed with the child who had taken them, and revealed information which the researchers say would not have been accessed by other means. In addition, 22 children were asked to draw their own mental maps of Kampala, showing places that were important to them, and the 'depots' where they slept. In another activity, 23 children were asked to produce three drawings of their everyday experiences, and in another, 22 children worked in a group to produce symbols of daily activities and to place them on a timeline showing a typical day. Again, the *discussions* about the maps, the drawings and the timeline – during and after their production – were a crucial part of the process, eliciting valuable information. The researchers note that their engaging, non-threatening and action-oriented methods resulted in a high level of participation by the children (p. 151), and meant that the children were able to communicate what was important to *them*, putting at the heart of the study material 'that would have been overlooked by an adult' (ibid).

Studying masculinity through making men's magazines

In the last of these visual sociology examples, we turn to the work of my own PhD student, Ross Horsley (completed 2006). In his study, Horsley sought to explore men's feelings about lifestyle magazines aimed at men, and changing ideas about masculinities. He asked 105 young people (83 men but also 22 women) in the UK, drawn primarily from high schools, colleges and a prison, to produce a front cover and a contents page for an imaginary men's magazine:

> The essential directions given asked participants to envisage 'a men's magazine that they would like to read, but which they also think would appeal to men in general', in the hope that this might inspire not only an interesting hypothetical product but also a creative and personal composition with the capacity to reveal something about its creator's own identity (as evidenced by what they would like to read) and their assumptions about wider notions of masculinity (evidenced by their attempts to appeal to 'men in general').
>
> (Horsley, 2006: 97)

All participants also answered a follow-up questionnaire about their experience, interpreting their own work. The magazine covers and contents pages that the participants produced mostly *looked* more or less like the published men's lifestyle magazines, such as *FHM* and *Maxim*, which have become popular since the mid-1990s, but with subtle differences; in addition, a small number (around 5 per cent) tried to offer a clear *alternative* to those titles. Horsley argues that most of the creations were intended to satirise the existing market, however, with varying degrees of irony, gusto and cheerfulness – whilst not actually being *opposed* to this magazine market, in most cases. In some cases he argues that a *playful* approach to masculinities and identities is on display.

One of Horsley's findings is what he calls 'the "identity-explaining" function of celebrities'. He notes that celebrities and celebrity gossip appeared to a surprising extent across the range of magazines proposed by participants, and argues that celebrities provide a 'reference point' through which personal identity can be understood. Here, Horsley summarises his own argument:

> In this study, a trend towards the incorporation of a great deal of celebrity- and gossip-related content was immediately apparent, going beyond the expected interest in glamour model types to extend to celebrities such as David and Victoria Beckham and their family, the contestants of the ITV 'reality' game show, *I'm a Celebrity, Get Me Out of Here!*, and pop singer Michael Jackson. It was argued that this newfound interest in celebrity lifestyles represented a shift in dominant constructions of masculinity, whereby men, recognising the widening spectrum of male roles and readings in popular discourses, empathised with the explicitly 'self-edited' faces of current celebrities; that is, they have become fascinated with the process by which a celebrity works to maintain a coherent persona to the world, recognising within it the processes through which they, as individual men, work to express their own identities to the people around them.
>
> (Horsley, 2006: 194)

Horsley's study also leads him to suggest that the knowingly stereotypical representations of women and men, in the magazines proposed by participants as well as in actual published magazines, have a social function as they offer a '"map" upon which explorations of identity may be charted' (ibid: 196). Furthermore, he argues that the process of creating a magazine revealed that a central part of magazine consumption, which men sought to put into their own magazines, was membership of a 'psychological community' of men. Not wholly certain about what 'being a man' means in contemporary society, they saw magazines playing a helpful socialising role, which included treating women in the way they would like to be treated – a point about which information was needed – as well as fitting into the 'social circle' of other men, often fuelled by joking and irony.

This was not straightforward, however. It is clear that published men's magazines manage to stretch themselves unconcernedly across a web of contradictions, in terms of what men can be expected to be (Gauntlett, 2002). In Horsley's study, where young men themselves – usually the audience rather than producer of these magazines – had to create a text which might be a vessel for such contradictions, we were able to see these struggles played out. Indeed, as Horsley suggests, the process of putting together a magazine mirrored, in some way, the process of identity construction:

> As the study progressed, it became increasingly clear that this process of writing, drawing, cutting, and pasting – whether on paper or with the use of computer software – in some way mirrored the procedures involved in piecing together one's own representation of the self and presenting this as a coherent persona to the outside world, and was therefore able to offer some insight into these behaviours . . . Magazines' ability to present contradictions simultaneously and alongside each other within the internal, psychological community they actively foster, it is argued, offers male readers a valuable way of experiencing the contradictions they must often deny in the outside world. In striving to present a coherent identity to others, men are encouraged to suppress the contradictions that exist in their own internal narratives, whereas magazines indulge the 'luxury' of contradiction, whilst also offering practical advice on how to go about constructing a more coherent identity in order to succeed in the external world.
>
> (Horsley, 2006: 199–200)

The creative visual research method used in this study enabled the researcher to arrive at these conclusions, which offer some of the most fruitful answers to the question of how and why it was that men's lifestyle magazines – previously thought of as a non-market – were suddenly able to take off and be massively popular in the past decade. Earlier researchers had only made rather banal observations about 'changing models' of masculinity; or proposed the view that these magazines had triumphed as part of a 'backlash' against feminism, which may have been one element of their origins, but didn't really explain why the magazines would sell so well month after month. By getting each participant to think through the meaning of the magazines by asking them to make one themselves, Horsley arrives at these more complex and insightful answers.

Visual culture

I should also note briefly that alongside the emergence of visual sociology, and interconnected with it, we have also seen the arrival of a discipline – or an interdisciplinary field of study – called 'visual culture'. Since the late 1990s, an array of books have been published presenting this new field to readers. Those readers could be forgiven for being rather confused about what 'visual culture' is, as so many approaches and definitions appear between the different books – or even between different chapters of the same books. Early collections such as *Visual Culture*, edited by Chris Jenks (1995), *The Visual Culture Reader*, edited by Nicholas Mirzoeff (1998, 2002), and *Visual Culture: The Reader*, edited by Jessica Evans and Stuart Hall (1999), gather cultural theories of 'the visual', usually in the style of cultural studies and often in the language of postmodernism. The many other and subsequent publications – which are discussed in Margaret Dikovitskaya's helpful 'bibliographic essay' (2005) – have continued along similar lines, whilst giving some obvious nods to new digital technologies. These books generally engage with 'practices of looking' in a wholly 'theoretical' way – in other words, by ignoring the experience of actual everyday viewers and inserting the speculations of the academic instead. This approach builds on the traditions of art history and literary studies, and can offer fruitful ideas in the not-very-common cases where it is done very well; however it is annoying that lip service is paid to the 'viewing subject' whilst these researchers generally pay no actual attention to real-life viewers. Discussing a number of the many 'visual culture' books in Gauntlett (2005), I concluded:

> Towards the start of such books it will be asserted that 'visual culture' emphasises that:
>
> • meanings are made in the minds of individuals in their encounters with visual material;
> • all aspects of visual culture – around the world and in different spheres – are equally important;
> • everyone interprets visual material in their own way.
>
> But when looking at what happens in practice, the reader comes to realise that 'visual culture' scholars typically:
>
> • emphasise the readings of 'experts', such as themselves (instead of being interested in the range of interpretations generated by actual everyday consumers);
> • select particular extraordinary examples which are deemed to be especially interesting (instead of looking at a typical spread of everyday examples);
> • set out specific methodologies for reading an image (instead of exploring ways of understanding other people's actual readings of images).
>
> (Gauntlett, 2005: 160)

To achieve their own stated goals, and develop a better understanding of their own claimed interests, researchers in the field of 'visual culture' therefore have something to learn from visual sociology, which also makes good use of social and cultural theories but (hopefully) ties such discussion to actual research regarding the use that people do, or can, make of images and the visual in everyday life.

Art and visual sociology

We should note that, in some cases, the work of socially engaged visual artists and the work of visual sociologists can look very similar. Many artists have used art to explore identity, memory and the construction of selfhood, as we saw in Chapter 2. Other contemporary artists have engaged in a more externally oriented art practice which involves 'ordinary' people in the making of work. Just as visual sociology sometimes blurs into something like art, in these projects, art expands into being a kind of visual sociology. There are many instances of such projects; here I will give just a few examples.

A project by the artist Per Hüttner, at Chisenhale Gallery, London, entitled *I Am a Curator*, gave 30 individuals or groups the opportunity to be 'Curator of the Day', over a period of six weeks (5 November–14 December 2003). Each day a new exhibition was assembled, using work by 57 artists that was made available in the gallery. As Hüttner explains:

> The premise of *I Am a Curator* was to let anyone be a curator for a day. Unfortunately, the exhibition was only open for 30 days, which meant that it was impossible to accommodate everyone who wanted this opportunity. The daily slots were administered through an application process through which we tried to give as many different people as possible (in relation to occupation, age, sex, social and ethnic background) the chance to be Curator for the Day. Quite often the Curator for the Day was in fact a small group and so in the end roughly 70 people were curators.
>
> (Hüttner, 2005: 13)

The curators were able to plan their exhibition using A5-sized plastic cards, each representing one artwork in the exhibition, which were slotted to fit together so that a structure could be simply assembled, and amended, to consider any number of combinations and relationships between works. They also made the actual exhibition, with the support of a 'gallery crew' team, in the large space (250m²) of the gallery.

Hüttner admits that at the beginning he had imagined that the project would produce '30 pretty clean-looking shows', and that the Curator of the Day would 'go through the "same" process every day', but it was found that, in practice, this was not the case at all (ibid: 23). Instead the project became an exploration of the process of exhibition-making. One Curator of the Day, for example, wanted the work to be selected democratically, and spent the whole day in discussions with gallery visitors. At the end of the day, he displayed only notes about the arguments made for each work, and how many votes each received (ibid: 43). On another day, two poets decided to use *I Am a Curator* as a resource to develop their own writing, rather than finishing an exhibition.

This project, then, engaged 'ordinary people' in creative work normally undertaken by a recognised 'artist' or 'curator', and therefore challenged or questioned perceptions of these roles. Its sociological questions are about the status of curators, museum directors and exhibition-makers as the formers of public knowledge and display (which are worthwhile sociological issues, even if they are obviously also dear to the hearts of art and artists). The project seems to have started as a punkish stab at the idea of curation, the assertive title *I Am a Curator* seemingly posing a challenge to the elite group who are 'officially' sanctioned curators. But in its realisation, it became more complex and subtle. Hüttner reflects, 'The project changed from saying "curation is easy" to stating "artwork and exhibition making is very complex – but come and have a go and see what you think"' (ibid: 19).

The power of everyday art

The artist Bob and Roberta Smith (actually one man) has similarly played with the status of art institutions by opening the Leytonstone Centre for Contemporary Art, which is a shed at the bottom of his garden in Leytonstone, a suburb in north-east London. International artworld figures would talk to him about the shows at his 'institution' without knowing that it was a shed which Bob would allow you into for 15p on Saturdays (Smith, 2004: 30). His list of projects has involved public participation in numerous ways. These include *Fight* (2002), a group show of artists from Manchester and London, reflecting the rivalry between the two cities, where the public were invited to vote out works they didn't like; *Make Boats* (1994, 1997), in which the public were given the opportunity to make boats; *Paint it Orange* (1997), in which gallery visitors were invited to paint objects orange; *Waiting* (2000), in which the public made cardboard cars, which were placed on a model motorway in an ever-expanding traffic jam; *New Language* (2000), in which gallery visitors were invited to make up and define words on pieces of card, to create 'a New Language for the New Millennium'; and many more such projects (see Smith, 2004). These are more witty art events, or challenges to the artworld, than they are 'visual sociology', but they reflect an interest in questions about whether art can really do 'good' socially, and how it can connect with people; and they are about giving people the chance to participate with art in accessible and compact ways, because Bob and Roberta Smith has a touching faith in the power of art:

It's embarrassingly evangelical, but I do think art is really powerful and transcendent. For instance, [during one period in my life] I had unbelievably awful jobs, which I won't go into. But the thing that really kept me going was the idea that somehow I was an artist, which is a sort of transcendent thought. Although I wasn't actually making any art, or was making it in a limited way, it gave me an identity that meant I could exist in a world of ideas and thoughts . . . More historical norms of art making activity have this idea that it is a bit like education. It's a mode of thinking and activity connected with action. Art brings the possibility of inventing who you are and who you want to be. When you see kids making art you witness them taking control of their world. As adults most people lose all that and end up being pushed around, or they become the ones that boss others around.

(Ibid: 127, 136)

Thus art-making offers a powerful, enabling way of being, which can help people to feel differently about their lives. Clearly here we are talking about any kind of art which a person makes and which gives them satisfaction – not (just) the officially sanctioned art of galleries and museums. These everyday artistic products are celebrated in the *Folk Archive* curated by Jeremy Deller and Alan Kane (touring exhibition, and book, 2005), a 'celebration of the creative life of Britain', a collection which includes all kinds of artefacts made by people who would not primarily call themselves artists, including decorated cakes, embroidered wrestling costumes, home-made badges, fancy dress, signs, graffiti, leaflets, flower arrangements, banners, stickers and sandcastles. This massive array of amateur art highlights the broad and diverse extent to which people enjoy making aesthetic things.

Similarly, *Drawing from Life: The Journal as Art* (New, 2005) brings together the journals kept by a range of people as part of their everyday lives. As the book's subtitle suggests, its aim is to *show* a selection of journals, rather than interpreting them (which is probably for the best), but it includes a number of interesting ideas about why people keep visual records of their lives. Jennifer New writes that while she was preparing and editing the book, she found that people whom she met by chance were usually happy to show and talk about their journals: 'Living in a shirt pocket, after all, makes a book an extension of oneself; pride is to be expected' (ibid: 8). She suggests that keeping a journal (or journals) over several years can help individuals retain a sense of their own biographical *narrative*. Looking at her own box of journals, she writes, 'There goes Blindly in Love at 19, followed by Depressed and Searching at 24, and Confused about the Motherhood Decision at 31' (p. 9). She recalls Joan Didion's essay, 'On Keeping a Notebook', in which the writer notes, 'I think we are well advised to keep on nodding terms with the people we used to be' (ibid).

Jennifer New also emphasises the *physicality* of drawing or writing by hand in a journal or notebook, and keeping everyday ephemera in the pages. The look and feel of these marks and objects can capture the spirit of a time, and a cultural milieu, much more powerfully than mere written records, she suggests. The journal keepers in her book 'are notably attached to the tactile quality of books' as opposed to technological alternatives:

> Though digital journals, especially blogs, are the fastest growing form of journal keeping, many visual thinkers prefer to work by hand. A pen and its slower pace ground them in the process more than the machinations of a computer . . . [and] most believe important lessons can be learned from drawing.
>
> (Ibid: 15)

The themes of constructing a narrative of the self and using the hands to think through a process of reflection on identity are ones which we will return to in the Lego identity study in the following chapters.

Reaching out beyond artworlds

Meanwhile, whilst considering visual sociology in its possible alternative incarnations, we should note the kinds of activity stimulated by public institutions. Public art galleries and museums typically have an education or outreach officer, or department, whose job it is to develop events and activities to accompany exhibitions. These frequently include workshops in which participants engage in creative activities related to the ideas in the show, and because the topic of 'myself' is something that everyone has some ideas about, such projects often involve explorations of identity or personal history. As if to illustrate this point, an example which it is easy for me to provide is one from my own personal history, which was a collaboration with Peter Bonnell at the Royal College of Art, London. The college was presenting an exhibition, *This Much is Certain* (March–April 2004), which involved contemporary art that explored the notion of 'truth' in documents and documentaries. For the accompanying workshops we considered ways in which individuals could consider documentation in relation to something they knew well – themselves. A basic document of selfhood internationally is the passport, and so we conceived a workshop called *The Passport of Me*, in which schoolchildren visiting the exhibition would complete a blank 'passport', including a Polaroid photo of themselves, collage about aspects of their lives and some biographical data. Therefore the children had the opportunity to use creative activities to consider the ways in which their existence could be documented. They were encouraged to challenge the 'documentary' nature of conventional passport photographs, by disguising themselves and altering their visible identities, and to take a playful approach to illustrating their own story. Later in the day the participants put their 'passports' together, in blank envelopes, and then selected someone else's at random, and were asked to imagine and draw what that person's bedroom might be like. This gave an opportunity to reflect on the writing, reading and rewriting of identities.

This workshop was not especially distinctive – art galleries do workshops and events like this all the time, a kind of personal visual sociology which is typically not analysed or used as data by sociologists, but is taken home or thrown away at the end of the day. Sometimes the projects become especially ambitious and outflank many visual sociology projects. For example, as I write this, Tate Britain in London is presenting an exhibition about *Nahnou-Together: Young People from London and Damascus in Visual Dialogue* (May–July 2006), a programme created to enable young people in London and Damascus to exchange pictures and share ideas through a website (www.nahnou-together.org) which is described as follows:

> How can pictures tell the story of who you are, what interests you, and what your culture means to you? . . . In Syria, art lessons are not an integral component of the school curriculum and there are no public examinations in art. However, young people in Damascus can take part in an ambitious, informal art programme offered outside of school at the Adham Ismail Centre, funded by the Syrian Ministry of Culture. Over the last academic year, students from the Adham Ismail Centre and from Quintin Kynaston School in St John's Wood, London, have been sharing their lives with each other through pictures. An artist exchange was arranged between the countries to introduce the students to new forms of art practice and to foster connections across cultures. Artists and educators set objectives, created a programme of activities and learnt how to manage the website. The Nahnou-Together display explores this visual dialogue.
>
> (Tate.org.uk, June 2006)

This project is an art-oriented community project which has much in common with the more academically oriented social science project CHICAM, discussed above, and other visual sociology studies. So we can note that artistic outreach projects, cultural citizenship education activities and sociological research projects can all be linked in a circle, involving some similar activities, but put to different uses depending on who is doing them and why.

Continuing my own journey: the *Drawing Celebrity* study

By this point in the book I have covered most of the steps which led me to the Lego study, which will be discussed in the following chapters. Although you

Figure 7.1 Examples of drawings of celebrities produced by teenagers in the study – clockwise from top left, Bob Marley, Delta Goodrem, Eminem, Christina Aguilera, David Beckham and Cameron Diaz

may not be interested in my own story *per se*, it's worth tracking the confluence of ideas which led me to arrive at a study that involves the apparently rather odd process of asking people to build metaphors in Lego. There is, then, one more stage to be mentioned.

In 2003–4, I did a study in which participants were asked to do *drawings*, as an alternative way of trying to access their thoughts or feelings about a particular issue. The issue in question was the relationship between young people and celebrities, and whether 'celebrity culture' was affecting young people's aspirations and their ideas about lifestyle and gender. The concept of 'celebrity' had become widely discussed in the media and had bounced onto the sociological radar, discussed in books such as Rojek (2001), Turner (2004), Cashmore (2006), and Holmes and Redmond (2006).

The participants were 100 young people, aged 14–15, at a number of schools in the south of England. I asked them to: 'Draw a star, celebrity or famous person who you would like to be. If there's nobody you'd like to be, at all, then choose someone who you think is good or cool.' The students were also asked to 'put them in a particular setting and/or doing something', and were reassured that their drawing skills were of no concern. I knew that it would be difficult for me to produce 'interpretations' of what each of these drawings 'meant' – indeed, in my own terms at least, such a task would be impossible, because I did not want to impose my own meanings onto what the participants had drawn. Ideally, then, I would have interviewed each of the 100 people about what they had drawn and what they felt it revealed. However, because I was working with quite large groups of school students and taking up their time, it was not possible to do this. Instead, I gave them a single-sheet questionnaire with three questions, which asked if they would like to be like their chosen celebrity, and *why*, and to note common themes between how the celebrity might be described and how they themselves might like to be thought of. These questions were 'open' and gave me qualitative written responses, but I would have gathered richer interpretations if I had been able to interview each participant about their drawing on a direct and one-to-one basis.

The findings of the *Drawing Celebrity* study are discussed in Gauntlett (2005). A number of the teenage male participants provided emotionally reflective responses, revealing a more sensitive side than other studies of young masculinities have tended to attract (Buckingham, 1993a; Frosh, Phoenix and Pattman 2001; Barker, 2005). I noted that this suggests either that young masculinities are changing, or that the drawing process itself gives research participants more *time*, and a little less constraint, to develop nuanced thoughts about the subject-matter. I believe that there is some truth to both of these explanations.

The process of giving the participant time to make an image, and to have the maker interpret their own work, owes something to the techniques of art therapy as they have developed over the past few decades (discussed in Gauntlett, 2005). As I was using drawings in this way in the celebrity study, it once again happened that someone in Australia was doing something similar, independently, at the same time. In this case, Marilys Guillemin, a health researcher at the University of Melbourne, used drawings to explore women's experience of the menopause, and of heart disease (Guillemin, 2004). Noting from her survey of relevant literature that 'the use of drawings as therapeutic tools and in social science has largely been limited to children' (p. 274), Guillemin nevertheless developed an apparently very fruitful approach for health researchers, in which participants were asked to 'draw how they visualised their condition' (p. 276). Participants were typically reluctant at first, but eventually they drew an image, 'sometimes hesitatingly and at times with such intent and force that I and they were taken aback' (ibid). Importantly, the researcher asked each participant to describe and explain their drawing, as well. The study revealed the many and diverse ways in which the women experienced these conditions. For example, menopause was represented as a life transition (such as one part of a staircase, or as 'a sun setting and the moon coming up'), or as a lived experience (often chaotic), or as loss and grief. Guillemin concludes:

As researchers, we take for granted word-based research methods without due consideration given to visual methodologies. The use of drawings as a research tool has enabled a broader and more in-depth exploration of the multiplicity of illness conditions. It offers not only potent visual products that offer insight into how people understand illness but is also simultaneously a process of knowledge production about the illness itself.

(2004: 287)

Like my celebrity drawing study, this project sought to 'bring to the surface' impressions and feelings about the subject-matter which a more conventional interview might not access. And because of its *particular* subject-matter – which was very personally meaningful and immediate for the participants – as well as the researcher's individual attention, and one-to-one discussion of the drawing, Guillemin's study achieved this more successfully than mine did.

Some points the drawing study reinforced

The experience of doing a drawing-based study led to a few more reflections on working with visual material. First, if research participants are asked to produce something visual (such as a drawing, collage, photography or a three-dimensional item), this enables them to circumvent the inherent linear mode of speech – one thing leading to another – and present a set of ideas 'all in one go'. In his book *Visual Thinking*, Rudolph Arnheim (1969) argues that the kind of 'intellectual thinking' that we organise into language 'dismantles the simultaneity of spatial structure', and makes the relationship between different concepts seem like 'the sort of event we represent by an arrow' (p. 246). Visual thinking, on the other hand, does not force ideas into a particular order. If we consider the notion of your 'identity', for example, the complex set of interconnected elements that might gather in your mind as you try to picture this would inevitably be different to a verbal account. The difference would not simply be one of form – as if the verbal description could be like a straightforward 'translation' of the pictured identity – but also of character, with each type carrying different implications, and the verbal account being much more likely to suggest a linear set of linkages.

Of course, as we saw in Chapter 5, the notion of having a picture 'in the mind' – the kind of thing which we might then seek to get 'down on paper' – is incredibly complex. Most people's brains don't carry round a ready-made diagram of their identity, or anything else, any more than they contain ready-to-go paragraphs of word-based description. Turning any of the information 'in' your head into something representable entails a task of arrangement and processing. And this means that any image you produce is the result of such work. As Arnheim says:

Every picture is a statement. The picture does not present the object itself but a set of propositions about the object; or, if you prefer, it presents the object as a set of propositions.

(1969: 308)

In the case of the celebrity-drawing study, it was not really possible to work out what the 'propositions' might be; of course, one could *guess* – a job which some colleagues in visual culture or film studies would call 'analysis' or 'interpretation' – but this would not be appropriate in sociological research. The task of extracting meaning from images is widely seen as a difficult one, as can be seen in this entry I made in a notebook whilst conducting the drawing study, in 2004:

> When people know that I am using images, they quite often ask if I will therefore be interpreting them using a psychoanalytic framework. But there is no more reason to psychoanalyse people's drawings than there is to psychoanalyse interviewee's answers. The argument for either is just as strong, or weak, depending on your view of psychoanalysis.
>
> (Notebook entry, 2004)

Ultimately, of course, in studies of this type I think we need a combination of (a) the process and thoughtful experience of taking time to make an artefact; (b) the artefact itself; and (c) the person's own interpretation of the artefact. A thorough implementation of this is arrived at in the next chapter, where we will see that the Lego study has multiple rounds of construction, interpretation, reconstruction and more interpretation.

Chapter 8

Building identities in metaphors

All the parts of this book so far have been building up, in different ways, to the presentation of the social research method in which people are asked to build metaphors of identity – or whatever other issue is being explored – using Lego. In this chapter I will finally set out exactly what this method involves, what it is based on and how it works. I will then go on to discuss metaphors, and why metaphor is a powerful tool for communication in general, and for use in social research in particular. Then I will consider some of the metaphorical elements which participants actually built in the Lego study. The chapter *following* this one and the Conclusion include analysis of the *whole* Lego metaphorical models which were built by participants in my identity research project.

Lego, and Lego Serious Play

Lego is one of the most-recognised brands in the world. As most readers will probably know, therefore, Lego is a construction toy aimed primarily at children, and produced by the Lego Group, based in Denmark. The company grew from humble origins in the Danish village of Billund, where a carpenter, Ole Kirk Christiansen, started making wooden toys in his workshop in 1932. He called his business Lego, from the Danish phrase *leg godt*, which means 'play well'. The company started making interlocking plastic bricks in 1949, but the familiar modern-day Lego brick was not invented until 1958. The range expanded in a number of directions during the following decades, its popularity being boosted by the introduction of the Lego minifigure in 1978. These little Lego people have appeared in ranges including town and space scenarios, as knights and pirates, and in popular *Star Wars*-themed sets. Importantly, all Lego pieces – including the double-sized Duplo for younger children, and the Technic sets for more mechanically minded teenagers – are part of an interlocking system. The company has remained in the family, and is presently owned by Kjeld Kirk Kristiansen, a grandchild of the founder.

The Lego company is corporately proud of its strong association with the concepts of creativity and learning, as well as play, and in recent years it has used these associations to promote a consultancy process for businesses and organisations, called Lego Serious Play. The research process discussed in this chapter is a variation of Lego Serious Play, used in a non-standard context. The work has been supported by Lego, but I have been 'free' to develop the research as I wished. (The initial connection was made in 2004 when the director of Lego Serious Play at the time, Per Kristiansen, heard about my research in which people were asked to *make* things, saw a connection and sent me an email.)

Lego Serious Play developed out of a problem within the Lego company itself. The story of its development that is told is as follows. In 1996–7, Kjeld Kirk Kristiansen was feeling disappointed that his staff meetings did not seem to be able to generate imaginative strategies for the future of the company. He knew that his employees were talented people, and so felt that some kind of tool was needed to unlock their imagination and creativity. During this time, he had discussions with Bart Victor and Johan Roos, both professors and consultants from the Swiss business school IMD, who had seen this kind of situation elsewhere. Together they realised that a solution to Lego's problems might be found in the Lego product itself: just as Lego had been telling children to 'build their dreams' for decades, so perhaps adults could be asked to *build* their visions for future strategy.

Since this was about people and ideas, the process should not be literal: it would be time-consuming, and not very imaginative, to be required to build Lego representations of office buildings and the people who worked in them. It would be just as unadventurous to have to construct standard strategy diagrams and flow charts using Lego materials. Instead, the idea was to invite participants to build symbolic or metaphorical representations, in a non-judgemental, free-thinking – and therefore *playful* – kind of environment. From these seeds, the Lego Serious Play process was born. The concept was developed over time, with Robert Rasmussen joining the team and playing a key role. Today, the company states that Lego Serious Play is:

> A groundbreaking process to realise, unlock and maximise the human potential in an organisation. Lego Serious Play enhances participants' insight, commitment and confidence by engaging them in a hands-on, minds-on experience. Worldwide, companies on five continents have used Lego Serious Play applications to improve strategic planning, manage successful projects and build better teams. In practical terms, Lego Serious Play is a concept and methodology that helps organisations have more effective meetings to solve complex strategic issues.
>
> (Lego Serious Play marketing material, 2006)

As it is based around a process in which individuals build metaphorical models, share their 'stories', and listen and work with each other, Lego Serious Play is unlike other consultancy interventions where an external 'expert' identifies problems and proposes solutions. Instead, Lego Serious Play begins with the notion that the answers 'are already in the room'. Every participant gets an equal opportunity to express their feelings or ideas, and the collaborative process means that – as long as the session is facilitated properly – individual contributions will be embraced within the broader overall vision which emerges during the consultancy process.

Lego Serious Play is based around a set of core ideas: constructionism (and being in 'flow'); play; and metaphor. I will discuss metaphor in some depth later in this chapter, but will focus on the others here.

Constructivism, constructionism and building knowledge

The developers of Lego Serious Play believed in the idea that we can use our hands to *construct* models of knowledge, and that using the hands in this way to build a three-dimensional representation of ideas and feelings opens up a new path for free, creative and expressive thinking. Neuroscientists found some time ago, for example, that a surprisingly large proportion of the brain's motor controls were dedicated to the hand (Penfield and Rasmussen, 1950). The brain has a continuous interactive relationship with the hands, which means that the hands are not simply a valuable place to get information 'from', or to manipulate objects 'with', but also that thinking with the hands can have meaning in itself.

Lego Serious Play makes use of the idea of constructivism, developed by Swiss psychologist Jean Piaget (1896–1980). Piaget argued that intelligence grows from the interaction of the mind with the world. In one interview, Piaget declared that the word 'constructivism' encompasses all of his work. He explains constructivism in the following way:

> Knowledge is neither a copy of the object nor taking consciousness of a priori forms pre-determined in the subject; it's a perpetual construction made by exchanges between the organism and the environment, from the biological point of view, and between thought and its object, from the cognitive point of view… The major problem in knowledge, since it isn't a copy of reality, a copy of objects, is the way it reconstructs reality. In other words, reality must be known, of course, but by recreating it through deduction and endogenous construction.
>
> (Piaget, 1980: 110–11)

The 'object' here does not necessarily mean a physical object, but any object of thought – anything you might think about – so it includes not only this book, or your father's face, but also what you did yesterday evening, getting older or the fear of being late. A student of Piaget, Seymour Papert, went on to use these ideas in his own notion of *constructionism* – a literal implementation of the idea of building knowledge. Papert says that constructionism might be summarised as 'learning-by-making', but is quick to assert that it is 'much richer and more multifaceted' than such a simple formula might suggest (Papert and Harel, 1991). Its origins are explained in this story that Papert tells about when he was a specialist in mathematics education, and was working on a project at a Junior High School in Massachusetts in the late 1960s. On his way to the math class, he walked past the art room each day:

> For a while, I dropped in periodically to watch students working on soap sculptures, and mused about ways in which this was not like a math class. In the math class students are generally given little problems which they solve or don't solve, pretty well on the fly. In this particular art class they were all carving soap, but what each student carved came from wherever fancy is bred, and the project was not done and dropped, but continued for many weeks. It allowed time to think, to dream, to gaze, to get a new idea and try it and drop it or persist, time to talk, to see other people's work and their reaction to yours – not unlike mathematics as it is for the mathematician, but quite unlike math as it is in junior high school. I remember craving some of the students' work and learning that their art teacher and their families had first choice. I was struck by an incongruous image of the teacher in a regular math class pining to own the products of his students' work! An ambition was born: I want junior high school math class to be like that. I didn't know exactly what 'that' meant but I knew I wanted it. I didn't even know what to call the idea. For a long time it existed in my head as 'soap-sculpture math'.
>
> (Papert and Harel, 1991: online)

In other words, Papert noticed that when students were making something with their hands (such as soap sculptures), they were in a deeply engaged state, whereas when they were making something rather abstract in their minds alone (such as solutions to math problems), they were much *less* engrossed. Papert therefore resolved to develop forms of learning, in different spheres, which would utilise the benefits of this 'hands on' process.

The level of fascinated engagement Papert noticed in the art class was that state which Mihaly Csikszentmihalyi would later call 'flow', as mentioned in Chapter 2. Lego Serious Play seeks to make use of both of these ideas, the 'hands-on, minds-on learning' proposed by Papert, and the state of flow outlined by Csikszentmihalyi, in a free-thinking, playful process. This brings us to the next theme.

Play

Lego Serious Play, as its name indicates, also makes use of the notion that adults can benefit from engaging in play. Although play is normally associated with

Figure 8.1 Participants in ten different groups, aged between 19 and 72, engaged in the Lego identity-building sessions

children, there is a growing body of literature, in both academic journals and popular paperbacks, which argues that behaving in 'play' mode offers creative possibilities, because it emphasises freedom and plays down responsibility, self-consciousness and shame. The non-judgemental environment of play, it is claimed, is more likely to foster surprising and innovative ideas (see Stephenson, 1988; Terr, 2000; Gee, 2004; Kane, 2005).

The booklet 'The Science of Lego Serious Play', published by the company, outlines their use of the concept as follows:

> We define play as a limited, structured, and voluntary activity that involves the imaginary. That is, it is an activity limited in time and space, structured by rules, conventions, or agreements among the players, uncoerced by authority figures, and drawing on elements of fantasy and creative imagination.
>
> (Lego Serious Play, 2006: 4)

The notion of 'play' is useful in a process like Lego Serious Play, although perhaps it works best as a fruitful *metaphor* for thinking freely and without constraints, a state where one is happy to try different things knowing that there is no right or wrong answer. This is not *quite* the same as play, as practised by children, which usually has no particular goals beyond those contained in the exercise itself. This is acknowledged in the booklet, which goes on to say:

> Adult play is not precisely the same as a child's play. When adults play, they play with their sense of identity. Their play is often, though not always, competitive. Adult play is often undertaken with a specific goal in mind, whereas in children the purposes of their play are less conscious. We have identified four purposes of adult play that are especially relevant to our discussion of Lego Serious Play: 1) social bonding, 2) emotional expression, 3) cognitive development, and 4) constructive competition.
>
> (Ibid)

It is argued that play is good for social bonding, as players have to collaborate and communicate; that it engages the emotions within a contained zone, where particular issues can be worked through; and that it fosters understanding between participants (Plato is supposed to have asserted that 'You can learn more about a person in an hour of play than in a year of conversation'). Finally, the idea of 'constructive competition' is not that anyone is concerned about 'winning', but rather that participants are encouraged to do their best when they can see that others are doing so.

The established Lego Serious Play processes

To become a certified Lego Serious Play facilitator, one has to complete a week of intensive training. (I did this in April 2005 at Hotel Legoland in Billund, Denmark.) This training is usually taken by people who are already business consultants, and who wish to be certified partners who will then be able to use the process, under licence, as part of their work. The week of training is necessary so that practitioners can become familiar with the carefully thought-out methods and ethos of Lego Serious Play. The process is learned by *doing* it, as well as hearing about and discussing it.

All Lego Serious Play sessions begin with 'Skills Building', during which participants become familiar (or reacquainted) with using Lego pieces, and are introduced to some of the key features of the process, including the hand–mind connection, and building in metaphors. This stage can easily fill two hours, and it has been found that this stage is *necessary* for the later processes to work well; it cannot be skipped to save time. This set of exercises would normally lead on to one (or more) of the Lego Serious Play applications themselves, the most popular of which are:

- 'Real Time Strategy for the Enterprise' – a sequence of activities in which participants build metaphorical models representing their organisation, and then combine these into a shared identity of the enterprise; then build 'agents' (any possible external entity which the organisation may have to connect or deal with) and place these on a landscape in relation to their main model; then build the different kinds of connections; then consider future scenarios; and ultimately arrive at 'Simple Guiding Principles', which emerge from the activity and help to make future decisions.
- 'Real Time Strategy for the Team' – a version more oriented towards team-building, in which participants begin by constructing models representing what they bring to the organisation; then create a part of a colleague's perceived identity which they have not included themselves; then are asked to review what has been built so far and to build a model representing 'the feel of the team'; then to build connections showing how the parts of the team relate; then to reflect on past ways of dealing with events to ultimately arrive at 'Simple Guiding Principles' for the team.
- 'Real Time Identity for You' – a simpler process in which individuals build a metaphorical model of their identity at work, then change it to show how they think they are perceived, and then again to represent an aspirational version, 'what you could be at your best', and to reflect upon the differences.

Note that every stage of these activities involves building with Lego, utilising the 'hand–mind connection'; there's never a point where participants merely sit back and write down, or chat about, the issues without *building* their response first. Therefore everything that is discussed comes from *out of* the building process, where the hand and mind engage to give visual, metaphorical shape to meaningful things, emotions and relationships.

My modified research process using Lego Serious Play

I used a version of Lego Serious Play to explore how people view their own identities, and what they feel are the strongest influences upon them. I conducted the following sessions, each at least four hours long, between September 2005 and February 2006:

- Group 1: Architects (8). Held at Allies & Morrison Architects, London.
- Group 2: Unemployed people (9). Held at RNLI building, Poole, Dorset.
- Group 3: Charity managers (7). Held at RNLI building, Poole, Dorset.
- Group 4: First year Scriptwriting students at Bournemouth University (7). Held at Bournemouth University.
- Group 5: All staff at the Study Gallery, Poole (10). Held at the Study Gallery.
- Group 6: Social Care workers, who were also second year students, at University of Winchester (8). Held at University of Winchester.
- Group 7: Norwegian students in Faculty of Arts, University of Oslo (7). Held at Intermedia, University of Oslo.
- Group 8: Norwegian academics, University of Oslo (8). Held at Intermedia, University of Oslo.
- Group 9: Unemployed people, Hackney, London (7). Held at Hackney Central, London.
- Group 10: Unemployed people, Hackney, London (8). Held at Hackney Central, London.

A total of 79 individuals took part. Most of the groups were recruited on an 'ad hoc' basis, through different contacts, and the Dorset unemployed people were recruited via Poole JobCentre. The intention was not to get groups to be representative of different professional sectors; rather, I just wanted a *range* of different kinds of people. After the first eight groups, there seemed to be something of an emphasis on middle-class arty types, and so two further groups of distinctly underprivileged unemployed people were recruited by a professional research recruitment company, Indiefield of London. This was funded by the Mediatized Stories project (University of Oslo and the Research Council of Norway). Most groups volunteered to take part, motivated by an interest in what the process might reveal, and were given refreshments and the opportunity to take and keep Polaroid photos of their model(s). The three unemployed groups were paid for their time (£50 for four hours), and some other groups were given 'thank you' gifts if they were giving up their leisure time rather than their work hours (for example, the architects all volunteered to do the session on a Saturday, and were given £25 gift vouchers as a 'thank you', whereas the charity managers and gallery workers were doing the session as part of 'staff development' within their work – as a way of getting to know each other better – and so were just given a nice lunch).

> Colour photographs from all of the sessions, and other additional material including interviews about the process, can be found at www.artlab.org. uk/creative.

I had a detailed 'script' for the four-hour process which I took each group through. This is an abbreviated description of the activities:

*   greeting and introduction to the session;
*   to get participants 'warmed up' with Lego construction, they were asked to build a tower each; these were 'tested' for stability, and I would cruelly break one or two of them, in order to demonstrate the emotional connection that we have with something we've built;
*   this was followed by a short introduction to the idea of the hand–mind connection, and then a short discussion to introduce the idea of metaphors.

Figure 8.2 A sloth-like creature (left) is transformed into a metaphor for Friday afternoons (right), with wheels, bright lights, and a wagging tail

- Participants were then asked to build a small creature; we would go round the table and see what everyone had built. Then I would say, 'In the next two minutes I want you to change the model into a *metaphor* for how you feel on Monday mornings. Or Friday afternoons'. (This was the crucial turning-point, where participants discovered that they were able to create metaphorical meanings with Lego after all.) As with every stage, we went around the table and heard each person's explanation of their model, looking at the parts and the whole.
- To further develop their ability with metaphors and telling a 'story' about a model, participants were then asked to build anything they liked, and then were unexpectedly asked to explain how their model was a 'perfect representation of' something else (random items chosen off little cards, such as 'marriage', 'paranoia' and 'genetic engineering').
- To gain experience of building a metaphorical representation of a person's identity, participants were then asked to build 'The boss from hell' (or in some cases, 'The boyfriend or girlfriend from hell'). They were told this should not represent one *actual* person, and of course would not *look* like a person, being a metaphorical model. (We found that, perhaps surprisingly, all participants 'got' this perfectly well.)
- After hearing about all these models (around two hours in), we would have a break.

All of the preceding activities were necessary exercises so that participants would be able to tackle the main identity-building task, which filled the second half of the session:

- I would introduce this part by saying 'Now I'm going to ask you to build *your* identity. Think about who you are and the different aspects of yourself that you bring to the world, and what you think are significant aspects of your identity'.
- Participants were reassured: 'This task doesn't mean you have to reveal the most private aspects of yourself; you don't have to "bare your soul"; rather, you are provided with an opportunity to say "This is how I would like you to be introduced to me"'.
- I would remind them about building in metaphors, and emphasise that 'This is all about *who you are*'. I would also say, more than once, 'If you don't know what to build, *start building*' – a standard Lego Serious Play encouragement – although generally participants were eager to race ahead with their constructions.
- Participants would have at least 20 minutes for this building stage, and then we would hear the 'story' of each model, taking another 15 minutes or so.
- Then I would say 'Now we're going to think about what feeds into you and affects who you are. Any of these things, these influences, we'll call

an "agent". We're not talking about something that just affects how you feel for a *moment*, like if it's raining, but things that actually have some kind of *influence* on how you live your life and the choices you make'. I would explain that the agents can be abstract or concrete, physical or psychological, obvious or subtle, near or far, large or small.

- Participants were asked to build three agents to begin with, and to position them in relation to the identity model; as always, we would then go round the table and hear about what had been added.
- Then we would have two more 'rounds' of adding 'two or three more' agents, and hearing about them.
- Finally, participants were asked to fill in a two-page questionnaire, on which they would record what elements of their identity they represented in their identity model, and how each part was represented in Lego; the same information about the agents (influences); and a couple of reflective and evaluation questions (which will be discussed in the next chapter).

Later in this chapter I will discuss some of the metaphors that were constructed, and the next two chapters will discuss the *findings* of the study. Before that, I will consider the use of objects to represent identities, and the use of metaphors.

A theory of identities understood through objects

We typically draw a line between the 'external' world of objects and the environment, and the 'internal' world of our experience, feelings and identity. However, it is also common to make a link when we say, for example, that shopping for clothes, music or even a car can be a way of expressing identity. It's worth taking a short detour here, then, to consider how objects (external items) can help us to understand identities (internal experiences).

Tony Whincup, in an article entitled 'Imaging the Intangible' (2004), discusses the connections between material aspects of our existence – such as objects we like, and the stuff in our homes – and more intangible dimensions of human activity. (In particular, he is concerned with ways in which photographs of the former can give us sociological information about the latter – although I'm not concerned with that here, and am using Whincup's arguments for other purposes.) He notes that we keep and display material things – objects such as gifts, souvenirs and cards – to make more 'real' the stuff which would otherwise only be in our minds: memories and feelings. The tangible objects are used to preserve the intangible memories. As Whincup notes (p. 80):

> It is not surprising that the nature of memory is of vital concern to individual and group alike. Memory, a slippery and fragile thing, is

constantly open to subtraction and addition. Inevitably, people have searched for strategies through which to restore the memory of these otherwise tenuous and transitory life events and socially agreed values.

Whincup offers examples – in the form of photographs of objects, with their owner's explanations of their meaning – to show how people imbue everyday objects with special meanings. A cheap toy or an empty champagne bottle, for example, can have massive amounts of sentimental meaning to one individual, because of the personal stories and memories they are associated with, even though the items would be worthless to anyone else.

> In the struggle to maintain memories by charging objects with their safekeeping, the relationship between the owner and the object changes … The personal mnemonic object becomes as priceless and unique as the memory to which it holds the key.
>
> (Ibid: 81)

Although such objects mean nothing to an outsider, they can be vital parts of their owner's construction of self, reminding them of significant differences or associations with others. These are usually positive, Whincup says:

Figure 8.3 Fridge doors often present everyday identity collages

As a group, mnemonic objects generally encapsulate the best of people's reflections about themselves. It is in these object attachments that a personal and 'advantageous' sense of self can be sustained. Objects as mnemonics are a complex business intertwined with edited past experiences, current constructions and orientations towards future aspirations.

(Ibid)

A set of objects deliberately placed in a personal or shared space, then – whether on a mantelpiece, bedroom wall or fridge door – is a 'presentation of self', but its central purpose, Whincup suggests, is not primarily that highlighted by Goffman's *The Presentation of Self in Everyday Life* (1959) – that is, a staged arrangement constructed to give a particular impression to an external audience. Although the autobiographical explanation of the set of objects *may* be one of its uses (to show what an interesting or sensitive person one is), these arrangements are primarily about creating a stable sense of self-identity for *oneself*. Whincup suggests that 'an awareness of self is arrived at, *retrospectively*, by witnessing consistent patterns revealed and maintained in the concrete expressions of our experiences' (2004: 81; my emphasis). This simple statement, therefore, proposes a whole theory of self-identity, in which people look back on their experiences and put together sets of visual mnemonics which say 'this is who I am', which may then provide markers or signposts for future orientations. As with most explanations of how self-identity is constructed, this doesn't need to be part of a conscious plan; an individual does not need to think to themselves, 'After breakfast I'll put together a visual representation of my identity using meaningful mnemonic markers of self'. Rather, this is something that people do anyway. If you think of the homes of your relatives and friends, it is likely that, in some way, they include some collections of photographs, objects, cards, souvenirs or other collected items, which tell us something about their owners – and which, as is being emphasised here, tell their owners something about *themselves*.

Whincup's study of the ways in which individuals and groups put together such objects suggests that people seek to assemble 'coherent and satisfying' combinations of items, 'with the emphasis upon a particular sense of unity' (ibid). This matches our experience in the Lego Serious Play study, in which participants – in every case, in fact – could be seen trying to assemble coherent, unified and balanced models of their identities. The desire for 'unity' – to clarify – was not that all the parts should be the same, or 'say' the same thing, but rather that the parts should add up to one meaningful whole. Some participants were apologetic if their model appeared 'schizophrenic' (i.e. apparently contradictory, or with non-unified parts – the commonplace but medically incorrect use of the word 'schizophrenic'), and typically sought to explain how the parts 'actually' fitted together and made sense as a unified whole.

Furthermore, Whincup makes use of the work of German philosopher Wilhelm Dilthey (1833–1911), who suggested that individuals come to understand the world and themselves by looking at the symbolic systems we create through personal expressions and interactions. In terms of our personal sets of meaningful objects, this means that our sense of self is clarified not only by making our own arrangements of symbolic items, but also through considering our own in relation to other people's. Such comparisons are not necessarily paranoid or insecure, but can be reassuring and positive – 'identity-affirming', if you like – in terms of both observed similarities and differences. For example, I might be pleased to see that my friend admires the artist Tracey Emin, as I do, so we have something in common there, but also I might be equally happy to note that I am *not* interested in collecting photographs of the actor Tom Cruise, as she is, and have spent my time on other things. Indeed, of course, the same kind of considerations will be made in the group Lego sessions when reflecting on one's own metaphorical identity model, and those made by other participants: I might be happy to see certain similarities, but equally be *relieved* to think that my identity is not burdened with the particular fears or insecurities highlighted by others. Having considered the relationship between objects and identities, I now move on to discuss the use of metaphors in communication.

Metaphors

We all use metaphors, in everyday language, all the time. When we use a metaphor, we say that something is something else – 'X is Y' – because we hope to create a better understanding of 'X' by connecting it with the notion of 'Y'. So, for example, I might say that 'John is a snake', to communicate the idea that he is cunning, sneaky and possibly a dangerous predator, although he is obviously not *literally* a scaly reptile. Or we might observe that Mary's face lights up when she sees you, making use of the idea of coming out of darkness into light, the warmth and pleasure of a light bulb coming on, without *actually* meaning that she would glow in the dark. Obviously, we use metaphors because they *add* something – an additional level of meaningfulness; otherwise we would just say the straightforward literal thing instead. Lynne Cameron states that:

> Metaphor appears to draw on a basic human cognitive capacity for noticing similarities between disparate entities, and on an affective capacity for enjoying playing with language and ideas. A metaphor is a kind of package which compactly brings together two concepts and their properties, entities, relations, connotations and evaluations.
>
> (Cameron, 2006: 49)

Metaphors are often taken for granted; we are not aware of any great linguistic achievement when we say 'I don't think you're following me' or 'His glass is always half empty' or 'Her ideas finally bore fruit'. In addition, metaphor is often taught in school: in England, for example, 14 and 15 year olds will typically spend some time learning that Hamlet said that all the world is a stage, or that Macbeth said he was stained in blood, not because they were really inaccurate speakers but because they were employing the power of metaphor.

Metaphor is not just a linguistic device – visual icons can be metaphorical too (though we might need to 'translate' the imagery into words before the metaphor becomes clear). I can still recall a day in 1984, when I saw a demonstration of a brand new Apple Mac computer, where a 'mouse' was used to pull 'documents' from a 'filing cabinet' onto a 'desktop'. Today, these metaphors seem completely natural to computer users, but at the time they were really striking, strange and impressive. Before that, my junior-nerd experience of computers was all about using programming codes, which were complicated and non-intuitive, and nothing at all like these neat metaphors. The idea that erasing data would be a matter of 'dragging' a 'file' into the 'waste basket', for example, was memorably brilliant and bonkers. And this, again, is the power of metaphors – making something more meaningful by equating it with something else.

Paul Ricoeur's survey of approaches to metaphor

Metaphor has been studied for centuries. The Greek philosopher Aristotle set out some principles of metaphor some 2,350 years ago. He argued that a metaphor (such as 'Achilles is a lion') is more powerful than a simile (to say that 'Achilles is *like* a lion') because it more potently creates the idea of one thing *as* another thing, conveying the knowledge in a way that produces a surprising mental image. Since Aristotle's time, a number of scholars have considered metaphor, treating it as an aspect of language. (In recent years, as we will see below, a 'cognitive linguistic' approach has seen metaphor as making connections between ideas and concepts, rather than language, which is perhaps what Aristotle was getting at all along.)

The French philosopher Paul Ricoeur dealt with many of the key traditional ideas in his exhaustive discussion in *The Rule of Metaphor* (2003; first published in French in 1975, in English, 1977). (Ricoeur's work on narrative and identity, incidentally, will play a significant role in the next chapter.) Ricoeur begins with Aristotle and then moves through approaches which see metaphor in terms of the individual word, to those which consider it in the context of a sentence, and then to viewing metaphor at the level of discourse. He easily shows that metaphor is not a matter of merely substituting one word for another, as had been suggested in the eighteenth and nineteenth centuries, as metaphors regularly depend on a whole phrase or sentence for their full meaning. Ricoeur then considers some twentieth-century theorists whom he generally finds useful up to a point, although he has some reservations about each of them.

The first of these is I. A. Richards. In *The Philosophy of Rhetoric* (1936), Richards argues that to use a metaphor is not simply to exchange the 'proper' word for an improper but figurative one, because words only gain their full meaning from the context in which they appear. Rather, a metaphor plays upon the tension between the words in a sentence and the use of an underlying idea – which Richards calls the *tenor* – and the thing which is a carrier of this underlying idea, which Richards calls the *vehicle*. Both the tenor and the vehicle, together, make up the metaphor. So when I say 'I do like Craig, but he's on another planet', the *vehicle* is the notion of him being 'on another planet', and the *tenor* (underlying idea) is the notion that he is difficult to communicate with. But the choice of vehicle adds additional meaning: the phrase 'on another planet' makes Craig seem distant, not a part of our world, and even points to associated metaphorical ideas like 'space cadet' or even, perhaps, 'high as a kite'.

Richards was also one of the first to point out that metaphors are not really an unusual or especially poetic mode of speech, but are a commonly used tool of communication. As Ricoeur puts it:

> Contrary to Aristotle's well-known saying that the mastery of metaphor is a gift of genius and cannot be taught, language [for Richards] is 'vitally metaphorical' … If to 'metaphorise well' is to possess mastery of resemblances, then without this power we would be unable to grasp any hitherto unknown relations between things. Therefore, far from being a divergence from the ordinary operation of language, it is 'the omnipresent principle of all its free action'.
>
> (Ricoeur, 2003: 92)

Ricoeur is impressed by Richard's contribution, and likes the questions it raises, but has some precise reservations about the detail (ibid: 94–6). He therefore moves on to make use of Max Black's work, *Models and Metaphors* (1962), in which the author argues that metaphors work by bringing into play a set of ideas which organise how we think about something, and deliver insight. The associations will inevitably vary between different individuals. So when I say 'John is a snake', to return to that example, different listeners might have a range of associations with the notion of the snake (some might see it as rather sexy, or cruel, or exciting, or frightening), but nevertheless the metaphor is likely to foreground some associations and play down others, and therefore 'organises our view' of the subject (in this case, John). As Ricoeur notes, 'Organising a principal subject by applying a subsidiary subject to it constitutes, in effect, an irreducible intellectual operation, which informs and clarifies in a way that is beyond the scope of any paraphrase' (Ricoeur, 2003: 101). A metaphor is therefore not just a short-cut, or a poetic bit of cleverness, but can add meaning in a *unique* way. However, Ricoeur is disappointed that this theory, which relies on a set of commonplace associations going with the vehicle, does not seem to account for cases where such associations do not already exist (ibid: 102).

Another view is put forward by Monroe Beardsley (1958), who suggests that metaphor is part of the strategy of literary composition, which also includes oxymoron and irony, in which the *meaning* of a phrase or sentence is incompatible with, or the opposite of, that which is stated. From the contradiction, in the particular context of a particular sentence, a new meaning emerges. Ricoeur is pleased with this proposal, as it does not rely on already-existing associations, and shows the power of metaphor as part of a *living* language which can add vibrantly to our experience of the world.

Through a series of lengthy discussions, then, only a few of which have been touched on here, Ricoeur builds towards his own view of metaphor. (Simms, 2003, offers a useful account of this discussion.) Ricoeur disagrees with the view that metaphor is about substituting one term for another, or that it hinges on single words. Rather, metaphorical meaning emerges from the 'live' process of the individual having to make sense of a statement which is not literally true. 'Metaphorical meaning', Ricoeur explains, 'is not the enigma itself, the semantic clash pure and simple, but the solution of the enigma, the inauguration of the new semantic pertinence' (2003: 254). The listener is forced to perform an act of interpretation in order make sense of a metaphor, and that is why Ricoeur finds metaphor exciting, because it shows us that language is *alive* and can generate new knowledge. He has said that metaphor offers 'a reshaping of our way of looking at things which, in a sense, is no longer description, and surely is no longer representational ... It is a creative referentiality' (Ricoeur, interviewed in Reagan, 1998: 107). Metaphor is therefore the most creative part of everyday speech.

The cognitive linguistic approach

Ricoeur, then, worked through a number of arguments about metaphor as an aspect of language, before reaching his own conclusion, which includes the idea of dynamic cognitive work taking place in both the composition and interpretation of metaphors. A few years later, George Lakoff and Mark Johnson published *Metaphors We Live By* (1980; new edition 2003), in which they argued that metaphors are not crucially about language at all, but are primarily *conceptual*, mapping one idea onto another. Lakoff and Johnson point out that there are basic conceptual metaphors (such as LIFE IS A JOURNEY) which can be expressed in a number of different instances of language (such as 'I don't know *where I'm going*', 'We're at a *crossroads*', 'I don't want to *get in your way*', 'She's really *going places*' and many more). The basic conceptual metaphor is the root idea, the basic 'X is Y' statement, which cannot be broken down further, and which lies at the heart of a range of metaphorical phrases. So, for example, the basic conceptual metaphor IDEAS ARE FOOD underpins everyday metaphors such as 'We don't need to *spoon-feed* our students', 'She *devoured* the book', 'This is an issue I can really *sink my teeth into*', and several others (2003: 46–7). I have here adopted the formatting style established by Lakoff and Johnson, where a basic conceptual metaphor is written in SMALL CAPITALS, and its expression, which can typically occur in a range of phrases, is shown in *italics*.

Because analysis of metaphors is important in this chapter and the next, it will be helpful to give a few more examples at this point (mostly adapted from Lakoff and Johnson, 2003: 46–51):

- Basic conceptual metaphor: ARGUMENTS ARE BUILDINGS
  – appears in phrases such as 'Your claims are *built* on really *shaky foundations*', 'Her whole argument *collapsed*' and 'We need to *prop up* the theory with something *solid*'.
- Basic conceptual metaphor: EMOTIONAL EFFECT IS PHYSICAL CONTACT
  – appears in phrases such as 'His mother's death *hit* him *hard*', 'I was *touched* by her letter' and 'Meeting her just *blew me away*'.
- Basic conceptual metaphor: LIFE IS A GAMBLING GAME
  – appears in phrases such as 'You'll be OK if you *play your cards right*', 'Where is she when the *chips are down*?' and 'It's the *luck of the draw*'.
- Basic conceptual metaphor: LOVE IS A PHYSICAL FORCE
  – appears in phrases such as 'There was *electricity* between us', 'They *gravitated* towards each other' and 'The *atmosphere* around them was *charged*'.

Of course, there are many more basic conceptual metaphors. Even on just one of these themes, such as love, we can also identify LOVE IS MADNESS, LOVE IS MAGIC, LOVE IS WAR, LOVE IS A PATIENT, and others. Nevertheless, the list of basic conceptual metaphors that are regularly employed is probably relatively short – a few hundred – whereas the list of expressive phrases which could make use of these concepts is almost infinite. (The 'index of metaphors' at the back of Lakoff and Turner's 1989 book on metaphors in poetry, for instance, lists just 90 basic conceptual metaphors, 20 of which are 'LIFE IS X', although of course poetry has made use of each of these ideas in a vast variety of ways.)

Mapping the source domain to the target domain

The cognitive linguistic approach asserts that metaphors derive their power from the link between concepts in the *source domain* and the *target domain*. The target domain is the thing that is being talked about, such as love, and the source domain is the source of a meaningful conceptual model through which we understand the target, such as a physical force, madness, magic or war. Typically the *target* is something more intangible – a feeling, or life itself – which we understand by reference to a more concrete *source*. For example, the basic conceptual metaphor LIFE IS A JOURNEY helps us to understand the rather abstract idea of our own lives, by connecting it with the idea of a journey, which is more familiar and less abstract.

In particular, metaphors work by mapping elements of the source domain onto the target domain. With LIFE IS A JOURNEY, for example, we get to import all of the 'furniture' of a journey onto our notion of a life. This is made very clear in this extract from Lakoff and Turner:

When Robert Frost says,

Two roads diverged in a wood, and I—
I took the one less traveled by,
And that has made all the difference,
        ("The Road Not Taken")

we typically read him as discussing options for how to live life, and as claiming that he chose to do things differently than most other people do.

    This reading comes from our implicit knowledge of the structure of the LIFE IS A JOURNEY metaphor. Knowing the structure of this metaphor means knowing a number of correspondences between the two conceptual domains of life and journeys, such as these:

- The person leading a life is a traveller.
- His purposes are destinations.
- The means for achieving purposes are routes.
- Difficulties in life are impediments to travel.
- Counselors are guides.
- Progress is the distance travelled.
- Things you gauge your progress by are landmarks.
- Choices in life are crossroads [or junctions].
- Material resources and talents are provisions.

(Lakoff and Turner, 1989: 3–4)

Each of these associations, as mentioned above, is a mapping of an aspect of the source domain onto an aspect of the target domain. So, for example, destinations are mapped onto purposes, and distance travelled is mapped onto progress. To take another example, with the metaphor LIFE IS A GAMBLING GAME we get to map the furniture of gambling – being dealt cards, throwing dice, holding aces, chips, bluffing, upping the ante, chances, odds, poker faces, luck of the draw, and all that – onto the twists and turns of everyday life. This set of metaphors provides us with a number of (mostly quite reassuring) ways of thinking about, and coping with, unexpected events in life. Of course, it would be perverse to *actually* treat life like a gambling game (although Luke

Rhinehart's 1971 novel *The Dice Man* shows what this would be like, to comic and chilling effect).

The importance of mapping is highlighted by the fact that some metaphors work intuitively, whilst others do not. The viability of a metaphor depends on whether the typical listener would be able to map elements of the source domain onto the target domain. So, for example, metaphorical phrases based on LIFE IS A JOURNEY are likely to be ones we can relate to, because we are very used to making those connections, but if we used an expression based on LIFE IS A TOMATO then it would probably leave the listener feeling bewildered. Any imaginative person can probably think of some reasons why LIFE IS A TOMATO could be a compelling basic conceptual metaphor, and we could derive metaphorical phrases from it – such as 'She's really trying to get to my pips' or 'He boiled my skin right off'. However, because LIFE IS A TOMATO is not one of the (relatively small) number of established basic conceptual metaphors for life, most listeners would struggle to make sense of it.

Metaphors for understanding everyday life

It is noticeable that the basic conceptual metaphors which underpin metaphorical expressions, such as 'LOVE IS A PATIENT' or 'ARGUMENTS ARE BUILDINGS' may appear strange and unusual – not phrases that you would actually say – although each one is the basis for several familiar and everyday phrases. Indeed, the 'everydayness' of metaphors is one of Lakoff and Johnson's main points:

> Metaphor is for most people a device of the poetic imagination and the rhetorical flourish – a matter of extraordinary rather than ordinary language. Moreover, metaphor is typically viewed as characteristic of language alone, a matter of words rather than thought or action. For this reason, most people think they can get along perfectly well without metaphor. We have found, on the contrary, that metaphor is pervasive in everyday life, not just in language but in thought and action. Our ordinary conceptual system, in terms of how we both think and act, is fundamentally metaphorical in nature.
>
> (Lakoff and Johnson, 2003: 3)

It is important to Lakoff and Johnson that many metaphors are used in everyday speech as a matter of routine, and are not deliberately generated *as metaphors*. Research by Lynne Cameron suggests that 'around 90 per cent' of metaphors are used in this conventionalised and non-deliberate way (Cameron, 2006: 48). The fact that many metaphors have become 'naturalised' in everyday language is fine for proponents of the cognitive linguistic approach – unlike Ricoeur, say, who was interested in metaphors for the *active* knowledge-production which occurs when we coin a *new* metaphor – because one of their central claims is that metaphors are central to *how we think about things*.

The notion that metaphors are central to how we think about life is not necessarily new. For example, the idea that metaphors frame how we perceive the world appears in I. A. Richards's *Philosophy of Rhetoric*:

> Our world is a projected world, shot through with characters lent to it from our own life … The processes of metaphor in language, the exchanges between the meanings of words which we study in explicit verbal metaphors, are super-imposed upon a perceived world which is itself a product of earlier or unwitting metaphor, and we shall not deal with them justly if we forget that this is so.
>
> (Richards, 1936: 108–9)

The phrase 'a projected world' illustrates very nicely the way in which we might apply mental concepts and metaphors to our experience of being in the world. Perhaps what Lakoff and colleagues really demonstrate is the extent to which this is so. Metaphors structure how we think about our experience of the world, and are indispensable to that understanding. As Lakoff and Turner say:

> Take, for example, PURPOSES ARE DESTINATIONS and TIME MOVES. It is virtually unthinkable for any speaker of English (as well as many other languages) to dispense with these metaphors for conceptualising purposes and time. To do so would be to change utterly the way we think about goals, and the future.
>
> (Lakoff and Turner, 1989: 56)

It is in this way that we see that metaphors *are* conceptual mappings. Although they can be *expressed* in language, the metaphor is not merely contained in the words, but is about the connection of concepts. It is for this reason that metaphors can also map images; to say that a woman is an 'hourglass' means that we map the narrow centre of the image of an hourglass onto the image of the woman's waist, but the words did not give us this information (ibid: 90); rather, it was the cognitive work of a metaphorical image-mapping.

Evaluating the cognitive linguistic approach

The approach of Lakoff and colleagues, which shifted the study from metaphors as flourishes of language to an approach which has to consider metaphors as concepts and ideas, might seem to 'reveal' something quite obvious. However, the publication of *Metaphors we Live by*, in 1980, apparently *was* a major turning-point and had a significant impact on the study of metaphor (see for example, Kövecses, 2002; Cameron, 2006). Of course, they were not the first to observe that metaphors involve linking one idea with another. However, their contribution was to establish very clearly that the potentially infinite number of metaphorical linguistic expressions which we can generate is underpinned by a much smaller group of basic conceptual metaphors, which are simple, irreducible and underpin numerous familiar phrases. Lakoff and colleagues have also explained in detail the mapping that occurs from one domain to another (see Lakoff and Turner, 1989: 62–5, for example, for a brilliant section which explains the schemas through which metaphors offer conceptual 'slots' to be filled with items in the source domain; LIFE IS A JOURNEY, for example, offers a range of slots to be filled: we might fill the PATH slot by characterising it as a racing track, a mountain pass or a minefield, and we might put in an optional VEHICLE which could be a car, horse or rocket, and each choice has implications for how the metaphor will frame the target).

Most importantly, perhaps, the approach has shown that metaphorical expressions, whether newly coined or very well established, stem from a

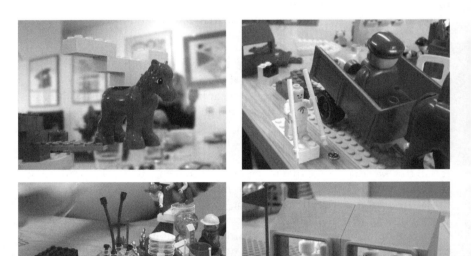

Figure 8.4 Metaphorical items in Lego – clockwise from top left: an aspirational winged horse; a man skiing around the other concerns in the model, representing a turning-point; lonely skeletons queuing up to enter the world with 'misplaced optimism'; and people under a transparent plastic container, representing people from the past

set of basic conceptual metaphors without which we would have difficulty thinking about such fundamental but intangible concepts as life, death, love, knowledge and time. Metaphors are therefore not merely 'useful' tools for communication; they are central to understanding human experience.

Using metaphor in social research

It should by now be obvious *why* we might want to use metaphor in social research. Metaphors enable people to capture complex ideas, often with a number of facets, in simple visual (or visualisable) form. When considering abstract or internal intangible concepts, in particular, such as *identity*, or *how a person sees their life*, metaphors provide a route through which individuals can express ideas or thoughts which they might not otherwise be able to put into words. (This point was emphasised in the evaluation comments from participants in the Lego study, some of which are quoted in the following chapter.)

For this reason, and because they are part of everyday communication, my study will not be the first to have used metaphors in social research. Indeed, Paul Sweetman commented to me that 'All sociology is, in a sense, metaphorical', which is a provocative thought – delightfully sweeping, but rather broad (!). On a more specific level, we know that deliberate and extended use of metaphors as an integral part of a research process is less common. Market researchers were perhaps the first to spot the simple communicative power of visual metaphors. Market research guru Gerald Zaltman (2003), for example, advocates a 'metaphor elicitation process' in which individuals are asked to gather pictures which represent their feelings about a topic (for example, their 'thoughts and feelings about being Hispanic in the United States today', p. 101). They bring these to an interview, in which they are asked 'probing' questions about the images, and their associated feelings, in order to reveal the 'stories' which they connect with particular experiences or brands. This simple idea seems to be an effective way of approaching an issue 'sideways', in order to reveal deeply held beliefs, anxieties or contradictions. Similarly, Russell Belk and colleagues have published studies in the *Journal of Consumer Research* in which participants have been asked to produce collages and other metaphorical images to represent the notion of consumer 'desire' (see, for example, Belk, Ger and Askegaard 2003).

Metaphors in Lego Serious Play

Now we can consider the results of my research project in 2005–6, which – as we saw at the start of this chapter – invited a range of people, in groups, to build metaphorical models of their identities in Lego. In the following sections I will discuss some of the metaphors which were constructed by participants. To give some idea of the kinds of things built by participants, I will begin with a few examples of metaphors from the many hundreds which went into the 79 participants' models. Some were quite straightforward:

- a dinner table, representing family;
- a dish with bright shiny coins, representing friendship;
- a sequence of hurdles presided over by a 'witch figure', representing work;
- a man paddling along in a kayak, representing meditation;
- a bird on the ground, representing responsibilities ('because I feel like a bird that wants to fly away, but can't');
- a headless walking dinosaur, representing a lack of goals and ambition.

Others were more complex:

- people under a transparent plastic container, representing people from past, who continue to have an influence but who cannot be accessed directly;
- nine bodies with tubes going up into one big head, representing different sides of the personality;
- a tiger underneath the main representation of personality, representing an underlying pride and defensiveness;
- a man skiing *around* the other concerns in the model, representing 'a ski trip that was a changing point, which caused me to be open to new ideas as opposed to shutting them out';
- a see-saw with a crowned king figure opposite an 'evil' person, representing yin and yang, and the choices to be made in life between good and bad behaviour;
- a huge spider climbing over the top of the entire identity model, representing a general fear of things going wrong;
- man reaching for money in a tray with a grenade in it, representing the lack of money but fear of monetary desires;
- a female figure standing on several bricks, holding a snake, covered by a net, representing the participant's ex-wife, a woman whom he 'put on a pedestal' (the bricks) but was ultimately 'poison' in his life (the snake), but is now safely in the past (the net);
- a wobbly ambulance with only three wheels, representing health problems.

These are just a few examples from the many imaginative metaphors which participants built to communicate aspects of their experience.

Summary breakdown of common elements

Participants built a wide *range* of aspects of identity (even with my best efforts to group similar items together, there were 128 different themes represented), and influences upon their identity (again, even when grouped together, there were 100 different kinds of influences). Note that, in this section, I am talking about *what* was represented, and not *how* it was represented. Although this was not designed as a quantitative study, it is worth noting the most commonly referred to aspects of identity (Table 8.1).

The diversity of the identity elements built by participants means that there were hardly any very common elements, and then a long list of less common (or unique) items. More than half of the participants included other people as part of their own identity (and everyone included others as *influences*, as we will see below). But the other themes are very diverse. The second most common theme, included by less than one quarter, is a grouping of 'self-worth' elements: strength, determination, confidence and pride. Other common themes, such as openness, the home and awareness of the past (including memories and roots), were included by fewer than one in five people. The main point here is that participants represented a very diverse range of things as elements of their identity.

It might be considered surprising that *work*, which takes up so much time in many people's lives, was included by so few people (9 per cent). This may partly be because half of my research groups were unemployed or students; but it is

Table 8.1

Aspects of identity	Number	%
People – family, partner, friends	44	56
Self-worth (confident, determined, strong)	17	22
Openness	14	18
Home	13	16
The past	12	15
Creativity and ideas	11	14
Happiness, optimism	15	19
Supporting and protecting others	11	14
Awareness and looking at the world	10	13
Unstable, lonely, lost, nomadic, insecure, worried	10	13
Lack of money, concern about money	9	11
Learning	8	10
Stressed – busy, overworked, chaotic	7	9
Security and stability	7	9
Travel	7	9
Work	7	9

A further 112 different aspects of identity were represented in the models (128 aspects in total), including ambition, goals and aspirations, being multi-faceted, being closed, being solitary, religion, helpfulness, music, seeking happiness, challenges, and many others. The full list can be viewed at www.artlab.org.uk/creative.

Table 8.2

Influence upon identity	Number	%
People – overall total	99	125*
People – family, inc partner, parents, and/or my children	47	59
People – friends and colleagues	36	46
People – parent(s) in particular	16	20
Music	13	16
Learning	9	11
Past	9	11
Religion	8	10
Travel	8	10
Work and workplace	8	10
Creativity and ideas	7	9
Dead relatives and friends	7	9
Fears	7	9

A further 87 different influences upon identity were represented in the models (100 influences in total), including career, life experiences, nature, dreams and the future, home, places visited, pop culture and TV, art, knowledge, religion, sport, colour, desire to be different, and many others. The full list can be viewed at www.artlab.org.uk/creative.
* This figure is 125% as some participants included more than one person or group.

also because participants tended to talk of their identity as being something at the core of themselves, which would then be manifested in, and interact with, a range of contexts. Therefore their identity would *go* to, and *respond* to, work, but work would not necessarily be built as a part of identity itself.

When asked to add *influences* upon their identities, the responses were also very varied (Table 8.2). Unsurprisingly, other people are the strongest influence on identity, the most significant specific grouping of people being the person's parents, included by 10 per cent of participants, and their own children, included by 8 per cent (although either or both of these may appear in other models subsumed under representations of 'family'). Again, though, these numbers are low, whilst the number of *different* influences represented was high.

This brief quantitative section merely gives a taste of which elements and influences were included in the models. The *overall* representations of identity will be discussed in the next chapter; now, though, I return to the discussion of metaphors built.

The range of metaphors for single ideas

As we would expect when using metaphors, the same notion was represented in a number of different ways. For example:

* *Supporting or protecting others* was represented by an elephant carrying people and animals, a person behind a shield, a safety net, a fence, a platform and food.

- *Learning* was represented as a tower expanding as it goes up, a staircase, a tree with books in it, silver tubes with yellow radar dishes at the top, a pink umbrella, flags, a bookcase and a big building. (Note, though, that most of these different constructions are united by the basic conceptual metaphor that Lakoff and Johnson would call LEARNING IS UP, linked also to GOOD IS UP.)

- *Work* was represented as a crocodile in the bushes with money attached, a wheelbarrow filled with many items, pipes and chimneys, a heavy trailer resting on the person's shoulder, hoops and hurdles and, as mentioned above, a sequence of hurdles with a witch.

- *Dreams and the future* were represented by a salad bowl, a door leading off the model, a grey tower, a tunnel (to the unknown future), a wheel of chance, a rainbow and a pot of gold.

- *Life experiences* were represented as a set of steps going up with flags, a 'trough with hats, steep slope up, and unstable see-saw', a cake with candles, a wheel of fortune, 'me trying to get up a rope', and animals on top of animals.

- *Isolation and loneliness* was represented variously as a desert with one green plant in the centre, 'myself peering into a separate side of the model filled with colours and dancing people', as the space between things ('self-inflicted loneliness'), and as a figure stuck between four walls.

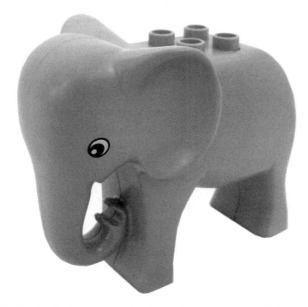

Figure 8.5 The Duplo elephant was variously used to represent ambition, strength, travel, overcoming fears, friends, supporting others and wisdom

- *Being multi-faceted* – playing a number of roles in life – was represented by a hatstand with different hats, different figures, three different animals in three different corners ('depending on what angle you come at me from, you may experience me differently'), skeletons queuing up to enter the world, lots of arches, and as mentioned above, nine bodies with tubes going up into one big head. (Note that these are particular *parts* of a model which refer to the idea of having multiple sides or roles. In addition, many of the models taken *as a whole* showed the multiple facets of a personality.)

Of course, some ideas were represented in mostly very similar ways. For example, people were very frequently used to represent *family*. A spirit of *openness* was represented by open doors, windows and transparent pieces. Participants often built houses to represent the importance of their *home* life, although 'pots and pans', a dog and a fenced-off area also represented this theme. *Happiness* was represented in various ways, but all were colourful.

Different metaphorical meanings of same objects

When introducing participants to the process, I would say reassuringly that 'It doesn't matter if you can't build some particular thing you have in your mind, because you can use anything to represent anything'. In fact, this is perhaps not quite correct. It is true that I *can* add to my model, say, a Lego sheep, and announce that it indicates my tendency towards conflict and fighting, but this is not likely to seem a very resonant metaphor, since the association between sheep and conflict is not one which is commonly made. Lakoff and Turner (1989: 200) argue that, although most people do have the ability to invent a metaphorical link between two random items, this 'does not mean that metaphor is completely unconstrained, that anything can map onto anything any old way'. The successful or memorable metaphor will be one which forms a bridge between aspects of the source domain and aspects of the target domain in an illuminating way. You can announce that the sheep is a *sign* for conflict in your model, and we can allow that and perhaps remember it because the link is so surprising, but it's not really a working metaphor, since metaphors should mean something to others with a similar cultural background.

Nevertheless, certain Lego elements were lent a wide range of meanings by participants. The Duplo elephant, for example, was used to represent, in different models, ambition, strength, travel, overcoming fears, friends, supporting others and wisdom. Different people built a boat on a sea to represent freedom, past history, adventures, a sense of being lost and drifting, or as a strong platform for friends and family united together on one boat. The tiger was used to represent ambition, pride, a driving force, work and a vehicle for the family. And a bridge was used to represent, variously, challenges, the chance to reach higher places, connecting people, fear, being a good manager, insecurities, openness, being reliable, risk-taking, seeking happiness, decisiveness, travel, being laid back, leadership and friendship.

In this chapter we have looked at some theories of metaphor, and seen that in the Lego study, all participants – from a wide range of backgrounds – felt able to construct metaphorical models of their own identities. We noted that similar ideas were represented in a range of different metaphors, and conversely that similar objects or representations were used to represent a range of different feelings and concepts. In the following chapter, I proceed to consider the overall metaphorical meaning of the whole models.

Chapter 9

What a whole identity model means

In the previous chapter I looked at the use of individual metaphors. First I considered the literature discussing the common linguistic form of metaphor, such as might be used within speech, and then gave some examples of the metaphors for particular elements of identity, and influences, which were built by research participants in my Lego study. In this chapter, we will expand the frame of reference to consider the meaning of the *whole* models, and what these might tell us about identity.

The whole model as a metaphor

In Lakoff and Turner's book about metaphor in poetry (1989), the authors dedicate one chapter to a discussion of a single poem, 'To a Solitary Disciple' by William Carlos Williams. They examine the metaphors employed, one by one, in some detail, but then move on to consider a 'global metaphorical reading' – seeing the *whole* poem as a metaphor. A non-metaphorical account of the whole poem would say that it presents to a young follower some advice on how to appreciate the pretty scene of a church in the early morning light. Most poetry readers would, however, suspect that the whole adds up to more than this: advice to a young poet on how to view the world, perhaps, or more likely the poem is a meditation on religious belief, and the relationship between institutionalised religion (the church, the 'squat edifice' described in the poem) and the divine (the sky and the 'jasmine lightness of the moon'). Different readers would have different interpretations of the whole, of course. One solution would be to ask William Carlos Williams what he *intended*, although he might not be willing to talk about it, and in any case he died in 1963, so this would be difficult. We also might feel obliged to consider the perennial debate about whether we need to know an artist's *intentions* in order to appreciate a work of art.

With the Lego identity models, however, we *do* have their creator's accounts of the whole, and we can be confident that their intentions are worthy of our consideration, since the models were clearly built to communicate something in particular – or a *set* of 'somethings' in particular – about that person's

Figure 9.1 Photographs of the 79 models, and what their creators said about them, arranged for analysis

identity. The stories about each model, shared with the group, were complex, developed in stages, and might be considered too long and too personal to be reproduced in full here. However an overview of each model was also brought out, in an interesting way, in the questionnaire (completed only at the end of each session), where each participant was asked to complete boxes saying 'I think that people see me as: ... ', followed by 'But in my Lego identity model, we can see me as: ... '

Many of the responses included the idea that the metaphorical model had revealed aspects of identity which were not normally on 'display'. For example, this unemployed woman felt that she faced more difficulties and was less confident than her friends would think:

> *I think that people see me as:*
> Very strong natured. Confident having a large family.
> *But in my Lego identity model, we can see me as:*
> Just a person with a family, struggling to live better. Carrying a great responsibility.
>
> (Female, over 35, London unemployed)

This architect felt that his model showed that he was much *less* isolated and cautious than people might expect:

> *I think that people see me as:*
> Remote and isolated, responsible and dutiful, ordered and safe.
> *But in my Lego identity model, we can see me as:*
> Engaged with people, free, carefree, random.
>
> (Male, 35, London architect)

Others also said that their model showed that they were almost the *opposite* of what others might expect:

> *I think that people see me as:*
> Optimistic.
> *But in my Lego identity model, we can see me as:*
> Pessimistic and bleak.
>
> (Male, 20, Bournemouth scriptwriting student)

> *I think that people see me as:*
> Menacing looking. People see me as trouble.
> *But in my Lego identity model, we can see me as:*
> Peaceful person. I just wish to get on with my life.
>
> (Male, 32, London unemployed)

In particular, some people felt that one of the most striking things about their overall model was that it showed how they actually took things seriously, even though they might normally be seen predominantly as a carefree or jokey individual:

> *I think that people see me as:*
> Less serious.
> *But in my Lego identity model, we can see me as:*
> More serious.
>
> (Female, over 50, Dorset art gallery worker)

> *I think that people see me as:*
> Maybe frivolous.
> *But in my Lego identity model, we can see me as:*
> More serious.
>
> (Male, 52, Dorset charity manager)

In what struck me as rather a sad case, this woman showed that she took her role as a good mother seriously, in spite of the strong negative terms which she thought others might attach to her:

> *I think that people see me as:*
> Stupid. Quiet. Scared.
> *But in my Lego identity model, we can see me as:*
> Mother.
>
> (Female, 40, London unemployed)

Several participants felt that their models revealed the anxiety which they normally kept hidden, for example:

I think that people see me as:
Carefree, don't know that I'm religious, confident.
But in my Lego identity model, we can see me as:
Slightly more stressed out, religious, worried about things.

(Female, 26, Winchester social care worker)

I think that people see me as:
Calm.
But in my Lego identity model, we can see me as:
Somewhat fearful.

(Male, 29, Oslo student)

I think that people see me as:
Very strong willed, level headed, good family provider, wise.
But in my Lego identity model, we can see me as:
Someone who maybe has dealt with a lot in the past and maybe tries to hide the fact that I'm not as strong as I might think. But putting on a brave face.

(Female, 30, London unemployed)

Some had quite a list of subtle contrasts:

I think that people see me as:
Managing to juggle many things. Professionally confident. Socially flexible and adaptable. Staying in touch with everyone I meet.
But in my Lego identity model, we can see me as:
Doing it with a certain sense of chaos. Needing to see and being surprised by what I achieve. Retaining the important people close to me only. Some people influence you but you move on without them.

(Male, 28, London architect)

I think that people see me as:
Confident, level-headed, organised, outspoken, reliable.
But in my Lego identity model, we can see me as:
Prepared to have a go and not worry about being right. Usually see more than one side to something. Will get the ball rolling. Not closed and am prepared to communicate. Know when to say yes and NO.

(Female, 43, Winchester social care worker)

Some participants felt that their models revealed that they were on a journey towards becoming more settled, which others might not be aware of; for example:

I think that people see me as:
Headstrong, helpful, stroppy, moody, direct.
But in my Lego identity model, we can see me as:
Transiting through Lego landscape to reach an eventual place to stop journeying.

(Male, 44, Dorset art gallery worker)

I think that people see me as:
Kind, loving, caring, generous.
But in my Lego identity model, we can see me as:
Myself and my two boys trying to see the light at the end of the tunnel.

(Female, 40, London unemployed)

Finally, we should note that some respondents felt that their Lego identity model represented them well, and that what it showed would *not* actually be a surprise to those who knew them:

I think that people see me as:
Holding back my feelings.
But in my Lego identity model, we can see me as:
I think probably as this. I think I'm quite a 'what you see is what you get' kind of person. Not sure if people see me as different.

(Female, 26, London architect)

I think that people see me as:
Very friendly, bubbly personality. Hardworking. Easy going.
But in my Lego identity model, we can see me as:
Busy, likeable, happy. I believe people see me relatively the same way.

(Female, 42, London unemployed)

The participants' feelings about the overall process also come out strongly in the evaluation comments. The questionnaire asked them 'What are your thoughts about today's session? Did you learn something?' and 'Did building a metaphorical model in Lego help you to think about your identity?' Almost all of the comments were positive. We have to recognise that many people are naturally 'polite' at the end of any kind of session like this, and may try to be 'nice' to the facilitator by giving positive feedback. Nevertheless, the emphatic, detailed and confessional comments which were provided seem to suggest that these people were not just being pleasant.

The sense of discovery and revelation is perhaps the most striking theme of these comments, and so I will quote a few:

[I learnt that] there's more to me than I have thought before. That all people have faults and fears. I think building a metaphorical model in

Lego surprised me – it wasn't a waste of time but in fact was a benefit in helping me engage with my own identity.

> (Female, 20, Bournemouth scriptwriting student)

Yes. I learned that deep inside I miss many people that are no longer here. I realise that I have many constants in my life which is comforting. I did not learn but reaffirmed that I have made many very good friends. I think I am reassured that I have lots to be thankful for. I did learn that I am stronger and have more confidence than I thought but that it can be fleeting depending on events. Therefore I can be vulnerable.

> (Female, 57, Dorset art gallery worker)

I did learn something. Using the Lego allowed me to relax and visualise my thoughts, although I found my answers to be surprisingly bizarre, but they made sense to me.

> (Male, 30, Dorset unemployed)

Very challenging, hard work (surprisingly). Made one think of areas of life that you normally don't have time to analyse or rationalise.

> (Female, 38, Dorset art gallery worker)

Today I have learnt how you can express so much about yourself by creating something and not just talking. Metaphors are not something I often use and so it has been great to use them and with Lego. I have learnt today about the issues, influences and important parts of myself, some of which I had not consciously thought about before.

> (Female, 26, Winchester social care worker)

The younger participants tended to emphasise the eye-opening nature of the process, confirming some things that they had thought about, but also surprising them in other areas:

I learnt that maybe I can express myself in different ways and it made me really think about myself and who I am. I really deeply realised that everything and everyone around me influences me in different ways. Also I know I put up a front but being able to express myself through Lego in this way was really interesting for me. I also realised that things may not be as they seem and looking at peoples perceptions of their models is different to what I may think.

> (Female, 19, Winchester social care worker)

It helped me think about the influences on my life and how they can affect me in both negative and positive ways. It also helped me think about the way I come across and how others see me. I identified one or two of my fears and how I probably need to get over myself and stop being Woody Allen and Bridget Jones's bastard love child.

(Female, 23, Bournemouth scriptwriting student)

I learnt more about myself and my identity. I don't normally think about who I am but by building metaphorical Lego models it has made me think about myself and what my identity is. I have also thought more about how factors in my life have influenced me and made me who I am.

(Female, 20, Winchester social care worker)

I realised what actually influences who I am. The session made me aware of the impact friends and family have had on my life. Building a metaphorical model helped to remind me about who and what is important in my life. Building the model helped to confirm what I already know about my identity. It made me think about all the different aspects of my identity and how these aspects affect the way I behave, such as being closed about certain aspects.

(Male, 22, Winchester social care worker)

The oldest of all participants, who came to the art gallery session thinking it would be some kind of staff meeting, and who was initially very self-conscious and apologetic about his Lego work, ultimately found the process somewhat magical:

I turned up to be polite – now I'm amazed at what Lego can do for anyone!

(Male, 72, Dorset art gallery volunteer)

A handful of people said that they had a good understanding of their identity already, but had found it interesting to build it. For example:

I think it told others more about me (I think I'm pretty clear on my own identity). To be able to build something you need to know it, so in that sense I did not learn any more about me … but I loved it.

(Male, 31, London architect)

To be a useful tool for social research, of course, the process does not need to also be a tool of self-discovery. Nevertheless, as we have seen, many participants indicated that they had found the process revealing to some extent, with a few indicating therapeutic benefits. For example, this participant thought that the process might help her to become reconciled with past events:

Building a metaphorical model helped me to think more about my identity and where I am at, in this stage of my life. Perhaps this session will help me to come to terms with my father's illness and my past.

(Female, 42, London unemployed)

On the process itself, in addition to the large number of positive comments, there were a few critical remarks. For example, this person felt that the four-hour session was perhaps too short:

Building Lego helped me to discover my identity in new ways, see things from a different angle but it was not easy to explain it in words. And I need more time to find or express the real me.

(Female, 38, Oslo academic)

Other critical comments:

I think Lego is still fun and may help to model your personality. Though I also see that Lego creation has limitations and may not reflect your true identity. I learned that I like to build Lego in peace and quiet to get good results.

(Male, 24, Oslo student)

Yes I learnt that it is a lot harder trying to describe what you and your life is like in Lego than what it would be by mouth.

(Female, 30, London unemployed)

The 'hands-on' process was generally praised, however:

I liked the idea of building because it helped to form words and thoughts that I might not have been able to come up with. I like doing hands-on stuff.

(Female, 43, Winchester social care worker)

It was also a very good method for visualising identity, because you can always go back to the construction and change, add or remove what doesn't fit. A lot easier than words.

(Male, 29, Oslo student)

Overall, then, the Lego identity-building process was seen to have worked well, and produced insights, from the perspective of the participants themselves. We will now take a step back from the empirical data, for a while, and consider how the work of Paul Ricoeur on narrative and identity can help us to take a sociological overview of this study.

Paul Ricoeur on time, narrative and identity

In this section we return to the work of Paul Ricoeur, whose study of metaphor was discussed in the previous chapter. After he published that book, Ricoeur moved on to consider how narratives are made meaningful in his three-volume *Time and Narrative* (1984, 1985, 1988), and then applied these ideas to the study of personal identity in *Oneself as Another* (1992). These ideas are fruitful ones both for interpreting the Lego study, and the question of *what identity means* in general.

Ricoeur characterises his philosophy as hermeneutics, which he explains as being about 'the task of interpretation', and 'the recognition that we can only have an indirect relationship to what is' (Ricoeur, interviewed in Reagan, 1998: 100). In other words, the world cannot be directly and instantly *known* and understood, but must always be *interpreted*. This is why Ricoeur is interested in the stories that we tell – ultimately including the stories that we tell about ourselves, which we call our 'identities'.

This does not mean that Ricoeur takes a cynical view of identity: seeing identity as a story is not the same as seeing it as a *fiction*. Rather, Ricoeur seeks to bridge the gap between the inner certainty of Descartes and the grand suspicion of Nietzsche. Descartes's famous assertion 'Je pense, donc je suis' (I think, therefore I am) takes personal consciousness as the absolute foundation for all knowledge, whereas Nietzsche argues that this is an illusion. Ricoeur characteristically wants to steer a dialectical course between these two poles, as neither view is wholly satisfactory in itself. In *Freud and Philosophy*, Ricoeur says, 'The first truth — *I am, I think* — remains as abstract and empty as it is invincible; it has to be "mediated" by the ideas, actions, works, institutions, and monuments that objectify it' (1970: 43). In this key statement, as Charles Reagan puts it, 'Ricoeur rejects the classical picture of consciousness as a veridical "mirror of nature" and says we gain self-knowledge through the long route of the interpretation of texts, monuments, and cultural forms' (1998: 75).

First, let us consider *Time and Narrative*. As space is limited, this will necessarily be a rather simplified discussion of the three-volume work, picking out the highlights which will be of most use to us. A philosophical discussion of narratives might seem out of place here, as we have been considering how people understand their lives in terms of self-identity, not literary fiction. However, in a 1982 interview, whilst the first volume of *Time and Narrative* was being written, Ricoeur said the following, which responds to this point, and sets out a key argument of *Time and Narrative* in general:

> I fight against the claim that texts constitute by themselves a world or a closed world. It is only by methodological decision that we say that the world of literature, let us say, constitutes a world of its own ... The distinction between the inside and the outside of the text is created by a methodological

decision, that of considering texts only as closed on themselves. I think that it is a task of hermeneutics to reopen this closure and to reinsert the world of literature between what precedes it, let us say a kind of naïve experience, and what succeeds it, that is to say, a learned experience.

(Ricoeur, in Reagan 1998: 108)

Reading a text – or watching a film, engaging with a soap opera, or any other kind of narrative art presumably – therefore is a way of developing understanding, and moving oneself from relative ignorance towards an informed engagement with experience. Ricoeur goes on:

It is in this sense that I speak of the hermeneutical arch through which the work of art is a mediation between man and the world, between man and another man, and between man and himself. So it is a mediating stage in a process of communication, man and man; referentiality, or man and the world; but also self-understanding, man and himself.

(Ibid)

This idea is developed more fully in volume one of *Time and Narrative*. Creating a narrative, Ricoeur says, is an act of *configuration*, pulling together different strands and elements into a particular order to tell a story. Prior to this there is *prefiguration*, a kind of basic practical knowledge of the world, and an everyday awareness that there are agents who engage in actions because of motives. This is the basic understanding of how things usually happen in the world, which a reader or viewer brings to a text in order to comprehend it (Ricoeur, 1984: 54–5). The *configuration* of a narrative involves *emplotment*, in which various elements are organised into a whole. This is the task of making *meaning* out of the available pieces. As Karl Simms puts it, 'This is not merely the same as organising events into a series; rather, it is the "thought" of the story, *that which stops us asking "But so what?"*' (Simms, 2003: 85; my emphasis). Ricoeur explains that:

Plot is mediating in at least three ways. First, it is a mediation between the individual events or incidents and a story taken as a whole. [In other words] it transforms the events or incidents into a story ... Furthermore, emplotment brings together factors as heterogeneous as agents, goals, means, interactions, circumstances, unexpected results ... Plot is mediating in a third way, that of its temporal characteristics. These allow us to call plot, by means of generalisation, a synthesis of the heterogeneous.

(Ricoeur, 1984: 65–6)

The arrangement of elements and events into a story gives it an important time-based dimension, which involves the arrangement of events into a sequence, on the one hand, and also the organisation of these elements into a whole narrative, with a start and a finish, which imposes an 'end point' from which the whole story can be viewed and which enables us to see the meaning of it all, the 'point' of the story, on the other. This temporal dimension is crucial to Ricoeur's argument. The configuration of a narrative is the 'grasping together' of items into a story. This process 'draws from this manifold of events the unity of one temporal whole' (Ricoeur, 1984: 66). It is therefore an act of judgement and, as we all know, different ways of telling a story – arranging a temporal sequence with different elements and emphases – can result in very different effects. In volume two of *Time and Narrative*, Ricoeur states this more explicitly, emphasising that configuration is an *act* – 'a judicative act, involving a "grasping together". More precisely, the act belongs to the family of reflective judgments ... To narrate a story is already to "reflect upon" the event narrated' (1985: 61). To clarify the role of configuration, Ricoeur says that 'We are following ... the destiny of a prefigured time that becomes a refigured time through the mediation of a configured time' (1985: 54). To put it another way, Ricoeur's interest is in how the telling of a story (configuration) gets us from unenlightened existence (prefiguration) to a new understanding (refiguration).

Refiguration, then, is 'the intersection of the world of the text and the world of the reader or hearer' (1985: 71), where what we have learned (in the broadest sense) from the narrative feeds into our understanding of the world of our lived experience. Ricoeur suggests that the potential stories offered by narratives we have previously engaged with can be taken up by individuals and used in establishing their own sense of identity (1985: 74). Indeed, one of Ricoeur's fundamental notions is the idea that we make sense of the passage of time in our lives by turning it into a personal biographical narrative, and this temporal arrangement of elements parallels the appeal of narratives in general:

> The world unfolded by every narrative work is always a temporal world. Or, as will often be repeated in the course of this study: time becomes human time to the extent that it is organised after the manner of a narrative; narrative, in turn, is meaningful to the extent that it portrays the features of temporal experience.
>
> (Ricoeur, 1984: 3)

There are clear pointers, such as this, throughout *Time and Narrative*, which link Ricoeur's thoughts about narratives to human experience in general. It is not surprising, then, that Ricoeur came to take his model beyond the traditional subject-matter of narrative studies, literature, and extended it to personal identity as well. The sequence of prefiguration through configuration to refiguration fits perfectly: a completely unanalysed life would be just a jumble of encounters and events (prefiguration), but as we process it into a sense of identity and autobiography (configuration) we arrive at a reasonably stable sense of a coherent self (refiguration).

There is a lot of detail in *Time and Narrative* which I have not been able to cover here, of course. To cut a very long story short, though, by the end of the third volume, Ricoeur has arrived at a 'practical' answer to the question of what identity means:

> To state the identity of an individual ... is to answer the question, 'Who did this?' 'Who is the agent, the author?'. We first answer this question by naming someone, that is, by designating them with a proper name. But what is the basis for the permanence of this proper name? What justifies our taking the subject of an action, so designated by [their] proper name, as the same throughout a life that stretches from birth to death? The answer has to be narrative. To answer the question 'Who?' ... is to tell the story of a life. The story told tells about the action of the 'who'. And the identity of this 'who' must therefore be a narrative identity. Without the recourse to narration, the problem of personal identity would in fact be condemned to an antinomy with no solution.
>
> (Ricoeur, 1988: 246)

In other words, we attach a proper name to a body, and then to make sense of this life across time we connect the points with narrative. The me of 1987 is the 'same person' as the me of 1997 and the me of 2007 because I have been given a name and can tell you a story which links my existence at these different points. *Without* this narrative, the whole sense of 'who' I am collapses. These thoughts are the starting-point for *Oneself as Another* (1992), in which Ricoeur shows how individuals put together their identity as a narrative (in an everyday cognitive version of *emplotment*) so that disparate elements are unified into a coherent whole and a narrative timeline.

We can note that this is also the process that takes place in the Lego Serious Play exercise, in the present study; each participant is required to consider the selection of important elements in their life, and then configure a model of their identity (and in this case, to actually *build* it, so that the process of configuration takes on a powerful literal putting-it-together dimension). The process of configuration is completed in the telling of the 'story' about the model, and refiguration is the new understanding gained from this reflective process.

If identity is shaped as a narrative, then we can see the *potential* influence of the stories we consume for pleasure, whether movies, TV drama, novels, videogames or comics. Ricoeur states that the 'narrative models of plots – borrowed from history or from fiction (drama or novel)' can be used to make life stories 'more intelligible' (1992: 114). It is likely that members of different cultures will come to view their *own* stories in different ways, connected to the popularity of different styles of storytelling in that culture. Fans of mainstream Hollywood movies may, therefore, be somewhat more likely to see themselves in terms of the heroic individualism so often celebrated by such films. Followers of community-oriented folk tales may correspondingly see their own identity-narrative in such terms, too – and so on.

Identity as sameness and selfhood

At the end of *Time and Narrative*, and then in *Oneself as Another*, Ricoeur fleshes out his own model of narrative identity. He notes that in Latin there are two terms for identity: *idem*, meaning 'being the same' – a more fixed notion of identity; and *ipse*, meaning 'self-same' or 'self-constancy' – a more flexible notion of identity, which allows for change over time, and which Ricoeur therefore links with narrative identity. This notion of self can be refigured by narrative configurations which account for changes over time. Nevertheless, it is important to most of us to feel that we are the 'same' person – that identity has some rootedness, and is not random, and so the *idem* meaning of identity plays a role as well. Identity is both selfhood and sameness, but selfhood is not sameness (1992: 116). Rather, Ricoeur says that narrative identity 'discloses itself … in the *dialectic* of selfhood and sameness' (1992: 140; my emphasis). On the one hand we each have a 'character' which we want to preserve as a constant, but on the other hand each of us may have 'diversity, variability, discontinuity, and instability' (ibid) in our behaviour, and even indeed in our thoughts, which can only be integrated with our more permanent sense of identity through emplotment.

Ricoeur's model of personal identity 'is inextricably bound up with a concept of the other and the relation between the self and the other', as Charles Reagan has put it (1998: 74), because the need to demonstrate self-constancy to others – by keeping promises and by being reliably coherent as a self – necessarily involves other people. This brings in an ethical dimension which is important to Ricoeur's argument. Narratives are not ethically neutral, he says, but typically prescribe (or at least suggest) something about the human condition, by giving us the opportunity to consider fictional individuals of 'good character' – or questionable character. Ricoeur suggests that human action is mediated through the triad: describe–narrate–prescribe. So narrative evaluates situations, and points toward the ethical dimension of what you 'should' do. In particular, continuity of character and 'keeping one's word' are important to an ethical life (Ricoeur 1992: 114–25). Fictional narratives, like life, involve *entanglements* of friendships, family life, commitments and disagreements, and fictions provide the ethical resources we need to configure a sustainable course for our narrative identity.

This also points to a role for our everyday media consumption, as Ricoeur suggests that literature – which we can take to mean all kinds of fictional narrative – is 'a vast laboratory for thought experiments in which the resources of variation encompassed by narrative identity are put to the test of narration'

(1992: 148). All possible ways of living life are played out in the stories that are told in a culture, and we learn from stories of greed, lust, hate, love, kindness and heroism, and develop our own narrative of self in relation to these templates.

Ricoeur and the Lego identity models

As I noted above, building a metaphorical model of one's identity in Lego is a literal enactment of the configuration process. We start off with piles of bits and pieces (*prefiguration*), and then we select from this range of pieces, attaching meaning to them and arranging them in a particular way, making connections between the parts and building a satisfying whole. This is obviously *configuration*. We then consider the model, tell the 'story' of what has been built, and potentially arrive at new insights about our identity through reflection on the configuration – and this is *refiguration*.

Indeed, building the model is like an embodiment of the point, described by Ricoeur, where the individual draws a line and declares 'This is where I stand!', as an answer to the more everyday 'tormenting question' of 'Who am I?' (Ricoeur 1992: 167–8). On the one hand the person knows that there is still the idea that 'I can try anything', but they can take pride in at least trying to pin down the story in a particular way, effectively declaring 'Here I am!' This would help to explain the sometimes quite extreme differences between how some participants felt they were perceived by others, and what they felt their model showed. Earlier in this chapter we saw, for instance, that a male student who thought that others would see him as 'optimistic' said that his Lego identity model revealed him to be 'pessimistic and bleak'; an unemployed man who felt that others regarded him as 'menacing looking' and 'trouble' could be seen in his model to be a 'peaceful person', just wanting to 'get on with my life'; and a few participants noted that their model showed them to be more serious, worried or cautious than others would expect. In Ricoeur's terms, these would all be instances of a person configuring a particular narrative which sweeps aside other people's misplaced beliefs or interpretations, discards the potentially infinite range of identities that one might claim to inhabit, and asserts 'Here I am!' in a particular and determined way.

Furthermore, Ricoeur writes of the search for 'the good life', an ethical dimension to narrative identity (1992: 171), and this could be seen in many of the Lego models, as participants had included their values and aspirations. These elements were typically *central* to their identity: rather than being like a tugboat, dragging an identity in a particular direction, this drive to seek a 'good life' would be a motor at the heart of the machine, driving the person.

The models also tended to emphasise the 'entanglements' with other people and diverse interests in life, with almost all models suggesting that a narrative identity was a complex construction which tied together a range of disparate elements. Indeed, the models made the range of connections with others vivid, reinforcing Ricoeur's point that identity is an 'abstract and empty' concept until it is mediated through actions, communications and objects. The Lego model of identity is an unusually deliberate mediation of identity itself; usually, of course, we disclose identity through a multitude of little signs and actions, not by building a plastic model.

The models also reflected 'the *dialectic* of selfhood and sameness' through which Ricoeur argues that narrative identity emerges. Often the explanation of a model would explain this bit, then this bit, then this bit, but then step back to explain the overall character of the model – the sameness which binds together the unique mix of components of selfhood.

Examples of whole identity models

It is clearly not possible, in this book, to discuss all 79 identity models in depth. Even single models could be discussed for several pages each. To give a mere *flavour* of what the models were like, I will outline four case studies briefly here. These models have been selected as 'typical' examples, and not for being 'special' or especially 'impressive'. They reflect common themes – although every model in the study was unique, and no two models were very similar.

In the examples below, participants' names have been changed to protect their anonymity. The descriptions of the models are, of course, based entirely on what each participant said about it themselves. I have found it easier to tell their stories in the present tense.

Case 1: Katie

Katie is a 33-year-old architect, working in London. The figure in the centre of the model is herself. Her face cannot be seen in this picture as she is facing towards her goals, which are ahead of her towards the top end of this photograph. She has not reached her goals, though; she only looks towards them. She is 'drifting' on a boat, with different sides of her personality represented by the figures to her left and right. Although she appears to be at the helm, her course is affected by these uncertain aspects pulling her in different directions. Behind her on the left – the skeleton in a house – is her previous life, which she has left behind and is moving away from. The couple under the arch on the right are her parents, who have been an influence upon her, but whom she is also heading away from.

On the left there is 'a skeleton adrift next to my boat', which represents 'a foreboding sense of time' passing in her life. The goal posts ahead of her represent 'striving to achieve happiness', but these are 'beyond a line I have to cross'. The archway of goals includes a dog (top left), representing her partner

Figure 9.2 Katie's identity model

(in a good way – loyal and reliable); a person on a pedestal with a looking glass (top right), representing 'learning and achieving'; a house, meaning 'stability and grounding'; and a 'sparkling trophy', representing 'career and creativity'.

Overall, Katie remarked that, although her friends might think she was 'happy to be floating around, and travelling', her model showed that she was really 'striving for some kind of stability'. She felt that the Lego exercise was 'useful in being able to distil what and who you are', and helped to see 'what you want and need in life'.

Case 2: Gary

Gary is 25 years old, and lives in Poole, Dorset. He is unemployed. His model shows 'many paths that could be chosen', although only one of them leads towards a desirable goal with two people and a 'happy home' (top left). There is 'a sheep following the obvious path', heading in the wrong direction; Gary's wish to *not* follow the sheep represents his 'desire to be different and unique'. In the bottom left corner a cowboy, representing 'hope', helpfully points in

Figure 9.3 Gary's identity model

the right direction. On the opposite side of the baseplate, crocodiles and authority figures represent fear and danger. Other figures, representing 'good friends and bad friends', mostly encourage him 'to take chances and go for gold', although one is 'holding me back'.

In the centre is a monkey climbing a tree, representing 'playfulness', but this is tempered by the career ladder, which runs up the tree – 'not necessarily pointing in the right direction', Gary notes. The big red brick represents passion. The '30' sign represents his 30th birthday, which he feels he will probably have to get past before he reaches his goals.

Overall, Gary commented that his friends might see him as 'Lethargic, easily distracted, not that fussed with getting on in life', as well as 'short-sighted, not able to see the big picture' and 'a dreamer with no grounding in reality'. However, in his model we can see that he is 'Career driven and keen to do the right thing' and 'Able to see my options and realise the pitfalls and drawbacks of decisions'. He also proudly mentions that the overall model reflects his 'intelligence' and 'wit'.

Case 3: John

John is 51 years old, and is employed as a manager at a social care charity in Dorset. He used to work in the church, which appears at the bottom left of this photograph, and as can be seen, a number of people have accompanied

Figure 9.4 John's identity model

him on his journey towards his current identity (represented on the main baseplate). In particular there are 'lots of little men', an allusion to his sexuality. The people and animals on the baseplate represent different aspects of his own personality. Apart from his parents, an influence 'in the background', there are no other people on the main baseplate itself; they are arranged around it. A number of fences around the edge of the base act as 'barriers making it difficult for people to get in'. Two special people 'had been inside, but were now on their way out'; they can be seen above the baseplate, moving away.

On the baseplate representing his identity today, there is a 'lion' (tiger) representing his 'Leo' personality, liking 'authority' and 'to be in control'. A panda means that he is 'warm and approachable, when you get to know me', but this represents two sides to his character – 'huggable, but still with claws'. The elephant represents 'wisdom and intellect'. The high tower represents 'inspirational, blue sky thinking'.

Overall, the model represents a warm but private person. John notes that other people see him as primarily 'in control'; in his Lego model we can see that he is 'in control, yes, but also more than that', with tensions between his private nature, his preference for independence, and his wish to be loved.

Case 4: Patrick

Patrick is over 50 and is a senior manager at a public art gallery. During the building process his model included a lot of empty space, and this remained mostly true of the final model seen here (even after 'influences' had been added). These spaces represent 'self-inflicted loneliness', and the blue baseplate represents feeling 'blue' as well as 'the sea'. Various adventure elements such as a dome tent, netting and 'navigation poles' represent travel and 'living rough'.

The importance of art in Patrick's life is shown by the 'abstract Barbara Hepworth sculpture' which dominates the model on the left. His partner is the 'figure leaning backwards', shouldering responsibilities, and she stands 'on the bridge between two territories'. His children also appear around the model. The sun is represented by the yellow radar dish on top of a tall stalk, and appears as an influence as it is 'life giving', helps to produce the 'best ideas' and 'inspires adventure'. The car and a map, and a boat and skidoo, also refer to the desire for outdoor adventure. The large book at the back represents art books – 'looking, more than reading'.

Considering the model overall, Patrick commented that, although others might see him as 'quite confident' and 'quite full of ideas', the model reveals him to be 'quite separated, almost anonymous' and 'on a rather nebulous journey'. Others might see him as 'abstract in thought' but 'quite chirpy most of the time', but the model shows him to be 'perhaps a bit torn between chirpy and quiet'. The large amount of space in the model reflects his 'quiet' nature, and the model shows him to be 'self-sufficient'. He said 'I think I have

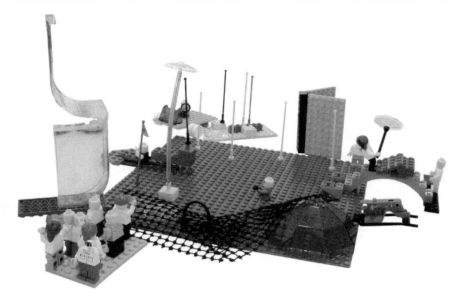

Figure 9.5 Patrick's identity model

represented one side of me which is not publicly shown very often. I think the design of the model says a lot about how I feel when not obsessed by work and making ideas work'.

Common themes

The four identity models discussed above were selected on an ad hoc basis, as 'typical' but not necessarily representative examples. Nevertheless we can identify five common themes, which can also be seen in the other models (although not necessarily crucial in all of them).

The sense of moving through a journey

Katie's model showed her 'drifting' along, but moving away from her past, towards her future and particular goals, such as a more stable home life; Gary's model included 'many paths that could be chosen', including a positive goal but also hazards and wrong directions; John's model reflected a journey away from the church, and towards his current life; and Patrick's model allowed a lot of space for his 'rather nebulous journey'. The theme of a journey could be seen in many of the models across the study.

Having goals

This is a corollary of the previous point, since journeys have destinations. We can see that these models were oriented towards future goals (in Katie and Gary's cases), or a 'better' place already arrived at (in John's case). A range of different goals could be seen in many models in the study. In the fourth example here, Patrick's path was wilfully ambiguous – which was unusual – but it still engaged with the idea of goals, whilst taking a more experimental attitude towards them.

Uncertainty and life stages

In the models by younger people, especially – which in this context is those under, say, 35 – we can see that, although they are likely to have goals, the route is uncertain, and may be challenged from both within and without. The models by older participants tended to be more settled, exhibiting both fewer future goals, and less anxiety about reaching them. In these four examples, we can see that Katie and Gary, both under 35, face more uncertain routes, whilst John and Patrick, both over 50, are more secure in the present.

Private and public sides of identity

All models in the study revealed something about their maker which would not have been immediately apparent. That, of course, is part of the idea. Nevertheless it is notable that participants highlighted quite considerable differences between their 'public' self and the more private identity revealed by their Lego construction. In these four cases, Katie's model reflected a desire for a more 'settled' life; Gary's model showed personal drive, a focus on career, and some related anxieties; John's model revealed a tension between his privacy and independence, and his relationships; and Patrick's model reflected a somewhat disconnected, quiet, lonely journey. All of these aspects were usually hidden from others (according to the participants' own accounts).

The individual and the social

None of these participants represented themselves in isolation; there are other people – friends and family – on each of their journeys. But each of these models involves a tension between the desire for individual distinctiveness – being on one's *own* journey – and the demands and pleasures of social ties with others. This common theme will be discussed further in the next, concluding chapter.

Some aspect of each of these themes could be found in every model in this study, although the significance of each theme, within each model, might vary from mild to strong.

Seven ways of telling identity stories

Finally in this chapter, an analysis of what we can call the 'primary story emphasis' in each of the 79 identity models revealed three types containing a total of seven different kinds of central story about identity. One third of the models showed the individual's identity primarily as a *traveller* (33 per cent), whilst just over half showed it as an *object* (54 per cent) – which does not necessarily mean the identity was seen as fixed or unchanging, merely that the snapshot of 'my identity now' did not primarily emphasise movement. However, the theme of the journey was still often found somewhere in these models. Between these two was a further type – *object seeking travel* (13 per cent) – as they built a home-rooted identity (like the object) which was still seeking dreams (like the traveller).

Having employed a process which reveals complex reflections on identity, I did not want to crudely simplify the participants into certain 'personality types'. This part of the analysis is only meant to show the primary (inevitably simplified) ways in which the identity stories were told.

The types which were identified are as follows:

Traveller models (33 per cent)

(1) Dream-seeker (16 per cent)

These models emphasised movement towards goals and dreams (although the route might be uncertain). The models included metaphorical items such as a winged horse, chasing rainbows, and towers reaching towards aspirations. In the examples above, Katie (on her drifting boat) is a dream-seeker, and Gary is a career-oriented dream-seeker.

(2) Traveller (11 per cent)

These models represented travelling through life – not necessarily geographical travel, although that was also popular amongst this group. These journeys were not so much about chasing dreams, but rather just the desire to move on and to experience new things. The models included metaphors such as the whole identity being built on a tractor or a boat moving contentedly forward, a journey towards God, and, in one case, handles on the base (to pick up the whole model and put it down somewhere else).

(3) Lonely traveller (5 per cent)

These models were typically spacious, and other people were not central to their story. The story told about the model emphasised an independent and isolated journey. Metaphors included skeletons queuing up to enter the world with 'misplaced optimism', and the individual as a rare plant in a dry and barren land. In the examples above, Patrick is a lonely traveller.

Object models (54 per cent)

(4) Unified independent (28 per cent)

These models were often based around a solid structure or web of connections, and represented a unified and independent sense of self, which would be self-contained (rather than being associated with home or family), although relationships with others were often an important aspect of the model. Some of the unified independent models – including that of John in the examples above – showed not only the unified self, but also the now-completed journey which brought the individual to that point.

(5) Home-rooted (24 per cent)

In these models the story was primarily about the home and family, and was also often based around a solid structure or web of connections. The home itself, or family members, were typically represented at or near the heart of the model, and were the hub of identity for these individuals.

(6) Chaotic independent (3 per cent)

In these cases (just two models), the emphasis was on chaos. Some sense of order was still visible, though: the parts would be diverse, but interconnected; and so the models were not completely 'random'. Ironically perhaps, the makers of 'chaotic' models also commented that the Lego-building process helped them to see their situation with more clarity.

Object seeking travel models (13 per cent)

(7) Home-rooted dream-seeker (13 per cent)

These models combined the 'home-rooted' and 'dream-seeker' themes, being based in the home but also looking towards dreams and the future. The metaphorical representations would therefore typically include aspects of home and family, but also towers, radars, or a staircase reaching towards aspirations, or an imagined (happy) future for the family.

As noted above, these are rather crude simplifications, based on reducing each model to 'one central story', when in fact each model tended to have a number of parallel, interconnected stories. However, they highlight the importance of unity, sociability and a journey, in how individuals think about identities.

In this chapter, we have seen that participants themselves often reported that their Lego identity model revealed aspects of their character which would not usually be seen by others, and which in each case was a unique mapping out of identity elements within an overall journey or story. The building process involved a sense of discovery and revelation, in several cases, which I linked with Ricoeur's argument that the reflective process of configuring an identity narrative would lead to new understandings, as participants marked out their position in relation to personal ethics, aspirations, and entanglements with others. We gained insights into how people carve out individual identities within a social context, the key strands of which will be outlined in the next, concluding chapter.

Chapter 10

Conclusion

Eleven findings on methods, identities and audiences

This book has considered a number of areas and approaches, including discussions about creativity, science, sociology, and consciousness, and studies of art, identity and social experience. In this concluding chapter I want to move beyond discussion of views, and to make some assertions about what we have found. Readers are always free to disagree with these arguments, of course – we learnt from Popper, way back in Chapter 3, that scientific understanding is advanced through researchers having the freedom to make any kind of claim, as long as it is concrete enough for others to test it and potentially disagree with it. The eleven findings are divided into three sections: 'Method', 'Understanding social experience and identities' and 'Media audiences'.

Method

Much of this book has been about methodology and approaches to social research, and so we should begin with this. These findings build on the outcomes of the research projects outlined in Chapters 6 to 9 of this book, and in particular on the Lego identity study discussed in Chapters 8 and 9.

Finding 1: Creative and visual research methods give people the opportunity to communicate different kinds of information

This book has discussed a number of studies which have used primarily visual and creative methods in order to elicit different kinds of responses from research participants. The argument is not that language-based approaches are necessarily redundant or inferior – they clearly have many positive uses. However, creative and visual methods offer a powerful alternative. Many people are inexperienced in transferring their thoughts about personal or social matters into the kind of talk that you would share with a researcher. It can also be difficult to talk instantly about abstract concepts such as identity or emotion. If participants are invited to spend *time* in the *reflective process* of making something, however, they have the opportunity to consider what is particularly important to them *before* they are asked to generate speech. (This time-based dimension is the focus of finding 3, below.)

The process of making a representational object or image encourages a considered *holistic* response, compared with language-based research methods. Imagine if we were to ask people to generate a verbal account of identity. (To be parallel with the Lego study, we might say 'Think about who you are and the different aspects of yourself that you bring to the world, and what you think are significant aspects of your identity . . . and tell me about them'.) A participant would have to outline and explain one aspect of identity, followed by another one, and another one, but then might get weary, self-conscious, or bored. In the hands of a skilled interviewer, they might feel comfortable explaining a few more. However, generally we would expect that items mentioned early in this linear sequence would get more attention, or questioning by the interviewer might highlight certain areas. By contrast, when preparing a visual presentation of identity – such as a collage, video or metaphorical Lego model – a person is given the opportunity to take time to prepare something which is then presented as a whole, and 'all in one go'. For instance, when making their Lego models, participants seemed to seek a kind of balance – thinking, 'If I've put on [this], I also want to put on [that]', or a more complex arrangement of unity and relationships, as in 'I've said that [this thing] is important to me, but also clustered around that are [x], [y], and [z], and these are all influenced by [something else] which is important too'. Language is not necessarily the best way to explain how a number of elements coexist and are linked together. As Rudolf Arnheim argued:

> Propositional language, which consists of linear chains of standardised units, has come about as a product of the intellect; but while language suits the needs of the intellect perfectly, it has a desperate time dealing with field processes, with images, with physical and social constellations, with the weather or a human personality, with works of art, poetry, and music.
>
> (Arnheim, 1986: 20–1)

Pictures or objects enable us to present information, ideas or feelings simultaneously, without the material being forced into an order or a hierarchy. Language may be needed to *explain* the visuals, but the image remains primary and shows the relationships between parts most effectively.

Finding 2: Metaphors can be powerful in social research

Social research is often concerned with complex and intangible concepts such as lifestyle, belief, identity, democracy, relationships or social forces. As these things do not have a physical existence, the social scientist is immediately faced with the problem of how we capture 'data' about them. The typical solution requires participants to translate feelings about the experience of such concepts into concrete language, which can be a challenge. This is where metaphors can be valuable. Individuals naturally use metaphors in everyday communication to capture a set of feelings and ideas within the simple envelope of a particular image, as discussed in Chapter 8. (I even did it there – the 'envelope' as a container for a set of ideas.) My identity study, based on the Lego Serious Play process, went further by actually *requiring* participants to transform all of their sense of 'identity' into a multi-faceted metaphorical model. This did not necessarily require conscious thoughts to be 'translated' into some plastic imagery; sometimes playing with the Lego elements would suggest fruitful bits of metaphorical identity expression which seemed to connect with previously not-quite-conscious ideas, giving the participants 'surprise' and satisfaction. A participant would typically pick up certain parts from the Lego boxes without really knowing *at that point* how they were going to come together to have metaphorical meaning – but then meanings would soon emerge when the building began. For example, a person might choose a tiger to represent pride and assertiveness, and then put the tiger on wheels to give it movement; but then would realise that the wheels could not be steered, so that the proud tiger tended to race forwards and crash into things; and then this characteristic became incorporated into the 'official' meaning of the model, because the person recognised that this was a good representation of her character. Metaphors would often appear by 'accident' in this way.

As well as the constituent parts being a set of meaningful metaphors, the *whole model* served as a metaphor on a different level, leading to the more general conclusions about identities discussed below. As well as the metaphorical bits and pieces of identity, in other words, we were able to see unity, or tensions, or a journey, in the *overall* model. This could be achieved because participants were being asked to generate a whole picture 'in one go', as discussed above, and their explanations of their models tended – without prompting – to begin as a tour of the constituent elements, but then conclude with an account of what the whole model revealed. Indeed, being able to look at the whole metaphorical construction meant that participants tended to evaluate the whole, in terms of their emotional response to what they had represented, as well. For example, 'Looking at my identity overall, I can see that I've got interests in lots of things, have strong connections with certain people, there's some uncertainty and it's a bit of a jumble, but I'm happy with it and I seem more secure than I might have expected'. Having built metaphors with their own hands, participants seemed to have a strong connection with them, and felt that the metaphorical items enabled them to share an imaginative understanding of emotional or psychological states.

Finding 3: Research participants need reflective time to construct knowledge

As mentioned in finding 1, visual and creative methods give participants *time* to generate a response. This reflective time is important and can lead to much more nuanced and authentic research data. People's brains do not usually contain ready-made lists of 'what I think' about any number of issues, as we saw in Chapter 5. The brain certainly *can* rise to the challenge of dynamically generating instant answers to an interviewer's questions, but it is not always likely that these responses will be wonderfully expressive, meaningful or 'true' to the interviewee's more precise feelings.

We saw in Chapter 2 that studies of creative people showed that they tended to find that their best and most authentic ideas and forms of self-expression followed a period of 'underground incubation', leading to ideas surprisingly 'popping up' when they were doing everyday chores or a mundane physical task. Creative and visual research methods seek to tap into this possibility, on a basic level, because they ask participants to spend a fixed amount of time addressing a task in a creative way – giving their brain time to work through an indirect response – rather than having to immediately form answers to direct questions in words. In Chapter 5, research from the field of neuroscience and the contemporary philosophies of consciousness suggested that there is no ready-made 'me' inside the brain, like a chief executive who responds to things coming in. Rather, processing happens across the brain, all the time, with consciousness just dealing with the 'highlights'. However, artistic and creative activities might give us the opportunity to 'dig' more deeply into the unconscious activities of the brain. This was suggested in the early twentieth century by Jung, who asserted that creative activity gives individuals the opportunity to work on deep psychological issues, potentially leading to breakthroughs which instantaneous speech may not have arrived at.

Furthermore, as Piaget and Papert contended (Chapter 8), we can help the brain to construct knowledge – in this case, knowledge about *themselves* – by giving people exercises in which they are able to 'put together' what they know. In the case of the Lego study, this obviously involved the actual construction of a symbolic model. Using the hands to explore and construct a model of identity opened up a different channel for the communication of experience. As one participant, quoted in Chapter 9, said:

> I liked the idea of building because it helped to form words and thoughts that I might not have been able to come up with.
>
> (Female, 43, Winchester social care worker)

As Ricoeur noted, the mere fact of existing and thinking is 'abstract and empty' until it is 'mediated' by 'ideas, actions, works, institutions, and monuments' that give it form and shape (1970: 43). Since we cannot just 'know' other individuals, in everyday life, we have to develop an understanding of them via the 'long route' of interpreting the stuff that they produce – which includes their speech, but also what they do with their appearance, clothing, and signs and symbols in their home or office, emails, messages and any other 'clues' we can gather. Creative and visual methods can intervene in this process in a deliberate way by asking participants to produce something specifically as part of a research project. In order to interpret this non-linguistic data, I argue that the researcher does need to ask the participant to provide their *own* interpretation of the thing they have made – in words. Language therefore comes back into the process, but at a later point, *after* time has been spent on the reflective, non-verbal exercise of thoughtfully making a two- or three-dimensional object which represents an often complex matrix of feelings and impressions.

Understanding social experience and identities

Finding 4: Recognition of 'identity'

It is worth noting that the notion of 'identity' was readily familiar to all participants in the Lego identity study. To be more specific, the notion that 'I' have 'an identity', which could be represented in some way (such as in Lego), was already accepted by all participants. Unsurprisingly, a number of participants initially thought it might be a difficult challenge to represent their identity in this way – their concerns were along the lines of 'What will I show?' and 'What will I use?' However, the more basic finding is: *the task made sense*. All participants took it for granted that they *did have* an identity, and that this could be represented in some way. Therefore, 'identity' is not merely an external theoretical construction of philosophers or sociologists, but is already embedded in everyday life.

I do not have the historical comparative data that I would need to draw upon in order to confidently argue that this shows 'the rise of "identity"' as a structuring term in everyday life. Nevertheless, the finding that all participants were already well able to work with the notion of a representable identity *lends support to* the argument that, in modern Western societies, individuals come to see self-identity as a personal project to be worked upon (as argued, for example, by Giddens, 1991, 1992; Beck, 2002).

The relative ease with which participants from different walks of life took to this task also seems to confirm the argument of Tony Whincup, building on the work of Wilhelm Dilthey (see Chapter 8), that individuals are well used to creating symbolic systems of objects to represent aspects of their identities, as part of everyday life. The collection of photographs and souvenirs attached to a person's fridge, for example, is already an informal and unsystematic way of expressing 'who I am', and is an everyday case of someone making a presentation *similar to* the Lego models which we asked people to make in this project. This leads to the next finding.

Finding 5: Identity theories are common currency

Sociologists and philosophers may like to think that their theories of identity, consciousness and everyday life have the status of 'superior' academic knowledge. This is understandable, as nobody wants to be putting forward a theory which seems completely commonplace – which people only react to by saying, 'Yeah, we knew that'. However, to be useful and successful, a theory needs to be *resonant* with actual experience. Only a few theorists, such as Giddens, have recognised that most people might be aware of *some* theories and discourses from the world of academia, and that their everyday practices might be informed or affected by them. Supposedly complex ideas such as postmodernism, for example, pop up regularly in movie reviews, and are knocked around in newspapers and TV shows. Academic theories about lifestyles and relationships, self-knowledge and self-fulfilment, are popularised in mass market paperbacks, lifestyle magazines and daytime TV shows, as well as more serious documentaries. Ideas about identity and self-presentation are worked through constantly in TV shows from *Smallville* to *What Not to Wear*, as well as popular movies, newspaper and magazine advice features, and the continuous media commentary about the personalities of politicians, royalty and celebrities.

It is therefore no surprise that the Lego identity models in this study, and their creators' accounts of them, revealed participants to be working with a set of ideas which sociologists like to think of as being their own. For example, it was recognised that identity was constructed from a set of relevant parts, some rather intimate and personal, some to do with external obligations and social ties; and that identity was established though a matrix of similarity and difference – acceptance of some categories and resistance of others. In particular we can note two core 'sociological' themes which were reflected by participants in their models:

- *The public and private presentation of self:* the essence of Erving Goffman's classic sociological argument – mentioned above in Chapters 5 and 8 – that people have to routinely generate a kind of social performance in order to appear competent and coherent in everyday life, was taken for granted by most participants. It was assumed to be normal and unsurprising that their identity models would include, for example, 'backstage' areas where the more private aspects of identity were to be found, and a more 'public face' which looked out to and interacted with the external world.
- *The reflexive narrative of the self:* Anthony Giddens's (1991) argument that individuals in contemporary Western societies have to construct

and maintain a personal biographical narrative of the self, in order to enjoy a coherent and stable existence, was recognised by the Lego study participants, who all took to the task of putting together their identity 'story' in a particular way, whilst acknowledging that there could be other ways of telling it. Giddens notes that pride and self-esteem – or, on the negative side, embarrassment and shame – are associated with our ability to tell a consistent and meaningful story of our self-identity; and indeed participants did seem distinctly *pleased* when they had constructed models representing their personal narrative in an attractive, reasoned and (literally) solid way. It is notable that the idea of identity being about assembling a coherent narrative has emerged at various points in this book, from different perspectives. Our study of neuroscience in Chapter 5, for instance, also led to the argument that brains can be seen as 'narrative-producing engines', continually generating drafts of stories and 'writing them down' in memory; and Paul Ricoeur's work discussed in Chapter 9 began as an examination of fictional narratives which then turned into a study of people's own identity narratives. This work points towards a way of understanding the role of media in the construction of identities, discussed in finding 11.

The central point here is not simply that certain sociological theories seemed to be 'proved' within the Lego exercise, but rather that these theories were *already known and accepted* in the participant's underlying assumptions about how everyday life is carried on. This reinforces the view that the typical social actor is sophisticated and knowing about the complex constructed nature of everyday life.

Finding 6: Identities are typically unified, not fragmented

This finding is straightforward, and may not seem especially surprising: all participants built their identity as *one thing*. Each model was complex, with many parts, but each one was seen to represent one whole. This is worth mentioning because it contradicts the claims of postmodernists that identities have become fragmented: a Lego postmodern identity would be an array of unconnected bits. But nobody built this. As mentioned above, it was common for participants to include – to different degrees – the idea of an exterior self-presentation which other people see, and a more private 'inner' identity which others may not be aware of (but which usually had some continuity with the outer parts). This notion of a more 'private' self and a more 'public' self-presentation is entirely conventional, and is not what postmodernists meant: Shakespeare, for example, covered this theme a lot, over 350 years before Goffman, and the fascination of superheroes with a secret identity, such as Batman and Superman, began in the 1930s.

The idea that identities in contemporary 'postmodern' society have become wholly fragmented, as Jean Baudrillard would argue (1988, 1994), or discontinuous and 'schizophrenic', as suggested by Fredric Jameson (1991), does not seem to be part of general experience for the range of twenty-first-century individuals in my study. Rather, as discussed in Chapter 8, participants tended to seek unity and balance whilst building their models of identity. Furthermore, in Chapter 9, a simplifying filter showed that we could identify seven ways of telling identity stories, which – in order of frequency – were as follows:

1 Unified independent (28 per cent)
2 Home-rooted (24 per cent)
3 Dream-seeker (16 per cent)
4 Home-rooted dream-seeker (13 per cent)
5 Traveller (11 per cent)
6 Lonely traveller (5 per cent)
7 Chaotic independent (3 per cent)

These 'core stories' also highlighted the importance of unity, sociability and the sense of a journey. Participants therefore did not believe that their identities were a fragmented mess – even the tiny minority in the 'chaotic independent' category presented their identity as a whole, even if it was somewhat messy and occasionally contradictory. Overall, with a remarkable degree of consistency, the participants in this study presented themselves as distinctive individuals, but whole identities, making their way on the journey of life. This may be a 'discourse' they have bought into, or a popular metaphor for experience which they have applied to themselves, but nevertheless we saw none of the painful 'fragmentation' which is supposed to be eating at (post)modern subjects (and which they are meant to be conscious of). There certainly *is* some uncertainty, but this is actively fought against by what we might call 'the will to coherence' – the desire to have solid stories about the self.

Finding 7: Relationship between the individual and society

The striking diversity of the Lego identity models suggests that individuals typically take their individuality to be important, and have sought to avoid becoming the stereotyped, homogeneous mass which critics such as Theodor Adorno established as a concern more than six decades ago (see Horkheimer and Adorno, [1947] 1979; Adorno, 1991). Indeed, in the Lego identity study we see people carving out their *individuality*, but within a *social sphere*. Both dimensions were given considerable weight – the distinctiveness of personal identity and the importance of social ties. There are connections here with the work of Georg Simmel (1858–1918), a social theorist whose wide-ranging work – published in books, journals and (unusually) newspapers and magazines – brought him fame in Germany and Europe at the start of the twentieth century, although the German academic establishment rebuffed him throughout his life. Simmel's reputation 'retreated into the shadows' during much of the century but then enjoyed a resurgence in the 1990s, as theorists rediscovered his prescient work which engaged with contemporary topics in cultural theory such as the emotions, gender, fashion and the challenges of 'modern' life (Scaff, 2000). Indeed, his work engages with many of the themes – and appeared in a style – which would often today be called 'postmodern', although Simmel would not have recognised the term.

The value of Simmel for us here is that he saw social experience in terms of a continuous tension between the individual and society, which seems to mirror the way in which participants represented their identities in the Lego study (Simmel, 1971, 2004). David Cheal neatly summarises Simmel's point about this tension as follows: 'On the one side, societies seek to shape each individual's life to fit the goals of society as they change over time. On the other side, individuals resist the shifting influences of society as they seek internal consistency in trying to realise their own values' (2005: 36). Indeed, Simmel argued that the friction generated by the need to establish similarity with others, and difference from them, is the driving force in both individual and social development. He even stated that 'the cultural history of humanity can be interpreted as the history of the struggle and attempted conciliation between' these two forces (Simmel, 1890, translated in Frisby, 2002: 83).

This is the 'double relationship' that is a core theme of Simmel's work. In his *Introduction to the Moral Sciences* (1893), it is defined as a state of being both inside and outside of the collective: 'On the one hand the individual belongs to a whole and is a part of it, while on the other hand s/he is independent and stands opposed to it' (translated in Scaff, 2000: 255). Almost a century before Bourdieu was writing about distinction – the cultural ways in which individuals mark themselves as different from others (discussed in Chapter 4) – Simmel was discussing the same theme, but underpinned by a more dynamic model which assigns a greater amount of agency to the individual:

> A human being is basically a differentiating entity. Just as we never perceive the absolute amount of a stimulus but only its distinction from the previous state of feelings, so too our interest attaches not to these contents of life that always and everywhere exist but to those through which each is distinguished from every other . . . For all practical interests, all that defines our position in the world, all utilisation of other human beings rests upon these distinctions between one human being and another, whereas the common ground on the basis of which this transpires is a constant factor.
>
> (Simmel, 1890, translated in Frisby, 2002: 77–8)

Simmel noted that in Europe in the eighteenth century individualism was seen in terms of *freedom* from external constraints, based on a spirit of equality. However, in the nineteenth century, emphasis came to be placed on *differences* between unique individuals (Simmel, 1971: 218–23), and therefore individuality became about inequality:

> As soon as the ego had become sufficiently strengthened by the feeling of equality and universality, it sought once again inequality – but this time an inequality determined only from within . . . The quest for independence continued to the point where individuals who had been rendered independent in this way wanted also to distinguish themselves *from one another.*
>
> (Simmel, 1971: 222)

In both cases, and indeed as we have moved forward into the present, 'the drive underlying this development remains one and the same': the individual is searching for 'a fixed and unambiguous point of reference', and cannot find it outside the self (ibid, p. 223). As social life becomes more complex, and different perspectives have to be taken into account, meaning does not come from external sources but needs to be achieved by the individual themselves, *in relation to* – but separately from – the social world of others. This process of establishing an individual self in a social context could be seen quite concretely in the process of constructing Lego identity models, as mentioned at the start of this finding; individuals tended to set up a network of elements which gave them a kind of stand-alone strength, but accompanied by ties and interactions, of varying levels of intensity, with other human beings.

One of Simmel's concerns was that as the external world of technology and culture became so complex, and much too vast to be fully accessed by one individual, so the individual's own participation would come to seem relatively fragmentary and insignificant (see chapter 6, 'The Style of Life', in Simmel, 2004). In the Lego identity models, we can see individuals engaging with this tension by *asserting themselves against it*, in this case literally building up a case for their own distinctiveness to shore up a defence against the powerful waves of consumer culture, information and fashion. The less 'walled in' models were often representations of a willingness to engage with this culture, whilst still retaining the crucial core of individuality.

We should also record, on a related note, that definite social constraints such as *lack of money* were included in a number of models. The participants' diverse constructions of self-identity were, of course, not able to release them from such practical constraints, although they produced a different set of relationships to them. The opportunities for free and pleasurable living were seen to be partly limited by lack of resources, or by the responsibility of having to go out to earn money to provide for a family. One participant summed up this dimension by building 'the stomper machine', a kind of robot which stomped around the edge of his model, representing these dismal everyday responsibilities and constraints, such as work and money.

Media audience studies

This project began as a development of media audience studies, but some readers may be wondering if this is a study about 'the media' or 'audiences' at all. This brings us to the first finding in this section:

Finding 8: Media studies is often too much about the media

All forms of media – from mass broadcast TV shows and popular magazines to blogs and individually crafted websites aimed at small numbers of people – play a part in social life, and become meaningful for academic study within that social context – as people consume, discuss and interact with them and embed them in their lives. Media studies, however, has a tendency to discuss 'the media' as an independently fascinating set of texts and technologies – which can be sufficient for half a study, but I would suggest that the relevant social context and issues also need to be addressed. This often does not occur, or does not occur fully and properly. (Linking *Buffy the Vampire Slayer* with social discourses about feminism, for example, is a decent (if predictable) start – rather than just discussing *Buffy* in reference to itself, or other TV shows – but would need also to be linked to the actual reflective consumption of *Buffy* by actual people in everyday life, and understood in the context of the fact that these people are consumers of a wide range of media, and not just one show in isolation.)

Research which does work with people (or 'audiences') themselves in some depth, such as the Lego identity study discussed in this book, and also studies such as Hermes (1995) and Gauntlett and Hill (1999), suggest that most people don't put any element of the media anywhere near the top of the list, when discussing their own social identities and what is important to them. This point will be discussed in finding 10 below; here, the main point is that some spheres of media studies could do with a substantial injection of social context.

Finding 9: Audiences are people, and people are complex

This finding sounds obvious, but is worth stating because the media studies literature on audiences has a tendency to acknowledge the diversity of audiences – that an audience may be comprised of a range of different people with different interests and backgrounds – but then proceeds anyway, as if talking about 'audiences' is fine as long as you mention this first. In fact, of course, it is the case that audiences are not only a diverse set of individuals, but that each individual is complex, internally diverse and often somewhat contradictory in attitudes, tastes and pleasures. The media engages with these interests, and makes a substantial contribution to satisfying them. Nevertheless, participants in my study generally did not include the media as a significant influence upon their fundamental sense of self, which brings us to the next finding.

Finding 10: People generally do not think the media influences their identity much

It is not necessarily the case that people would be *aware* of ways in which the media influenced their thoughts or behaviour. On the one hand, it seems highly likely that the media must influence how we see relationships, for example, and the purpose of life and how to spend one's time on the earth, *in some way*. We consume so many stories about these things; it doesn't seem far-fetched to suggest that they must have some impact on our consciousness. On the other hand, it is incredibly difficult for researchers to isolate what this 'effect' might be, as discussed in Chapter 1. A different solution would be to ask people themselves, directly, about media influences, but this carries with it the problem that the media is presented as a possible influence at the start. This study therefore took a different approach, and invited people to reflect upon the influences on their identities, but without mentioning the media – or anything else – in particular.

The finding from this was that very few people mentioned the media at all. Remembering the warning about generalisability discussed at the start of Chapter 3, I have to note that this study did not utilise a scientifically constructed representative sample, and so I should be somewhat cautious about making generalising claims. However, the ten groups did represent a diverse range of people from people in professional jobs to those who were unemployed, with a balance of women and men, and 19 per cent from black and minority ethnic groups.

The numbers of people who included media influences are generally too slight to be of great significance. Music was included in the identity models most often (by 16 per cent of participants), but popular culture and television were included by just 8 per cent, most of whom were media scriptwriting students whose interest in such things was so pronounced that it had directly contributed to their choice of degree. A number of people mentioned an engagement with, and interest in, the wider world, and mass media are likely to be an important source of information about the world beyond direct experience – but was not mentioned in particular. A thirst for knowledge (5 per cent), interest in different places (6 per cent), sport (5 per cent), technology (5 per cent), art (5 per cent) and a dislike of George W. Bush (3 per cent) were all likely to be satisfied in some way by the media, but I wouldn't want to clutch at straws. In general the clearest finding is that, when asked to consider influences upon their identities, the participants did not usually think of media products or technologies.

Finding 11: A role for media in thinking about identity

This study still points to a role for the media in construction of identities, however. As we saw in Chapter 9, Paul Ricoeur argued that narratives provide their audiences with the opportunity to consider ethical questions. We can see the stories in popular media as today's most commonly engaged-with dimension of the 'vast laboratory for thought experiments' mentioned by Ricoeur (1992: 148). These narratives include television drama and soaps, movies, comics, video games, and even the 'true' narratives about celebrities and reality TV stars which appear in a range of media forms. Such narratives give people the chance to think about what constitutes a 'good life' or a desirable identity. Many dramatic stories are about characters who, in one way or another, face failure in their journey towards potential happiness, but then learn – or are tragically unable to learn – from their mistakes. (This may sound formulaic, but writers who have analysed numerous myths and stories, such as Campbell (1993), Vogler (1999), McKee (1999) and Booker (2005), insist that humans down the ages have been drawn to a small number of basic archetypal stories which we find especially inspiring.)

Such stories are *resources* which can be drawn upon as an individual constructs their own narrative identity – linking with the theme of the reflexive narrative of the self discussed in finding 5 above. Stories which emphasise the importance of love, family and keeping one's word – themes which are at the heart of numerous popular movies, for example – help individuals to orient themselves towards what is important in life, if you share this cultural view; or more cynical entertainments are preferred by others as offering something more 'challenging' to reflect upon. Responses to different kinds of stories can change over time, and life-stages are significant here, but – whatever their content – media narratives offer their audiences models to respond to as they refine their own sense of self-identity, and *navigation points* as they steer their own personal routes through life (Gauntlett, 2002: 250). Since participants *themselves* recognised that they were assembling identity in the style of a narrative (finding 5), and sought unifying themes (finding 6), it seems highly likely that the network of influences upon their identity-storytelling will have included a sampling from the media stories which are so prevalent in their social and cultural worlds, and which are the mainstream place (along with published novels and biographies) where 'the story of a life' is commonly presented.

This finding, which relies on the phrase 'it seems highly likely', may seem relatively weak; but since individuals are highly *unlikely* to say that they have based their narrative identity on a particular story, or a particular role model – because everyone wants to feel more 'individual', complex and distinctive than such a formula would suggest – it is perhaps as close to empirical confidence as we can get. Media influences are inevitably very complex, and intertwined with many other influences and aspects of personality. Nevertheless, this study has shown that people in everyday life *do* generate reflexive narratives to describe their identity, and are well able to create a representation of their own unified story. I would suggest that this will almost *inevitably* have been affected by the stories and values which we encounter so regularly in popular media, although on this particular point further research which turns the spotlight back onto people's relationship with media narratives will be needed.

In conclusion

The idea of 'identity' can seem vague and abstract. Academics have found it difficult to establish what identity means, so that at times it has been reduced to a set of categories such as gender, ethnicity and physical ability (each of which becomes more fuzzy itself when inspected closely). In this book I have preferred to approach the concept by seeing *what identity means to people themselves*. I was surprised to find the degree of clarity with which a wide range of people could picture their own 'identity', on their own terms, and share this story with others. It has also been heartening, if not so surprising, to find that people are philosophers on the state of their own lives *before* the social theorists come along.

We have followed a number of paths to arrive at a set of findings about personal identities, and how they might be studied. In particular I have proposed a visual and creative research method which encouraged participants to spend time reflecting on their identity, through asking them to build a metaphorical model of it in Lego. This challenge required the hands and mind to be working together in unison, playing with different pieces until conscious or previously-not-quite conscious ideas emerged in the formations of Lego shapes, figures and animals. I found Lego to be a colourful, appealing and straightforward medium, which almost all of the participants loved – and which, unusually for an art or craft material, meant that everybody was able to produce something with which they felt satisfied – but this kind of approach could, of course, use any of a wide range of potential techniques or materials.

The identity models that were built were complex and often rather beautiful. Although we continue to hear about 'fragmented' postmodern identities in academic publications, the view from this research was quite the opposite. I was struck by 'the will to coherence' – the desire to assemble a solid and unified view of self-identity. It was also possible to see participants asserting their own distinctiveness within the context of an increasingly globalised and mainstream fashion-led culture. The role of the media emerged as the provider of stories – ethical resources which people use to orient themselves towards aspirations. We saw that the sense of a *journey* was common, with each person as the hero of their own story, often moving away from historical ties towards greater stability, fulfilment and engagement with the world. Despite the dominance of consumer culture – of which popular media are a part – these goals were not about possessions gained, but about social connections, inner happiness and a life well lived.

References

Adams, Matthew (2006), 'Hybridizing Habitus and Reflexivity: Towards an Understanding of Contemporary Identity?', *Sociology*, 40(3): 511–28.

Adolphe, Bruce (2001), 'With Music in Mind', in Karl H. Pfenninger and Valerie R. Shubik (eds), *The Origins of Creativity*, Oxford: Oxford University Press.

Adorno, Theodor W. (1991), *The Culture Industry: Selected Essays on Mass Culture*, London: Routledge.

Ang, Ien (1985), *Watching Dallas: Soap Opera and the Melodramatic Imagination*, London: Methuen.

Ankori, Gannit (2005), 'Frida Kahlo: The Fabric of her Art', in Emma Dexter and Tanya Barson (eds), *Frida Kahlo*, London: Tate.

Aristotle (2004), *Poetics*, tr. Malcolm Heath, London: Penguin.

Arnheim, Rudolf (1969), *Visual Thinking*, Berkeley: University of California Press.

Arnheim, Rudolf (1986), *New Essays on the Psychology of Art*, Berkeley: University of California Press.

Baars, Bernard (2005), interviewed in Susan Blackmore (ed.), *Conversations on Consciousness*, Oxford: Oxford University Press.

Banks, Marcus (2001), *Visual Methods in Social Research*, London: Sage.

Barker, Gary T. (2005), *Dying to be Men: Youth, Masculinity and Social Exclusion*, London: Routledge.

Barker, Martin, and Brooks, Kate (1998), *Knowing Audiences: Judge Dredd, its Friends, Fans and Foes*, Luton: University of Luton Press.

Baudrillard, Jean (1988), *America*, London: Verso.

Baudrillard, Jean (1994), *Simulacra and Simulation*, Ann Arbor: University of Michigan Press.

Beardsley, Monroe C. (1958), *Aesthetics*, New York: Harcourt, Brace & World.

Beck, Ulrich (2002), 'A Life of one's own in a Runaway World: Individualization, Globalization and Politics', in Ulrich Beck and Elisabeth Beck-Gernsheim (2002), *Individualization*, London: SAGE.

Beckmann, Max (1968), 'On my Painting' (1938), in Herschel B. Chapp (ed.), *Theories of Modern Art: A Source Book by Artists and Critics*, Berkeley: University of California Press.

Belk, Russell W., Ger, Güliz and Askegaard, Søren (2003), 'The Fire of Desire: A Multisited Inquiry into Consumer Passion', *Journal of Consumer Research*, 30(3): 326–51 .

Bell, Julian (1999), *What is Painting? Representation and Modern Art*, London: Thames & Hudson.

Berkeley, George (1709), *An Essay Towards a New Theory of Vision*, ed. David R. Wilkins, 2002, Trinity College, Dublin. http://www.maths.tcd.ie/~dwilkins/Berkeley/Vision/.

Black, Max (1962), *Models and Metaphors: Studies in Language and Philosophy*, Ithaca, NY: Cornell University Press.

Blackmore, Susan (2003), *Consciousness: An Introduction*, London: Hodder Arnold.

Blackmore, Susan, ed. (2005), *Conversations on Consciousness*, Oxford: Oxford University Press.

Bloustein, Gerry (1998), '"It's Different to a Mirror 'cos it Talks to you": Teenage Girls, Video Cameras and Identity', in Sue Howard (ed.), *Wired up: Young People and the Electronic Media*, London: UCL Press.

Bohm, David (1998), *On Creativity*, London: Routledge.

Booker, Christopher (2005), *The Seven Basic Plots: Why we Tell Stories*, London: Continuum.

Bourdieu, Pierre (1977), *Outline of a Theory of a Practice*, Cambridge: Cambridge University Press.

Bourdieu, Pierre (1984), *Distinction: A Social Critique of the Judgement of Taste*, London: Routledge & Kegan Paul.

Bourdieu, Pierre (1990), *In Other Words: Essays Towards a Reflexive Sociology*, Cambridge: Polity.

Bourdieu, Pierre and Wacquant, Loic J.D. (1992), *An Invitation to Reflexive Sociology*, Chicago: University of Chicago Press.

Bower, Robin (1992), 'Media Education as an Essential Ingredient in Issue-Based Environmental Education', in Manuel Alvarado and Oliver Boyd-Barrett (eds), *Media Education: An Introduction*, London: British Film Institute.

Brown, Tara (2005), 'In Loving Memory', transcript of *60 Minutes* report, broadcast 24 July 2005, Channel Nine (Australia), at http://sixtyminutes.ninemsn.com.au/sixtyminutes/stories/2005_07_24/story_1454.asp.

Buckingham, David (1993a), 'Boys' Talk: Television and the Policing of Masculinity', in Buckingham, David (ed.), *Reading Audiences: Young People and the Media*, Manchester: Manchester University Press.

Buckingham, David (1993b), *Children Talking Television: The Making of Television Literacy*, London: Falmer Press.

Buckingham, David, and Bragg, Sara (2004), *Young People, Sex and the Media: The Facts of Life?*, Basingstoke: Palgrave Macmillan.

Buckingham, David, and Sefton-Green, Julian (1994), *Cultural Studies Goes to School: Reading and Teaching Popular Media*, London: Taylor & Francis.

Calvin, William H. (1989), *The Cerebral Symphony: Seashore Reflections on the Structure of Consciousness*, New York: Bantam.

Cameron, Lynne (2006), 'Metaphor in Everyday Language', in Janet Maybin and Joan Swann (eds), *The Art of English: Everyday Creativity*, Basingstoke: Palgrave Macmillan.

Campbell, Joseph (1993), *The Hero with a Thousand Faces*, London: Fontana.

Cartwright, Nancy (1999), *The Dappled World: A Study of the Boundaries of Science*, Cambridge: Cambridge University Press.

Cashmore, Ellis (2006), *Celebrity/Culture*, London: Routledge.

Cech, Thomas R. (2001), 'Overturning the Dogma: Catalytic RNA', in Karl H. Pfenninger and Valerie R. Shubik (eds), *The Origins of Creativity*, Oxford: Oxford University Press.

Chalmers, David (2005), interviewed in Susan Blackmore (ed.), *Conversations on Consciousness*, Oxford: Oxford University Press.

Chaplin, Elizabeth (1994), *Sociology and Visual Representation*, London: Routledge.

Cheal, David (2005), *Dimensions of Sociological Theory*, Basingstoke: Palgrave Macmillan.

Chodorow, Joan (1997), *Jung on Active Imagination*, Princeton: Princeton University Press.

Clark, T. J. (1999), *The Painting of Modern Life: Paris in the Art of Manet and his Followers*, revised edn, London: Thames & Hudson.

Claxton, Guy (2006), *The Wayward Mind: An Intimate History of the Unconscious*, London: Abacus.

Clottes, J., and Féruglio, V. (2004), *The Cave of Chauvet-Pont-d'Arc*. Website at http://www.culture.gouv.fr/culture/arcnat/chauvet/en/. Paris: Ministère de la culture et de la communication – Mission de la recherche et de la technologie.

Collier, John (1967), *Visual Anthropology: Photography as a Research Method*, New York: Holt, Reinhart & Winston.

Cousins, Mark (2005), 'Introduction', in Sigmund Freud, *The Unconscious*, London: Penguin.

Csikszentmihalyi, Mihaly (1997), *Creativity: Flow and the Psychology of Discovery and Invention*, New York: Harper Perennial.

Csikszentmihalyi, Mihaly (2002 [1990]), *Flow: The Classic Work on How to Achieve Happiness*, revised edn, London: Rider.

Dahlgren, Peter (1988), 'What's the Meaning of This?: Viewers' Plural Sense-Making of TV News', *Media, Culture and Society*, 10(3): 285–301.

Damasio, Antonio R. (2001), 'Some Notes on Brain, Imagination and Creativity', in Karl H. Pfenninger and Valerie R. Shubik (eds), *The Origins of Creativity*, Oxford: Oxford University Press.

Danto, A. C. (1981) *The Transfiguration of the Commonplace: A Philosophy of Art*, Cambridge, MA: Harvard University Press.

De Block, Liesbeth, Buckingham, David, and Banaji, Shakuntala (2005), *Children in Communication about Migration (CHICAM): Final Report*, funded by the European Commission (Contract No: HPSE – CT2001-00048), available at www.chicam.net/finalreports.

De Bono, Edward (2000), *Six Thinking Hats*, revised and updated edn, London: Penguin.

Deese, James (1983), 'Foreword', in Carole Peterson and Allyssa McCabe, *Developmental Psycholinguistics: Three Ways of Looking at a Child's Narrative*, New York: Plenum Press.

Deller, Jeremy, and Kane, Alan (2005), *Folk Archive: Contemporary Popular Art from the UK*, London: Book Works.

Dennett, Daniel (1984), *Elbow Room: The Varieties of Free Will Worth Wanting*, Oxford: Clarendon Press.

Dennett, Daniel (1991), *Consciousness Explained*, London: Penguin.

Dennett, Daniel (2004), *Freedom Evolves*, London: Penguin.

Dennett, Daniel (2005a), *Sweet Dreams: Philosophical Obstacles to a Science of Consciousness*, Cambridge, MA: MIT Press.

Dennett, Daniel (2005b), interviewed in Susan Blackmore (ed.), *Conversations on Consciousness*, Oxford: Oxford University Press.

Dewey, J. (1980 [1934]) *Art as Experience*, New York: Perigee.

Dikovitskaya, Margaret (2005), *Visual Culture: The Study of the Visual After the Cultural Turn*, Cambridge: MIT Press.

Dowmunt, Tony (1980), *Video with Young People*, London: Inter-Action Inprint.

Duff, Leo (2005), 'Introduction', in Leo Duff and Jo Davies (eds), *Drawing: The Process*, Bristol: Intellect Books.

Durkheim, Emile (1938 [1895]), *The Rules of Sociological Method*, New York: Free Press.

Durkheim, Emile (2002 [1897]), *Suicide: A Study in Sociology*, London: Routledge Classics.

Easton Ellis, Bret (1991), *American Psycho*, London: Picador.

Edelman, Gerald M. (2005), *Wider than the Sky: A Revolutionary View of Consciousness*, London: Penguin.

Edwards, Betty (2001), *The New Drawing on the Right Side of the Brain: Expanded and Updated*, London: HarperCollins.

Eldridge, Richard (2003), *An Introduction to the Philosophy of Art*, Cambridge: Cambridge University Press.

Elkins, James (2003), *Visual Studies: A Skeptical Introduction*, London: Routledge.

Ellenberger, Henri F. (1970). *The Discovery of the Unconscious: The History and Evolution of Dynamic Psychiatry*, New York: Basic Books.

European Graduate School (2005), 'European Graduate School Faculty: Tracey Emin: Resources', available at http://www.egs.edu/faculty/emin-resources.html.

Evans, Jessica and Hall, Stuart (eds) (1999), *Visual Culture: The Reader*, London: Sage.

Falk, Dan (2005), *Universe on a T-Shirt: The Quest for the Theory of Everything*, London: Arcade.

Feyerabend, Paul (1993), *Against Method: Outline of an Anarchistic Theory of Knowledge*, London: Verso; 1st published 1975.

Foucault, Michel (1990), *The Care of the Self: The History of Sexuality Volume Three*, tr. Robert Hurley, London: Penguin.

Foucault, Michel (2000), *Essential Works of Foucault 1954–1984: Ethics*, ed. Paul Rabinow, London: Penguin.

Frazer, Elizabeth (1987), 'Teenage Girls Reading Jackie', *Media, Culture and Society*, 9: 407–25.

Freud, Sigmund (2005), 'In Defence of the Unconscious', in *The Unconscious*, tr. Graham Frankland, London: Penguin; 1st published 1915.

Frisby, David (2002), *Georg Simmel*, revised edn, London: Routledge.

Frosh, Stephen, Phoenix, Ann, and Pattman, Rob (2001), *Young Masculinities: Understanding Boys in Contemporary Society*, Basingstoke: Palgrave Macmillan.

Gardner, Howard (1993), *Creating Minds: An Anatomy of Creativity Seen through the Lives of Freud, Einstein, Picasso, Stravinsky, Eliot, Graham, and Gandhi*, New York: Basic Books.

Gardner, Howard (2001), 'Creators: Multiple Intelligences', in Karl H. Pfenninger and Valerie R. Shubik (eds), *The Origins of Creativity*, Oxford: Oxford University Press.

Gauntlett, David (1995), *Moving Experiences: Understanding Television's Influences and Effects* (1st edn), London: John Libbey.

Gauntlett, David (1997), *Video Critical: Children, the Environment and Media Power*, London: John Libbey.

Gauntlett, David (1998), 'Ten Things Wrong with the "Effects Model"', in Roger Dickinson, Ramaswani Harindranath and Olga Linne (eds), *Approaches to Audiences*, London: Arnold.

Gauntlett, David (2001), 'The Worrying Influence of "Media Effects" Studies', in Martin Barker and Julian Petley (eds), *Ill Effects: The Media/Violence Debate* (2nd edn), London and New York: Routledge.

Gauntlett, David (2002), *Media, Gender and Identity: An Introduction*, London: Routledge. .

Gauntlett, David, and Horsley, Ross, eds (2004), *Web.Studies, Second Edition*, London: Arnold.

Gauntlett, David (2005), *Moving Experiences, Second Edition: Media Effects and Beyond*, London: John Libbey.

Gauntlett, David, and Hill, Annette (1999), *TV Living: Television, Culture and Everyday Life*, London: Routledge.

Gauntlett, David, and Holzwarth, Peter (2006), 'Creative and Visual Methods for Exploring Identities', *Visual Studies*, 21(1): 82–91.

Gee, James Paul (2004), *What Video Games have to Teach us about Learning and Literacy*, New York: Palgrave Macmillan.

Giddens, Anthony (1976), *New Rules of Sociological Method: A Positive Critique of Interpretative Sociologies*, London: Hutchinson.

Giddens, Anthony (1984), *The Constitution of Society*, Cambridge: Polity.

Giddens, Anthony (1991), *Modernity and Self-Identity: Self and Society in the Late Modern Age*, Cambridge: Polity.

Giddens, Anthony (1992), *The Transformation of Intimacy*, Cambridge: Polity.

Giddens, Anthony and Pierson, Christopher (1998), *Conversations with Anthony Giddens: Making Sense of Modernity*, Cambridge: Polity.

Gilbert & George (1997 [1986]), *The Words of Gilbert & George*, London: Thames & Hudson.

Gilot, Françoise (2001), 'A Painter's Perspective', in Karl H. Pfenninger and Valerie R. Shubik (eds), *The Origins of Creativity*, Oxford: Oxford University Press.

Goffman, Erving (1959), *The Presentation of Self in Everyday Life*, London: Penguin.

Grady, John (2004), 'Working with Visible Evidence: An Invitation and Some Practical Advice', in Caroline Knowles and Paul Sweetman (eds), *Picturing the Social Landscape: Visual Methods and the Sociological Imagination*, London: Routledge.

Graham-Dixon, Andrew (2001), *Howard Hodgkin*, revised and expanded edn, London: Thames & Hudson.

Grahame, Jenny (1991), 'The Production Process', in David Lusted (ed.), *The Media Studies Book: A Guide for Teachers*, London: Routledge.

Gray, Ann (1992), *Video Playtime: The Gendering of a Leisure Technology*, London: Routledge.

Greene, Brian (2000), *The Elegant Universe: Superstrings, Hidden Dimensions, and the Quest for the Ultimate Theory*, London: Random House.

Guillemin, Marilys (2004), 'Understanding Illness: Using Drawings as a Research Method', *Qualitative Health Research*, 14(2): 272–89.

Harper, Douglas (1998), 'An Argument for Visual Sociology', in Jon Prosser (ed.) *Image-Based Research: A Sourcebook for Qualitative Researchers*, London: RoutledgeFalmer.

Hawking, Stephen W. (2006), *The Theory of Everything: The Origin and Fate of the Universe*, London: Phoenix.

Hayes, John R., and Flower, Linda S. (1983), 'Uncovering Cognitive Processes in Writing: An Introduction to Protocol Analysis', in Peter Mosenthal, Lynne Tamor and Sean A. Walmsley (eds), *Research on Writing: Principles and Methods*, New York: Longman.

Hegel, Georg Wilhelm Friedrich (2004), *Introductory Lectures on Aesthetics*, tr. Bernard Bosanquet, ed. Michael Inwood, London: Penguin.

Hermes, Joke (1995), *Reading Women's Magazines: An Analysis of Everyday Media Use*, Cambridge: Polity.

Hill, Annette (1997), *Shocking Entertainment: Viewer Response to Violent Movies*, London: John Libbey. .

Hill, Annette (2001), '"Looks like it Hurts": Women's Responses to Shocking Entertainment', in Martin Barker and Julian Petley (eds), *Ill Effects: The Media/Violence Debate*, London: Routledge.

Hockney, David and Joyce, Paul (2002) *Hockney on 'Art'*, London: Little Brown.

Holliday, Ruth (2004), 'Reflecting the Self', in Caroline Knowles and Paul Sweetman (eds), *Picturing the Social Landscape: Visual Methods and the Sociological Imagination*, London: Routledge.

Holmes, Su, and Redmond, Sean, eds (2006), *Framing Celebrity: New Directions in Celebrity Culture*, London: Routledge.

Holzwarth, Peter, and Maurer, Björn (2003), 'CHICAM (Children in Communication about Migration): An International Research Project Exploring the Possibilities of Intercultural Communication through Children's Media Productions', in M. Kiegelmann and L. Gürtler (eds) *Research Questions and Matching Methods of Analysis*, Tübingen: Ingeborg Huber Verlag.

Horkheimer, Max, and Adorno, Theodor W. (1979), *Dialectic of Enlightenment*, London: Verso; 1st published 1947.

Horsley, Ross (2006), 'Men's Lifestyle Magazines and the Construction of Male Identity', PhD thesis, Leeds: University of Leeds.

Hüttner, Per (2005), *I am a Curator: One Project by one Artist Incorporating Thirty Exhibitions by Curators with No Previous Experience in Exhibition Making*, Stockholm: Föreningen Curatorial Mutiny.

Illuminations, eds (2002), *Art Now: Interviews with Modern Artists*, London: Continuum.

Jackson, Peter, Stevenson, Nick, and Brooks, Kate (2001), *Making Sense of Men's Magazines*, Cambridge: Polity. .

James, William (1950), *The Principles of Psychology*, New York: Dover; 1st published 1890.

Jameson, Fredric (1991), *Postmodernism, or the Cultural Logic of Late Capitalism*, London: Verso.

Jenks, Chris, ed. (1995), *Visual Culture*, London: Routledge.

Jenkins, Richard (2002), *Pierre Bourdieu*, revised edition, London: Routledge.

Johnson, Paul (2003), *Art: A New History*, London: Weidenfeld & Nicolson.

Jung, Carl Gustav (1997 [1931]), 'The Aims of Psychotherapy (from *The Practice of Psychotherapy*)', in Joan Chodorow (ed.), *Jung on Active Imagination*, Princeton: Princeton University Press.

Jung, Carl Gustav (1997 [1961]), 'Confrontation with the Unconscious' (from *Memories, Dreams, Reflections*), in Joan Chodorow (ed.), *Jung on Active Imagination*, Princeton: Princeton University Press.

Jung, Carl Gustav (1998 [1939]), 'Conscious, Unconscious, and Individuation', in *The Essential Jung*, ed. Anthony Storr, London: Fontana.

Kane, Pat (2005), *The Play Ethic: A Manifesto for a Different Way of Living*, London: Pan.

Knowles, Caroline, and Sweetman, Paul (2004), 'Introduction', in Caroline Knowles and Paul Sweetman (eds), *Picturing the Social Landscape: Visual Methods and the Sociological Imagination*, London: Routledge.

Kövecses, Zoltán (2002), *Metaphor: A Practical Introduction*, New York: Oxford University Press.

Kuhn, Thomas S. (1996 [1963]), *The Structure of Scientific Revolutions*, Chicago: University of Chicago Press.

Lakoff, George, and Johnson, Mark (2003), *Metaphors we Live by*, revised edn, Chicago: University of Chicago Press.

Lakoff, George, and Turner, Mark (1989), *More than Cool Reason: A Field Guide to Poetic Metaphor*, Chicago: University of Chicago Press.

Latham, Alan (2004), 'Researching and Writing Everyday Accounts of the City: An Introduction to the Diary-Photo Diary-Interview Method', in Caroline Knowles and

Paul Sweetman (eds), *Picturing the Social Landscape: Visual Methods and the Sociological Imagination*, London: Routledge.

Lego Serious Play (2006), *The Science of Lego Serious Play*, Billund: Lego.

Lewis-Williams, David (2002), *The Mind in the Cave: Consciousness and the Origins of Art*, London: Thames & Hudson.

Libet, Ben (1985), 'Unconscious Cerebral Initiative and the Role of Conscious Will in Voluntary Action', *Behavioural and Brain Sciences*, 8: 529–66.

Lord, John Vernon (2005), 'A Journey of Drawing: An Illustration of a Fable', in Leo Duff and Jo Davies (eds), *Drawing: The Process*, Bristol: Intellect Books.

Lumsden, Charles J. (1999), 'Evolving Creative Minds: Stories and Mechanisms', in Robert J. Sternberg (ed.), *Handbook of Creativity*, Cambridge: Cambridge University Press.

McEwan, Ian (2005), *Saturday*, London: Vintage.

McGrath, Melanie (2002), 'Something's Wrong: Melanie McGrath on Tracey Emin', *Tate: International Arts and Culture*, 1 (Sept.–Oct.), available at http://www.tate.org.uk/magazine/issue1.

McKee, Robert (1999), *Story*, London: Methuen.

Mirzoeff, Nicholas (1998, 2002), *The Visual Culture Reader*, London: Routledge.

Mirzoeff, Nicholas (1999), *An Introduction to Visual Culture*, London: Routledge.

Morrison, Ken (1995), *Marx, Durkheim, Weber: Formations of Modern Social Thought*, London: SAGE.

Moss, Gemma (1993), 'Children Talk Horror Videos: Reading as a Social Performance', *Australian Journal of Education*, 37(2): 169–81.

Néret, Gilles (2003), *Édouard Manet: The First of the Moderns*, Cologne: Taschen.

New Scientist (2006), 'The Science of You: The Ultimate Guide to Self-Knowledge', cover story, 19 Aug.

New, Jennifer (2005), *Drawing from Life: The Journal as Art*, New York: Princeton Architectual Press.

Nietzsche, Friedrich (1967 [1872]), *The Birth of Tragedy and the Case of Wagner*, New York: Random House.

Okasha, Samir (2002), *Philosophy of Science: A Very Short Introduction*, Oxford: Oxford University Press.

Papert, Seymour, and Harel, Idit (1991), 'Situating Constructionism', in *Constructionism*, Norwood: Ablex Publishing. Available at http://www.papert.org/articles/SituatingConstructionism.html.

Payne, Geoff, and Williams, Malcolm (2005), 'Generalization in Qualitative Research', *Sociology*, 39(2): 295–314.

Penfield, Wilder G., and Rasmussen, Theodore (1950), *The Cerebral Cortex of Man: A Clinical Study of Localization of Function*, New York: Macmillan.

Pfenninger, Karl H., and Shubik, Valerie R., eds (2001), *The Origins of Creativity*, Oxford: Oxford University Press.

Piaget, Jean (1980), *Conversations with Jean Piaget*, interviews by Jean-Claude Bringuier, Chicago: University of Chicago Press.

Pink, Sarah (2001), *Doing Visual Ethnography*, London: Sage.

Pink, Sarah, Kürti, László, and Afonso, Ana Isabel, eds (2004), *Working Images: Visual Research and Representation in Ethnography*, London: Routledge.

Plucker, Jonathan A., and Renzulli, Joseph S. (1999), 'Psychometric Approaches to the Study of Human Creativity', in Robert J. Sternberg (ed.), *Handbook of Creativity*, Cambridge: Cambridge University Press.

Popper, Karl (2001 [1972]), 'The Logic and Evolution of Scientific Theory', in *All Life is Problem Solving*, London: Routledge.

Popper, Karl (2002), *The Logic of Scientific Discovery*, London: Routledge.

Proctor, Robert W. and Capaldi, E.J. (2006), *Why Science Matters: Understanding the Methods of Psychological Research*, Oxford: Blackwell.

Prosser, Jon, ed. (1998), *Image-Based Research: A Sourcebook for Qualitative Researchers*, London: RoutledgeFalmer.

Radley, Alan, Hodgetts, Darrin and Cullen, Andrea (2005), 'Visualizing Homelessness: A Study in Photography and Estrangement', *Journal of Community and Applied Social Psychology*, 15(4): 273–95.

Reagan, Charles E. (1998), *Paul Ricoeur: His Life and Work*, Chicago: University of Chicago Press.

Rhinehart, Luke (1971), *The Dice Man*, New York: William Morrow.

Richards, I. A. (1936), *The Philosophy of Rhetoric*, Oxford: Oxford University Press.

Ricoeur, Paul (1970), *Freud and Philosophy: An Essay on Interpretation*, tr.Denis Savage, New Haven: Yale University Press.

Ricoeur, Paul (1984), *Time and Narrative,* vol. 1, tr. Kathleen McLaughlin and David Pellauer, Chicago: University of Chicago Press.

Ricoeur, Paul (1985), *Time and Narrative,* vol. 2, tr. Kathleen McLaughlin and David Pellauer, Chicago: University of Chicago Press.

Ricoeur, Paul (1988), *Time and Narrative,* vol. 3, tr. Kathleen McLaughlin and David Pellauer, Chicago: University of Chicago Press.

Ricoeur, Paul (1992), *Oneself as Another*, tr. Kathleen Blamey, Chicago: University of Chicago Press.

Ricoeur, Paul (2003), *The Rule of Metaphor: The Creation of Meaning in Language*, tr. Robert Czerny with Kathleen McLaughlin and John Costello, SJ, London: Routledge Classics.

Rojek, Chris (2001), *Celebrity*, London: Reaktion Books.

Rose, David (2006), *Consciousness: Philosophical, Psychological, and Neural Theories*, Oxford: Oxford University Press.

Sacks, Oliver (1985), *The Man who Mistook his Wife for a Hat*, London: Duckworth.

Scaff, Lawrence A. (2000), 'Georg Simmel', in George Ritzer (ed.), *The Blackwell Companion to Major Social Theorists*, Oxford: Blackwell.

Schratz, Michael and Steiner-Löffler, Ulrike (1998), 'Pupils Using Photographs in School Self-Evaluation', in Jon Prosser (ed.), *Image-Based Research: A Sourcebook for Qualitative Researchers*, London: RoutledgeFalmer.

Searle, John R. (1997), *The Mystery of Consciousness*, London: Granta.

Simmel, Georg (1971), *On Individuality and Social Forms*, Chicago: University of Chicago Press.

Simmel, Georg (2004), *The Philosophy of Money*, 3rd enlarged edn, ed. David Frisby, tr. Tom Bottomore and David Frisby, London: Routledge.

Simms, Karl (2003), *Paul Ricoeur*, London: Routledge.

Smith, Bob and Roberta (2004), *Make your own Damn Art*, London: Black Dog Publishing.

Stent, Gunther S. (2001), 'Meaning in Art and Science', in Karl H. Pfenninger and Valerie R. Shubik (eds), *The Origins of Creativity*, Oxford: Oxford University Press.

Stephenson, William (1988), *The Play Theory of Mass Communication*, New Brunswick, NJ: Transaction Books.

Sternberg, Robert J., ed. (1999), *Handbook of Creativity*, Cambridge: Cambridge University Press.

Sturken, Marita, and Cartwright, Lisa (2001), *Practices of Looking: An Introduction to Visual Culture*, Oxford: Oxford University Press.

Sweetman, Paul (2003), 'Twenty-First Century Dis-Ease? Habitual Reflexivity or the Reflexive Habitus', *Sociological Review*, 51(4):. 528–49.

Terr, Lenore (2000), *Beyond Love and Work: Why Adults Need to Play*, New York: Touchstone.

Tibol, Raquel (2005), 'Pain – Love – Liberation: Frida Kahlo's Words', in Emma Dexter and Tanya Barson (eds), *Frida Kahlo*, London: Tate.

Tolstoy, Leo (1960), *What is Art?*, tr. Aylmer Maude, Indianapolis: Bobbs-Merrill.

Tulloch, John, and Jenkins, Henry (1995), *Science Fiction Audiences: Watching Doctor Who and Star Trek*, London: Routledge.

Turner, Graeme (2004), *Understanding Celebrity*, London: SAGE.

Van Gogh, Vincent (1958), *The Complete Letters of Vincent van Gogh*, vol. 3, Greenwich, CT: New York Graphic Society; 1st published 1889.

Vogler, Christopher (1999), *The Writer's Journey*, 2nd revised edn, London: Pan.

Wearing, Deborah (2005), *Forever Today*, London: Corgi.

Weber, Max (1949), *The Methodology of the Social Sciences*, New York: Free Press.

Weber, Max (1978), *Economy and Society* (vols 1 and 2), Berkeley: University of California Press.

Whetton, N. M. and McWhirter, J. (1998), 'Images and Curriculum Development in Health Education', in Jon Prosser (ed.), *Image-Based Research: A Sourcebook for Qualitative Researchers*, London: RoutledgeFalmer.

Whincup, Tony (2004), 'Imaging the Intangible', in Caroline Knowles and Paul Sweetman (eds), *Picturing the Social Landscape: Visual Methods and the Sociological Imagination*, London: Routledge.

Whyte, Lancelot Law (1979), *The Unconscious Before Freud*, London: Julian Friedmann.

Williams, T., Whetton, N. M. and Moon, A. (1989a), *A Way In*, London: Health Education Authority.

Williams, T., Whetton, N. M. and Moon, A. (1989b), *A Picture of Health*, London: Health Education Authority.

Young, Lorraine, and Barrett, Hazel (2001), 'Adapting Visual Methods: Action Research with Kampala Street Children', *Area*, 33(2): 141–52.

Zaltman, Gerald (2003), *How Consumers Think: Essential Insights into the Mind of the Market*, Boston: Harvard Business School Press.

Index

Related titles from Routledge

Media, Gender and Identity
An Introduction

David Gauntlett

David Gauntlett explores the gender landscape of contemporary media and draws on recent theories of identity negotiation to understand the place of popular media in people's lives. Discussing a range of examples from films such as *Charlie's Angels, What Women Want,* and *Tomb Raider,* men's and women's magazines from *FHM* and *Maxim* to *Cosmopolitan* and *Glamour,* primetime television programmes, and pop music, *Media, Gender and Identity* shows how the media are used in the shaping of individual self-identities.

Media, Gender and Identity includes:

- A comparison of gender representations in the past and today, with many examples drawn from 1998–2002
- An introduction to theorists such as Anthony Giddens, Michel Foucault and Judith Butler
- A discussion of queer theory and the idea of gender as performance
- A study of 'girl power' role models such as Destiny's Child and Britney Spears
- A website with extra articles, interviews and selected links, at www.theoryhead.com/gender

ISBN13: 978-0-415-18959-0 (hbk)
ISBN13: 978-0-415-18960-6 (pbk)

Available at all good bookshops
For ordering and further information please visit:
www.routledge.com

The Media Student's Book
Fourth Edition

Gill Branston and Roy Stafford

The Media Student's Book is a comprehensive introduction for students of media studies. It covers all the key topics and provides a detailed, lively and accessible guide to concepts and debates. This fourth edition, newly in colour, has been thoroughly revised, re-ordered and updated, with many very recent examples and expanded coverage of the most important issues currently facing media studies. It is structured in four main parts, addressing key concepts, media practices, media debates, and the resources available for individual research.

Individual chapters include: Interpreting media * Narratives * Genres and other classifications * Institutions * Questions of representation * Ideologies and power * Industries * Audiences * Advertising and branding * Research * Production organisation * Production techniques * Distribution * Documentary and 'reality TV' * Whose globalisation? * 'Free choices' in a 'free market'?

Chapters are supported by case studies which include: Ways of interpreting * *CSI: Miami* and crime fiction * J-horror and the *Ring* cycle * Television as institution * Images of migration * News * The media majors * The music industry, technology and synergy * Selling audiences * Celebrity, stardom and marketing * Researching mobile phone technologies * Contemporary British cinema.

The authors are experienced in writing, researching and teaching across different levels of pre-undergraduate and undergraduate study, with an awareness of the needs of those students. The book is specially designed to be easy and stimulating to use with:

- marginal terms, definitions, references (and even jokes), allied to a comprehensive glossary
- follow-up activities, suggestions for further reading, useful websites and resources plus a companion website to supporting the book at www.routledge.com/0415371430
- references and examples from a rich range of media forms, including advertising, television, films, radio, newspapers, magazines, photography and the internet.

ISBN 13: 978-0-415-37142-1 (hbk)
ISBN 13: 978-0-415-37143-8 (pbk)

Related titles from Routledge

Beyond Subculture

Pop, Youth and Identity in a Postcolonial World

Rupa Huq

'An extremely accessible, comprehensive and, above all, enjoyable book. Huq's grasp of youth culture studies is impeccable as is her knowledge of the myriad musics and styles that characterise youth culture at the beginning of the twenty-first century. A highly valuable resource for both students and experienced academic researchers.'

Andy Bennett, Professor in Communications and Popular Culture, *Brock University*

'This book extends the study of music subcultures into the twenty-first-century globalised world ... ideal for students.'

Mica Nava, Professor of Cultural Studies, *University of East London*

'*Beyond Subculture* reinvigorates youth culture studies at just the right time. After the postmodern turn of the 1990s threatened to bury youth culture, and its theorists, forever, there are new, young writers shouting from the streets and the lecture theatres. Just as pop music and its culture is roaring back with a vengeance at festivals and live gigs, along comes a text for the twenty first century study of youth culture.'

Steve Redhead, Professor of Sport and Media Cultures, *University of Brighton*

Beyond Subculture addresses contemporary popular music cultures alongside the political possibilities of youth and youth culture and considers whether in today's diverse, globalised world it is possible to label any one type of music the 'authentic' voice of youth.

Beyond Subculture investigates a series of musically-centred global youth cultures, including:

- hip-hop; rap
- electronic dance music; grunge
- bhangra; Britpop

Drawing on first hand case studies and interviews with musicians and producers, including Talvin Singh and Noel Gallagher, Rupa Huq reexamines the link between music and subcultures. As youth culture becomes more diverse and the effects of globalisation become stronger, the late twentieth-century definition of 'Generation X' is becoming redundant.

Rupa Huq is Senior Lecturer in the School of Social Sciences at Kingston University.

ISBN13: 978-0-415-27814-0 (hbk); ISBN13: 978-0-415-27815-7 (pbk)
ISBN13: 978-0-203-49139-3 (ebk)

Available at all good bookshops
For ordering and further information please visit:
www.routledge.com